THE 15 MINUTE DAILY ACTORS WORKOUT

SIX MONTHS
VOLUME ONE

_____
_____
_____

Copyright © [2024] #1209505
by [Victor Zinck Jr] First Edition
Printed in [Canada]

All rights reserved. No part of this publication may be reproduced, distributed, or transmitted in any form or by any means, including photocopying, recording, or other electronic or mechanical methods, without the prior written permission of the publisher, except in the case of brief quotations embodied in critical reviews and certain other noncommercial uses permitted by copyright law.

LEGAL DISCLAIMER

This book is intended as a resource for actors and provides exercises and techniques related to emotional development, imagination, script analysis, character observation, animal work, physical and vocal warmups, and other aspects of actor training. The content within is for informational and educational purposes only. The exercises and techniques described in this book are based on the author's experience and knowledge in the field of acting and theatre education. They are provided with the intent to assist actors in their personal and professional development. However, they are not a substitute for professional training or advice. Readers are advised to use their own judgment and should consider their physical, emotional, and mental capabilities before undertaking any of the exercises or techniques described in this book. It is recommended to consult with a professional in the field of acting and theatre education if you have any concerns or doubts about the suitability of any exercise or technique.
The author and publisher make no representations or warranties with respect to the accuracy, applicability, fitness, or completeness of the contents of this book. They shall not be liable for any damages or injury arising out of or in connection with the use of, or reliance on, any content contained in this book.
The exercises and techniques in this book are diverse and may involve physical activity. Therefore, readers are advised to approach them with caution and be aware of their own physical limitations. The author and publisher are not responsible for any injuries or damages that may occur as a result of practicing these exercises.

INDEX

CHECKLIST..18,19

WHY THIS BOOK WAS WRITTEN 5,6
WHAT THIS BOOK WILL CONSIST OF...7
TIPS FOR SUCCESS 8-17

PERFORMANCE STRATEGY............ 21, 51, 81, 111, 141, 171, 201, 231, 261, 291, 321 351, 381

ALL-AROUND ACTORS WORKOUT...... 23, 53, 83, 113, 143, 173, 203, 233, 263, 293, 323 353

SCRIPT ANALYSIS - RELATIONSHIPS & SPECIFICITY.... 25, 55, 85, 115, 145, 175, 205 235, 265, 295 325, 355

IMAGINATION - WORLD BUILDING MEDITATION.... 27, 57, 87, 117, 147, 177, 207, 237 267, 297, 327 357

OBSERVATION - CHARACTER STUDY............ 29, 59, 89, 119, 149, 179, 209, 239, 269 299, 329, 359

VOICE & DICTION..31,61, 91, 121, 151, 181, 211, 241, 271 301, 331, 361

SUBTEXT..33,63, 93, 123, 153, 183, 213, 243, 273 303, 333, 363

EMOTION..35, 65, 95, 125, 155, 185, 215, 245, 275 305, 335, 365

WRITE A LETTER IN CHARACTER.........................37,67, 97, 127, 157, 187, 217, 247, 277 307, 337, 367

VERBAL IMPROVISATION IN CHARACTER.....39, 69, 99, 129, 159, 189, 219, 249, 279 309, 339 369

SELF AWARENESS DISCOVERY............................. 41, 71, 101, 131, 161, 191, 221, 251, 281 311, 341, 371

IMPROVISED STORYTELLING & WORLD EXPLORATION....43, 73, 103, 133, 163, 193 223, 253 283, 313, 343, 373

COLOUR & MUSIC FOR ANCHORING YOUR CHARACTER....45, 75, 105, 135, 165, 195 225, 285 315 345, 375

HISTORICAL EVENT/PERSON RESEARCH......... 47, 77, 107, 137, 167, 197, 227, 257, 287 317, 347, 377

BELIEF..49, 79, 109, 139, 169, 199, 229, 259, 289 319, 349, 379

GOING FORWARD..382
RECOMMENDED BOOKS & RESOURCES...383

WHY THIS BOOK WAS WRITTEN

This is not revolutionary in any way; it's very basic. As actors, we don't have a daily practice in our craft. In almost all jobs, you undergo some form of training, and then when you're finished, you practice your skills every single day at work. That day-to-day practice is invaluable in becoming highly proficient and successful. So, as an actor, unless you're in full-time school, auditioning every day, or working on set every day, we have so much downtime without practicing our craft consistently. We're waiting... No more waiting.

No matter how long you've been in the industry, one of the biggest challenges is there's almost no structure in this lifestyle. No consistency and no set schedule, even when you're working. Everything is always changing, which we've all embraced, but how do you get better every day? How do you keep growing and evolving as an actor so that when the time comes and your phone rings, you're not shaking off the dust, but you are so prepared that you can deliver something great?

You can tell the difference between someone who doesn't exercise and someone who does. Someone who works out twice a week and someone who works out five. Do you think they have more time than you? The answer is almost always no. The difference is they have made a specific choice that exercising *that* much, is a must in their life. Not a "should", "try to", or find every excuse in the book to say why they can't. If it's THAT important to you, you will make it a must.

It's the exact same with actors. But there's no gym for the actor. No workout routine for emotions, creativity, physicality, script analysis, voice, imagination. So, I created one. A daily exercise routine, focusing on some of the most important skills any great actor needs and I could tell a difference immediately—not just in my auditions, but in my creativity, my excitement, and especially in my focus.

Your tools as an actor are either getting sharper or becoming dull. It's one or the other. A professional athlete trains every day. A doctor goes to school for almost a decade and then practices their craft while they work. They consistently train their skills and improve their methods, day in, day out. Success in any high-level career hinges on one crucial habit: consistent practice.

That is our aim with these workouts.

WHY THIS BOOK WAS WRITTEN

This book is for those of you who know how great you can be and want to become masterful at your craft. For those of you who want to be ready when that opportunity comes, so that one day when they say how lucky you are, you know the truth...

"Luck is what happens when preparation meets opportunity." Seneca

And remember, have patience with yourself as you're growing.

"You don't yell at a bud because it's not a flower yet." Larry Moss

WHAT THIS BOOK WILL CONSIST OF

There are 14 different exercises with 125 variants, outlining a 15-minute workout for you to follow every day for six months.

THE 14 EXERCISES

1: ALL AROUND ACTORS WORKOUT
2: SCRIPT ANALYSIS - RELATIONSHIPS & SPECIFICITY
3: IMAGINATION - WORLD BUILDING MEDITATION
4: OBSERVATION - CHARACTER STUDY
5: VOICE & DICTION
6: SUBTEXT
7: EMOTION
8: WRITE A LETTER IN CHARACTER
9: VERBAL IMPROVISATION IN CHARACTER
10: SELF AWARENESS DISCOVERY
11: IMPROVISED STORYTELLING & WORLD EXPLORATION
12: COLOUR AND MUSIC FOR ANCHORING YOUR CHARACTER
13: HISTORICAL EVENT or PERSON RESEARCH
14: BELIEF - YOUR BELIEF ON A SUBJECT & EMBODYING SOMEONE ELSE'S

PERFORMANCE STRATEGY & REVIEW

After every 14 days/exercises, there is a structured performance strategy and review that will go over your ongoing goals, your why, strengths, weaknesses and action plan. This helps us stay focused and train like a professional.

CHECKLIST

A DAILY, WEEKLY & MONTHLY CHECKLIST for those who like to have a specific goal and check off accomplishments as you go on this journey.

TIPS FOR SUCCESS
HOW TO MAKE THIS BOOK AS EFFECTIVE AS POSSIBLE

CONSISTENCY IS KEY: We are our habits. Change your habits and you change who you are.

Dedicate just 15 minutes a day and <u>commit</u> to regular practice. Train with the dedication of a professional.

Darren Hardy has an incredible book called "The Compound Effect" (New York: Success Books, 2010), he says initially, a train requires significant energy to start moving. Much like the initial stages of pursuing a goal or creating a new habit, it demands considerable effort with minimal visible results. However, as the train gains speed, it moves more effortlessly becoming almost unstoppable.

When people say "Oh, that's just who they are"; is an example of a seemingly unstoppable train, but all it takes is a new habit to change who we are. It will start slow but soon you will become unstoppable in this new version of yourself.

SPECIFICITY: The more specific you are with the exercises, your imagination and your goals; the more powerful and effective you will be as an actor and the faster you will grow. This will be better explained with examples soon.

JOURNAL YOUR PROGRESS: *Write it down!* Writing has a powerful effect on our clarity, focus and understanding. It's almost like etching into stone. I've given space to write for each exercise but it is limited. **Get yourself a journal** or write it in your notes on your device. When you look back on what you've accomplished, you'll see your journey and how much you've grown. The more you journal <u>your</u> thoughts and ideas on a subject, the closer you will get to knowing who you are and what kind of artist you are.

ENJOY THE JOURNEY: Acting is as much about the journey as it is about the destination. Celebrate small victories, learn from challenges, and enjoy every moment of the process. "Happiness is not a destination, it's a way of travel." - Ralph Waldo Emerson.

REMEMBER: Take these exercises and tweak them to *your style*. Decide what works for you and discard what doesn't. Be open to trying everything and through the process of elimination, you will begin to discover yourself as an artist.

TIPS FOR SUCCESS
HOW TO MAKE THIS BOOK AS EFFECTIVE AS POSSIBLE

FINDING A GOOD SPACE: This is more important than you think. Depending on our space, we can feel uncomfortable being too loud, "weird", making others uncomfortable or embarrassing ourselves while we rehearse. These worries or insecurities hold us back from our creativity and success. Find a place where you can be completely present, comfortable and creatively free. A space to explore what works and especially what doesn't.

If you don't have a space like that or you are on the go while you're using this book, then make do with what you have. Stay quiet or get comfortable being explorative around people. **Tip:** Headphones are perfect. People just think you're talking to someone on the phone.

MENTAL REHEARSAL: Actual practice has been proven to have the best results in our performance but mental rehearsal was surprisingly close.

There was a study by psychologist Alan Richardson referred to as mental rehearsal or mental practice that has been tested in the field of psychology and sports science.

In Richardson's study, participants were divided into three groups:

- Group A *physically practiced* free throws in basketball every day for 20 days.
- Group B only *mentally rehearsed* and visualized themselves successfully making free throws every day for 20 days.
- Group C, the control group, *did not practice* or engage in any mental rehearsal.

The results of the study showed that Group A, which *physically practiced*, improved their free throw shooting skills as expected. Surprisingly, Group B, the group that only engaged in *mental rehearsal*, also showed significant improvement, *although not as much as Group A*. Group C, the control group, showed no improvement.

"I visualize about a month or so in advance of what could happen, what I want to happen and what I don't want to happen. So, I was prepared for it all. In 2008, in the 200m fly, my goggles fell off in the first 25m, so I swam blind for 175m. I reverted back to what I did in training and counted my strokes. I know how many strokes I take in the first, second, third and fourth 50m of all my best 200m flies. I was ready for that because I mentally prepared for it." - Michael Phelps (Most decorated Olympian of All-time)

TIPS FOR SUCCESS
HOW TO MAKE THIS BOOK AS EFFECTIVE AS POSSIBLE

MENTAL REHEARSAL: It's like creating a detailed movie in your mind. Close your eyes and vividly imagine yourself performing a specific skill, task or *audition*. *Practice this no matter what*, but remember in those times you don't have a good space to rehearse properly, *mental rehearsal* is the perfect solution.

This technique will also strengthen your imagination which I think, is the most powerful skill we can have as an actor.

COURAGE: "A great actor stays around 6 years old." Christopher Walken

The reason why children are so fascinating and magical to watch is because they are so playful and imaginative. Still so malleable, but as you age, life teaches you to "be quiet", to "grow up" or be "cool". Children don't need courage to be creative because that is our natural state. You can get back to that. You just have to have *the courage* to break the habit of not wanting to look "silly" or whatever "it" is for you.

If you become so focused on being a great actor, you won't have any time to think about your insecurities.

Also, you are an _actor_. You're playing dress up for a living. You have to have the courage to be free. Free to be ugly and weird and magical. As soon as you embrace *this*, your imagination will ignite and you as an artist starts to emerge. It can be embarrassing and uncomfortable at first, but fairly quickly you will understand how powerful this change is.

"Have the courage to do whatever you need to do, to get where you want to go."

WORKOUTS
Following this 15-minute daily structure is a great starting point to help get you in *the habit of practice*, but remember: Take control. Spend more time on one exercise than the other, make the workouts longer and begin forming *your* own specific practice routine.

EXAMPLE
15-MINUTE WORKOUT

MY WHY: (You write your own here) Example: "I want to make comedies to make the world laugh! Laughter is the cure to so many things."

GOAL:[Be as specific as you can] Example: "I want all my characters to have a powerfully vibrant way of looking at the world. An intense point of view. And I want to not mumble. A very clear and resonant voice." Book a supporting role.

PHYSICAL WARMUP - 1 minute [Set Timer]
Freeform Dance: Put on some music and engage in freeform dancing. Allow your body to move spontaneously and without inhibition. This can help you tap into your creative instincts and develop physical expressiveness. **Tip**: Try music you've never listened to.

VOCAL WORK - 3 minutes [Set timer]
Lip Trills: Close your lips together lightly, like you're going to blow a raspberry. Then, blow air through your closed lips while making sounds. You should feel a tickling sensation.

EMOTIONAL RECALL - 5 minutes - [Set Timer]
Romantic Nostalgia:
Select a personal memory from your own life that evokes feelings of romantic nostalgia. Vividly recreate the chosen memory. Imagine the setting, the people involved, and the details of the situation. Use all your senses to immerse yourself in the memory. **Tip:** Trust your body. Allow the emotions to wash over you and let your body react and move in whatever way it wants to and speak any dialogue or words associated with the memory out loud as if you were speaking to the person in the memory. Now close your eyes and take a few deep breaths to relax— Focus and begin your recall.

ANIMAL WORK -
Research - 2 minutes [Set Timer] Exercise - 3 minutes [Set Timer]

FLAMINGO
Research - 2 minutes - Go to Google or YouTube etc and search flamingo. If you don't have internet access, take this time to recall when you've seen a flamingo either in person, images, tv. You don't have to be exact.

Animal Exercise - 3 minutes - Morph your body into this creature as much as possible. Walk, make their sounds, and imagine how they see the world. Beauty, Danger etc. Let your imagination take you. Once you believe yourself— slowly evolve yourself into human form but DON'T lose the slight, almost imperceptible characteristics of your animal. Now walk and talk like a regular human and see how embodying this animal affects everything. Your voice, movement, the way you look at the world. **Tip**: This is your playground. Have the courage to have fun!

Discovery Journal - 1 minute [Set Timer]
3 Main Characteristics: Pink, quick movements, mate for life. (Whatever stands out to YOU to embody their essence)
[Journal what you took from today's workout. What you want to remember. What you want to work on, expand on]

WORKOUT COMPLETED ✓

EXAMPLE
15-MINUTE WORKOUT SCRIPT ANALYSIS

Title: The Unspoken
INT. OLD CHURCH HALLWAY - DAY
The hallway is dimly lit, filled with hushed tones and somber faces. LUCAS (mid-30s, stoic and introspective) stands alone, looking at a family photo. ELLA (early 30s, resilient but visibly emotional) approaches hesitantly.

ELLA
Lucas?

Lucas turns, surprised. A moment of recognition, then a guarded expression settles in.

LUCAS
(after a moment)
Ella?

Ella nods, the weight of the moment heavy on her.

ELLA
I know... I didn't expect my first meeting with my brother to be—

LUCAS
At our parents' funeral...

Ella steps closer, a mix of hope and uncertainty.

ELLA
Yeah. That.
(Long beat)
Did you know?

LUCAS
Did I know what?

ELLA
About me. That I existed?

Off of her surprise, Lucas hugs her tight.

LUCAS
Of course not. I don't know why they kept it—You, from me either.

ELLA
I do.

Clearly, it's not a happy story. Lucas can see Ella has been through so much. After a tense moment.

ELLA (cont'd)
But.. Maybe today isn't the best—

LUCAS
No. It's okay. I want to hear it. If... You want to tell me.

Ella has never trusted someone so quickly... She doesn't say anything just nods and they walk down the long path through the cemetery... A lifetime to talk about.

WORKOUT COMPLETED [✓]

RELATIONSHIP and SPECIFICITY

INT. OLD CHURCH: Same church I was baptized. Same musty smell too. I used to like this place... Not today.
DAY: Feels like the longest day in the world. I just want it to be night so I can go to sleep.
Dimly Lit: Matches the way I feel... People just look like "shadows."
Hushed tones and somber faces: People crying. Holding each other. Looking at me and talking about me.
Family photo: This is all I'm looking at though. I remember that day at the zoo. On my dad's shoulders. My mom biting my foot pretending to be a lion because I was so sad the enclosure was closed. She made me laugh so much... I loved this day.
ELLA: I was told about her yesterday by my aunt. My dad had a child before I was born with another woman. My mom knew, apparently too and they never told me. WHY wouldn't they tell me...
Surprised: This woman is just staring at me... Wait.. My aunt showed me a picture of Ella and...
Recognition: That's her. She has my dad's nose.
Guarded expression: It hurts to see my dad in you. I don't know what to say or how to do this. Especially today.
First meeting: Overwhelmed with so many emotions and thoughts.
My brother: I always wanted a sibling. To hear someone say "my brother" means a lot. When my parents died I thought it was only me now, but there's *you*.
Parent's funeral: The worst day of my life. They died in a car crash. Died on impact apparently. On the way back from their favourite vacation spot. I'm really grateful they were together... Closed Caskett because the bodies were too mangled.
That I existed: Of course I didn't. I would have found you.
I do: Woah... I can tell this isn't good. I'm scared to hear it.
I want to hear it: I don't care how scared I am. I'm your big brother. You're my little sister and I want you in my life. That feeling beats my fear.
Nods: Relief and Joy on the darkest day. She wants to be family.
OBJECTIVE: Get through this day as fast as possible. **WIN or LOSE:** Lose, but for a wonderful reason. I get to get to know my sister. **WHO** is in the scene: I am Lucas. Ella, extended family, a bunch of people I don't know, my parents, Sarah and Neal, in their closed casket.
WHAT is happening: My parents have died suddenly in a brutal car crash and my sister who I didn't even know about till yesterday, showed up at the funeral. **WHERE:** Back in my home town I haven't been to in 10 years. The Church I was baptized in. **WHEN:** Present day. 1 pm in the afternoon. Time has never moved so slowly. **EXTRA:** My secret is I don't know why I hate my parents at this moment... For leaving me alone? For lying to me for my whole life that I have a sister?

TIPS FOR SUCCESS
HOW TO MAKE THIS BOOK AS EFFECTIVE AS POSSIBLE

COMMITMENT TO THIS DAILY WORKOUT: Professional athletes spend on average, 20-40 hours <u>a week</u> training. Youth athletes spend 5-10 hours.

It looks like an intimidating number, but it's the truth. Now ask yourself and be honest: *"How many hours a week do I practice?"* and *"How good do I want to be?"*

These are 15-minute workouts. Seven days a week adds up to a total of 1.75 hours per week. That's it. But, after six months you'll have an extra 45 hours of training.

Our training as actors include classes, workshops, audition prep, auditions, working on set or stage, even watching TV/film/documentaries intentionally, etc This career can be extremely difficult to train *that* many hours, especially on our own. So, what do we do? We have to create a structure for ourselves. Allow this book to help.

Simply **having a goal** and **following a checklist** can have a powerful effect on our success. Goals give us direction and purpose. They can act as a compass, guiding your actions and decisions towards a defined endpoint. Without goals, efforts can become scattered and unproductive, but with them, every step you take is a step closer to your dream. The checklist provided gives us measurable progress and accomplishment. Even if it's only a small checkmark every day.

Just like the train metaphor, it will start slow but you will gain momentum if you continue to move forward every day. Success is also a habit. Start small—Only a simple checkmark and watch how the momentum of "every day" affects your career.

TIP: THERE WAS A STUDY AND THEORY BY DR. EDWIN LOCKE AND DR. GARY LATHAM THAT <u>SETTING HIGH, CHALLENGING GOALS</u> (SOMETIMES PERCEIVED AS UNATTAINABLE) ENCOURAGES GREATER EFFORT, FOCUS, PERSISTENCE, AND MOTIVATION, LEADING TO BETTER PERFORMANCE OUTCOMES. **THESE TYPES OF GOALS CAN PUSH INDIVIDUALS OUT OF THEIR COMFORT ZONES, FORCING THEM TO INNOVATE AND THINK CREATIVELY.**

TIPS FOR SUCCESS
HOW TO MAKE THIS BOOK AS EFFECTIVE AS POSSIBLE

DREAM BIG: Don't be afraid to make an audacious goal. **REMEMBER:** If you don't achieve it, take a step back and *look at what you did achieve*. If your goal was audacious and almost certainly unattainable, you'll most likely have accomplished a lot more than you would have if your goal was "realistic". *Sometimes,* you'll even surprise yourself and achieve that "unattainable" goal and you will realize the purpose of a goal and the power of a dream.

"Combine your GOAL with your WHY and you have a recipe for motivation and success."

YOUR "WHY": One of the most effective and important tools is finding your WHY and reminding yourself of it every day. Especially the days that get tough. When your WHY is clear and specific, it has the most profound effect on your focus and drive. "He who has a why to live can bear almost any how" - Friedrich Nietzsche

GENERAL VS SPECIFIC: My 'why' is I want to be a movie star and win an Oscar. *OR*: I want to give people what movies gave me. Hope, love, fantasy and escape. I want someone to walk up to me, shake my hand and say, "Thank you for helping me." When I win my Oscar, I see my wife, kids and mom sitting in the front row."

Be as specific as you can.
Write it out fully then simplify it into a few words or a sentence.
Change it as it evolves.

MY WHY

_____
_____
_____
_____
_____
_____
_____
_____
_____
_____
_____

TIPS FOR SUCCESS
HOW TO MAKE THIS BOOK AS EFFECTIVE AS POSSIBLE

GOALS: Goals help us focus. *They are lighthouses.* There are so many ways to reach the lighthouse and every journey will change, but you will always know where you are headed if you have a goal. Without it, you can become a ship lost at sea. The more specific you become with your goals, the journey becomes simple. Not easy; nothing worth it is, but *simple*. It's like putting on horse blinders. **The more specific your goal, that's all you can see.**

GOAL EXAMPLES: > Work on my memory > Strengthen my emotions > New headshots
ACTION STEP(s) are how and what you will do to achieve this goal.
 > Buy memory book Moonwalking with Einstein > Set daily alarm to do an emotional exercise > Call Ashleyross Studios and set up an appointment

In order of Importance
MY GOALS

1.

    Action Step(s):

2.

    Action Step(s):

3.

    Action Step(s):

4.

    Action Step(s):

TIPS FOR SUCCESS
HOW TO MAKE THIS BOOK AS EFFECTIVE AS POSSIBLE

PERFORMANCE STRATEGY 14-DAY REVIEW
Every 14 workouts/days there will be a *Performance Strategy and Review*. You will fill it out before the first workout in order to help with focus and your awareness of yourself as an artist.

I found that most self-help, educational books I've read, give you a wonderful idea and a powerful transformation tool, but rarely give you the practical application to apply their concept to your day-to-day life and create a new habit.

Anders Ericsson has a brilliant book called PEAK (Ericsson, K. Anders, and Robert Pool. 2016. Peak: Secrets from the New Science of Expertise) where he talks about "deliberate practice." It's about pushing beyond one's comfort zone, receiving immediate feedback, and <u>continuously refining one's technique.</u> It's not just repetition but a mindful and systematic approach to skill improvement.

This **Checklist, Daily Discovery Journal and 14-Day Strategy Review** will help with that style of skill improvement with an ongoing evaluation of *where you are now, where you are going and how you will get there.* It will also help you develop the new habit of *"sharpening your tools".*

I love that story of the two men chopping wood. One worked non-stop all day, not even a break for lunch. The other chopped steadily but took a brief break every hour. The first man thought to himself, he would surely chop more. However, at the end of the day, the second man had chopped significantly more wood. Confused, he asked, "How!? You were taking breaks and I worked so much harder and longer!" The second man replied, "I wasn't just taking breaks. *I was sharpening my axe."*

Taking the time to maintain your tools/skills can lead to greater efficiency and better results. It's not always the quantity of work but the quality and effectiveness of that work that matters most.

TIPS FOR SUCCESS
HOW TO MAKE THIS BOOK AS EFFECTIVE AS POSSIBLE

CREATING A NEW HABIT: They say a habit takes 21 days to form and 66 days to become automatic. Turn this quick workout into a daily habit and make it a part of your lifestyle. You may have a strategy that works best for you but here is a great starting point to add to your daily routine.

- [ ] After you find your **WHY** and have your specific **GOALS, write them again on a separate piece of paper** and **make sure you can see them every day.** "Out of sight, out of mind." Simple but powerful.

- [ ] **Set a daily alarm** on your phone, *reminding* you to workout.

- [ ] **Use the CHECKLIST** on the next page as you go through these workouts. This visual representation can be a powerful motivator when you see your accomplishments build over time.

- [ ] **Use the PERFORMANCE STRATEGY 14-DAY REVIEW** diligently. Like a map to your ultimate goal and be as specific as you can. Clarity will make your path simple; Again, not easy, but simple, if you know where you are and where you want to go.

Eventually, this will become automatic.
Success is also a habit.

TIP: USE THIS STRATEGY IN ALL ASPECTS OF YOUR CAREER, ESPECIALLY FOR YOUR TEACHERS / COACHES / DIRECTORS. TALK TO THEM BEFORE AND BE AWARE AND VULNERABLE ENOUGH TO LET THEM KNOW EXACTLY WHO YOU ARE AND WHAT YOU ARE WORKING ON RIGHT NOW AS AN ACTOR. IT WILL HELP YOU BE DELIBERATE IN YOUR WORK AND ALLOW THEM TO DO THEIR JOB THE BEST THEY CAN. **REMEMBER**: YOU ARE A BEAUTIFULLY IMPERFECT INSTRUMENT. KNOW YOUR INSTRUMENT AS BEST YOU CAN SO YOU CAN CREATE SYMPHONY BETWEEN YOU AND YOUR TEAM.

Now get after it!! It's going to take work but go get your dreams.

CHECKLIST

GOAL
WORKOUTS PER WEEK: ☐

MONTH ONE
- ☐ WEEK 1
- ☐ WEEK 2
- ☐ WEEK 3
- ☐ WEEK 4

MONTHLY GOAL
ALL 4 WEEKS ☐

MONTH TWO
- ☐ WEEK 1
- ☐ WEEK 2
- ☐ WEEK 3
- ☐ WEEK 4

MONTHLY GOAL
ALL 4 WEEKS ☐

MONTH THREE
- ☐ WEEK 1
- ☐ WEEK 2
- ☐ WEEK 3
- ☐ WEEK 4

MONTHLY GOAL
ALL 4 WEEKS ☐

MONTH FOUR
- ☐ WEEK 1
- ☐ WEEK 2
- ☐ WEEK 3
- ☐ WEEK 4

MONTHLY GOAL
ALL 4 WEEKS ☐

MONTH FIVE
- ☐ WEEK 1
- ☐ WEEK 2
- ☐ WEEK 3
- ☐ WEEK 4

MONTHLY GOAL
ALL 4 WEEKS ☐

MONTH SIX
- ☐ WEEK 1
- ☐ WEEK 2
- ☐ WEEK 3
- ☐ WEEK 4

MONTHLY GOAL
ALL 4 WEEKS ☐

BELIEVE

PERFORMANCE STRATEGY

DAY ONE CHECK IN

TAKE A MOMENT OF REFLECTION AND BREAKDOWN WHERE YOU ARE RIGHT NOW IN YOUR CAREER AND AS AN ACTOR.
THE MORE SPECIFIC YOU ARE THE MORE CLEAR YOU CAN SEE WHERE YOU ARE NOW SO YOU CAN GET TO WHERE YOU WANT TO GO FASTER

★ ★ ★ ★ ★

Viola Davis, growing up in poverty and facing numerous challenges, honed her acting skills in theatre. Her perseverance and talent led to breakthrough roles in film and television, making her the first black actress to win the Triple Crown of Acting: an Oscar, an Emmy, and a Tony.

DATE:

BREAKDOWN WHERE YOU ARE RIGHT NOW AS AN ACTOR - WHAT YOU ARE GREAT AT, WHAT YOU ARE WORKING ON NOW OR NEED TO WORK ON ETC.

STRENGTHS:

WEAKNESSES:

IMPROVEMENT STRATEGY
HOW CAN YOU IMPROVE ON THESE AREAS FOR THE NEXT 14 DAYS:

GOAL FOR THE NEXT 14 EXERCISES
THE MORE SPECIFIC YOU ARE THE GREATER THE RESULT

Action Step(s):

If you hook into the character's belief system and you believe it 100%, there is no way the audience won't.
Meryl Streep

MY WHY:

GOAL(s):

PHYSICAL WARMUP - 1 minute [Set Timer]
Freeform Dance: Put on some music and engage in freeform dancing. Allow your body to move spontaneously and without inhibition. This can help you tap into your creative instincts and develop physical expressiveness. **Tip**: Try music you've never listened to.

VOCAL WARMUP - 3 minutes [Set Timer]
Humming Waves: Hum an 'M' sound gently, starting at a low pitch and sliding up to a high pitch and back down. **Tip**: Feel the vibration in your lips and face, which helps to warm up the resonators.

EMOTIONAL RECALL - 5 minutes [Set Timer]
Childhood Wonder: Recall a moment from your childhood when you felt a sense of wonder and awe. **Tip:** Let your imagination reignite as you re-experience this moment through a child's eyes.

ANIMAL WORK - CAT

Research - 2 minutes [Set Timer]
Use this time to observe/research a cat's behaviour, movements, and sounds.

Animal Exercise - 3 minutes [Set Timer]
Begin by embodying the cat, from its quiet stalking to its sudden pounces and relaxed lounging. Transition gradually into human form while retaining feline grace and alertness.

Discovery Journal - 1 Minute [Set Timer]
3 Main Characteristics: (Whatever stands out to YOU to embody the essence)

_____
_____
_____
_____
_____
_____
_____
_____

WORKOUT COMPLETED [ ]

To live truthfully onstage and effectively
perform your action you must learn to
embrace each moment as it actually occurs,
NOT as you would like it to be.
A practical handbook for the actor

SCRIPT ANALYSIS for **RELATIONSHIPS & SPECIFICITY** - 15 minutes [Set Timer]
Choose your character then **circle everything in this script you have a relationship with**. That includes people, places, things, smells, time of day etc. On a separate piece of paper **write what your relationship with those items are** and **be specific**. The more specific and fun you have with your relationships, the more interesting your characters will be and the more fun the audience has. **Tip:** Everything isn't necessarily in the scene. Use your imagination to what you could add that would help the scene, <u>only if</u> it's contextually appropriate, helping tell the story. **Extra:** Write your > **Objective**, if you **win or lose**. Who What Where When and Why. **Who** is in the scene, **what** is happening, **where** are you, **when** does this take place(year, time of day) and **why** is your character doing what they are doing? Like in so many auditions, If it's not clear, make it up and be specific.

Title: **The Final Edition**
INT. NEWSROOM - EVENING
The newsroom is a hive of activity. Phones ring, keyboards clack. MORGAN (mid-30s, focused and assertive) is at their desk. TAYLOR (enthusiastic and determined) rushes in

TAYLOR
Morgan, you need to see this. I've got something big.
Morgan continues working, not looking up.
MORGAN
If it's not the Pentagon calling to surrender, it can wait.
TAYLOR
It's about the mayor. I found something...
Morgan finally looks up...
TAYLOR (cont'd)
Look at these transactions. There's a pattern of kickbacks.
MORGAN
Jesus. You're talking about accusing the mayor of corruption.
TAYLOR
Yes. We have a responsibility.
MORGAN
Responsibility. Do you know what happens if we're wrong? We don't just lose credibility, we lose everything.
TAYLOR
But if we're right, we change the game. Isn't that why we're here?
Morgan stands, circling the desk.
MORGAN
Idealism is a luxury, Taylor. This is the real world. It's messy and complicated.
TAYLOR
And that's exactly why we need to pursue this. To untangle the mess... We can't ignore it anymore.
MORGAN
You remind me of myself, once. But here's a lesson - truth is a double-edged sword. It protects and it pierces.
TAYLOR
I'd rather hold the sword than be cut by it.
Morgan is on a tightrope. The weight of morality on his shoulders. After a long moment...
MORGAN
Okay. We run with your story. But we do it right. No shortcuts.
TAYLOR
You won't regret this.
Morgan half-smiles, a hint of worry.
MORGAN
I already do.

WORKOUT COMPLETED [ ]

If you do the things that others won't,
you'll have everything they never will.
DAD - 2006
Victor Zinck Sr.

IMAGINATION

We have a lot of tools in our arsenal as actors but **I believe imagination is the most powerful.** "If you hook into the character's belief system and you believe it 100%, there is no way the audience won't." - Meryl Streep "Imagination is more important than knowledge for knowledge is limited. - Einstein. Everyone has an Imagination but it must be worked out to get stronger. Think of your imagination as a limitless playground. In this space, you can be anyone, go anywhere, and do anything. **Have the courage to allow yourself to play!**

Solo Imaginary World Exploration - 6 Minutes [Set Timer]

Find a quiet space to relax and focus. **Close your eyes** and **let your imagination run wild. Tip:** Engage all your senses to explore this environment. Touch, taste, smell etc. Allow your emotions to guide you. **Extra:** After you establish this world in your imagination, you could introduce characters and have a dialogue with them. Are they friends or foes?

IMAGINARY WORLD: Underwater Atlantis: A breathtaking underwater city filled with shimmering bioluminescent plants, mysterious ancient ruins, and curious sea creatures.

JOURNAL YOUR EXPERIENCE - 2 Minutes [Set Timer]

___
___
___
___
___
___
___

Your Characters Filter - 5 Minutes [Set Timer]

Everyone including the characters you play see the world through their own specific perspective/filter. I like to use the word filter because you can take out a filter, clean it, change its style, colour, an optimist or a pessimist, comedian or a nihilist, etc. **Find a quiet space** to focus. **Close your eyes and let go of your personal thoughts and emotions** to make space for your characters. **Open your eyes, and allow the filter provided to affect everything around you. Tip**: Explore wherever you are and interact with the objects. **Extra:** How does *this* character walk and move in their world?

FILTER: Eternal Optimist: Sees the good in everything and every situation, no matter how dire or mundane. There is always something positive and exciting.

JOURNAL YOUR EXPERIENCE - 2 Minutes [Set Timer]

___
___
___
___
___

WORKOUT COMPLETED [ ]

Stay true to yourself and your artistic vision. Don't compromise your authenticity for anyone or anything.
Tom Hardy

CHARACTER STUDY "PEOPLE WATCHING"

Actors are required to portray characters that are believable and relatable. You don't have to agree with them but you have to understand them. Walk like them, talk like them, see the world like them. So, in order to fill our toolbox, we have to **go out into the world and study.** Then practice them over and over so we can "walk in their shoes', comfortably and confidently. Study their movements, mannerisms, the "vibe" they give off, the clothes they wear etc. **Fill your toolbox with the rhythms and idiosyncrasies of human behaviour.**

OBSERVATION CHARACTER STUDY - 15 Minutes [Set Timer]

Find a busy place where you can **sit and observe.** Choose anyone you find interesting. **Write down what stands out about them**. *The way they sit, drink their coffee, walk, talk, interact with others etc.* **Tip: Mirror them immediately**. This will help memorize the feeling of that character so whenever you come back to these characters you're discovering, your body will remember. **Extra:** Before you go to sleep, read over the characters from today and reenact their movements.

_____
_____
_____
_____
_____
_____
_____
_____
_____
_____
_____
_____
_____
_____
_____
_____
_____
_____
_____
_____
_____
_____

COLOURS: We as humans respond to colours like frequencies. If you pay attention closely, you can see everyone has their own 'colour' that defines their core. An essence that informs how they operate and move through the world.

WHAT COLOUR ARE THEY:

WORKOUT COMPLETED [ ]

What if I fall? Oh, but my darling,
what if you fly?
Erin Hanson, We Bought a Zoo

VOICE & DICTION

I wish I had learned this earlier; the confidence to communicate clearly and powerfully is a game-changer for you as an actor. **Think of your voice as a musical instrument that needs regular tuning. This workout is your daily tuning session,** ensuring that your instrument is always ready. "The word 'theatre' comes from the Greeks. It means the seeing place. It is the place people come to see the truth about life and the social situation." - Stella Adler. Embrace this workout as a key to unlocking and portraying *that* truth by letting your voice be the vehicle that transports your audience into the heart of your story.

READ PASSAGE - 30 Seconds [Set Timer]
Speak the passage and take note of its quality. **Tip**: Record Audio to compare afterward.

> "In the heart of the valley, where the river flows gently beneath the sunlit sky, the echoes of nature's symphony create a melody of peace and serenity. Amidst the rustling leaves and the chirping birds, there lies a world untouched by time, a sanctuary where every whisper of the wind tells a timeless tale."

RELAXATION - 1 Minute [Set Timer]
Deep Breathing: Sit and Inhale deeply through your nose, filling your lungs, then exhale slowly through your mouth. Imagine stress leaving your body with each breath.

Nay Nay Nay - 1 Minute [Set Timer]
Pick a song and sing the word "Nay" repeatedly. Start with a comfortable pitch and gradually move the sound from your nose to your chest, ensuring each "Nay" is clear and resonant. Stretch your range as best you can to strengthen.

Sustained 'S' - 2 Minutes [Set Timer]
Inhale deeply and then exhale slowly, making a continuous 's' sound. Keep the sound as even and steady as you can. Always push a little longer than you think you can.

Vowel Pronunciation Drill - 2 Minutes [Set Timer]
Slowly go through each vowel sound **(A, E, I, O, U), holding and exaggerating each sound. Combine them with consonants** (e.g., ba, be, bi, bo, bu). Pay attention to the clarity and sharpness of each sound. Repeat a few times before moving to the next.

Lip Trills - 3 minutes - [Set timer]
Close your lips together lightly, like you're going to blow a raspberry. Then, blow air through your closed lips while making sounds. You should feel a tickling sensation. Pick a song and Lip Trill the whole along with it. **Tip**: Stretch your range as much as you can and pick a song you've never listened to.

The Cork Exercise - 4 Minutes [Set Timer]
Place a cork between your teeth and try to read a passage aloud. This forces your articulation muscles to work harder. If you don't have a cork, bite down gently on your thumb. You can use the following text for this exercise:

READ PASSAGE AGAIN - 30 Seconds [Set Timer]
Speak the passage and take note of its quality. **Tip**: Record Audio to compare.

Discovery Journal - 1 Minute [Set Timer]

_____
_____
_____

WORKOUT COMPLETED [ ]

You don't yell at a bud because it's
not a flower yet.
Larry Moss

SUBTEXT

Subtext is what lies beneath the surface of our words. It's the hidden layer of meaning, driven by the character's internal thoughts, emotions, desires, and motivations. Subtext is one of my favourite things as an actor because so much can be said with one simple line of dialogue. The power of "Hello" can be exciting if you told that person years ago "If I ever see you again, I'll kill you. Maybe it's the most beautiful person you've ever seen. Now, say "hello". *Subtext* shows the audience what your relationship with the characters/places/situations are, without having to explain it. We experience it every day and it is our job to create characters that interact as we do.

VOCAL WORK - 3 minutes - [Set Timer]

Lip Trills: Close your lips together lightly, like you're going to blow a raspberry. Then, blow air through your closed lips while making sounds. You should feel a tickling sensation. Pick a song and Lip Trill along with it. **Tip**: Stretch your range as much as you can and pick a song you've never listened to.

SUBTEXT PRACTICE

Use the line of dialogue provided and practice each of these subtexts **out loud.** Move on to the next, only when you believe yourself. Trust that you will know when *that* is. Before you begin, **pick a spot to look at and imagine** in detail, **who you are speaking with**. **Tip**: *Sometimes* we mean exactly what we are saying. Look for that too. **Extra**: Substitute someone you have a strong relationship with in real life, good or bad, and see it's affect.

Initial Line: "Did you hear about the park renovation downtown?"
Your Response Line: "Yeah, I heard. It's interesting, isn't it? Turning that space into something... I don't know, alive. It kind of reminds me of when we were kids, all the time we spent there. Maybe we should check it out once it's done, for old times' sake?"

SUBTEXTS - 6 Minutes [Set Timer]
[ ] Plotting revenge: You know they slept with your spouse.
[ ] Sarcastic: You're unimpressed and find the hype overblown.
[ ] Enthusiastic: You can't wait to try it out and love new places.
[ ] Apathetic: You don't really care about new places in town.
[ ] Skeptical: You doubt it'll be as good as people say.
[ ] Your Own Subtext

RELATIONSHIP SUBTEXTS - 6 Minutes [Set Timer]
[ ] Proud Sibling: You're bursting with pride that they designed the renovation!
[ ] Rival Classmate: You're competitive and feel a bit outdone by their success.
[ ] Inspiring Teacher: You're fulfilled to see your guidance come to fruition.
[ ] Indifferent Neighbour: You acknowledge their success but don't really care.
[ ] Unsupportive Partner: You've always been critical of their writing ambitions.
[ ] Your Own Subtext

Discovery Journal

_____
_____
_____

WORKOUT COMPLETED [ ]

Stay hungry for knowledge and always seek to expand your skills. The more you learn, the more versatile you become.
Mahershala Ali

EMOTIONS

The 'moment before', **the emotional preparation, is the most important key to a great scene.** If you start any scene <u>without</u> an emotional preparation it feels like trying to drive a car in neutral. The preparation is the uphill climb of every rollercoaster; Once you grind all the way to the top, the chains let go and the rest of the ride takes care of itself. "No one wants to see a play or a movie and look at technical proficiency. You want to be moved, you want a human experience, you want to feel less alone" - Viola Davis. **Practice your emotions over and over** so when it's time, you aren't worried "Will I get there?" **You're imagination and emotions should be a tinderbox, so easy to light up. All it take is half a spark.**

EULOGY - 12 Minutes [Set Timer]

Find a quiet comfortable space. Choose someone in your life who is alive and important to you. Create an imaginary reason for why they have died. Now start from the point of the phone call— Imagine who calls, what they say and what you say. Eventually find yourself at the funeral, about to begin the eulogy. See the casket, is it open or closed?? What is that person wearing and any other details for yourself. Before you begin to speak, look into the audience and see who is there- Family, friends etc **Then begin the eulogy.** **Tip**: <u>Be as specific as you can with everything.</u> **Inside of specificity is where you will find the triggers to your heart.** Let your imagination take you wherever you want in this exercise. **Example**: Placing her favourite sheep stuffed animal in the casket, tucked under her arm like she always held it, then kissing her goodbye one last time.

DISCOVERY JOURNAL - 3 Minutes [Set Timer]

Make sure to **include the specific triggers** you experience because you can use these **TRIGGER MOMENTS** in the future instead of repeating the *entire* exercise.

WORKOUT COMPLETED [ ]

The more risks you take, the more you'll learn about yourself and your craft. Don't be afraid to step outside of your comfort zone.
Rachel McAdams

THE CORK EXERCISE - 4 Minutes [Set Timer]
Place a cork between your teeth and read a passage aloud. This forces your articulation muscles to work harder. If you don't have a cork, bite down gently on your thumb. You can use the following text for this exercise:

> "As twilight falls, the bustling city begins to wind down. Streetlights flicker on, casting a warm glow on the pavements. In the distance, the gentle hum of traffic blends with the evening breeze, creating a symphony of urban life. Shadows lengthen, embracing the city in a cloak of dusk, while the stars above start to twinkle, heralding the arrival of night."

WRITE A LETTER - 10 Minutes [Set Timer]
Get a piece of paper or write this in your device. **Take a moment to let this situation and relationship sink in**. Then let your imagination run wild and **write them a letter.**

Your Character: Jordan, a once-aspiring artist who chose a stable career in law, now filled with regret and resignation.
Other Character: Alex, your younger sibling, a passionate and struggling artist, who feels betrayed by your decision.

Relationship: Jordan and Alex were once united in their shared dream of artistic success. However, Jordan's shift to a practical career path in law caused a deep divide between them, with Alex viewing this as a profound betrayal.

Context of the Letter: Seeing Alex's continued struggle and wanting to spare them further pain, you decide to write a letter. In this letter, you assertively express your belief that Alex should abandon their artistic dream for a more secure and stable career. It's a message born from your own experiences and the desire to protect your sibling, even if it means challenging their dreams and aspirations.

Discovery Journal - 1 minute [Set Timer]
_____
_____
_____
_____
_____
_____
_____

WORKOUT COMPLETED [ ]

I had to give up on their remedies. They kept trying to make me less angry. But I refuse to surrender my rage. So now I love my tinderbox heart. So easy to light up. All it takes is half a spark.
Nikita Gill

VOCAL WORK - 3 minutes [Set timer]
Lip Trills: Close your lips together lightly, like you're going to blow a raspberry. Then, blow air through your closed lips while making sounds. You should feel a tickling sensation. Pick a song and Lip Trill along with it. **Tip**: Stretch your range as much as you can and pick a song you've never listened to.

VERBAL IMPROV - 10 Minutes [Set Timer]

Find a space where you are comfortable and free to express yourself. Take a moment to **let this situation, character and prompt, sink in**. Then let your imagination run wild: **Picture who you are talking to** then **begin with the prompt** and **continue to verbalize everything** this character would say. **Tip**: This is exploration! There is no "getting it right". BE BRAVE to explore and discover.

Character: Jordan, a long-suffering assistant who has been loyally covering for their boss's repeated mistakes and unprofessional behaviour. After a particularly egregious incident that threatened Jordan's own job security, they've reached their limit and are confronting their boss for the first time.

Prompt: "You know what? I'm done making excuses for you."

Who are you talking to:

Describe them in two specific words:

Discovery Journal - 2 minutes [Set Timer]

_____
_____
_____
_____
_____
_____
_____
_____
_____
_____
_____
_____
_____

WORKOUT COMPLETED [ ]

Simplicity is the ultimate sophistication.
Leonardo da Vinci

SELF AWARENESS
The more you understand yourself, the more you are able to understand and develop your characters. Like you, your characters have thoughts, beliefs, traumas, passions etc. When you become aware of your own and start to see how those experiences and beliefs have shaped your life, how you operate and view the world, then you can develop your characters that are much more rich and vivid.

PHYSICAL WARMUP - 2 minutes [Set Timer]
Freeform Dance: Put on some music and engage in freeform dancing. Allow your body to move spontaneously and without inhibition. This can help you tap into your creative instincts and develop physical expressiveness. **Tip**: Try music you've never listened to.

CURRENT EMOTIONAL INVENTORY - 3 Minutes [Set Timer]
Write down and **record your current emotions**. Identify what you're feeling at this moment and why. **Tip**: Be as specific as you can, **don't disregard anything.** You can also **scan your body** to see how and where your current emotion is affecting you. Your posture, the way you walk, bouncing foot, sore neck etc

CURRENT EMOTIONAL STATE:

SELF DISCOVERY QUESTIONS - 10 Minutes [Set Timer]
I suggest a journal or writing it in your phone's notes so you don't run out of space here.

What are three words I would use to describe myself?

What are my strongest emotions, and how do they influence me?

WORKOUT COMPLETED [ ]

If I had asked people what they wanted,
they would have said faster horses.
Henry Ford

IMAGINATION

We have a lot of tools in our arsenal as actors but I believe imagination is the most powerful. "If you hook into the character's belief system and you believe it 100%, there is no way the audience won't." - Meryl Streep. Everyone has an Imagination but it must be worked out to get stronger. Think of your imagination as a limitless playground. In this space, you can be anyone, go anywhere, and do anything. **Have the courage to allow yourself to play!**

VOCAL WORK - 2 Minutes - [Set timer]
Lip Trills: Close your lips together lightly, like you're going to blow a raspberry. Then, blow air through your closed lips while making sounds. You should feel a tickling sensation. Pick a song and Lip Trill along with it. **Tip**: Stretch your range as much as you can and pick a song you've never listened to.

IMPROVISED STORYTELLING - 5 Minutes [Set Timer]
Speak out the scenario provided and continue the story! Focus on vivid details, character development and how the main character overcomes the main obstacle. **Tip**: Try not to stop speaking so you don't have time to "think". Allow your imagination to keep moving forward without interruption. **Tip:** Record these stories on your device, in case it's great but more importantly to see your progress as you go on.

STARTING POINT: You are Alex, a young aspiring photographer who has just inherited a mysterious, old camera from your late grandfather, a renowned but reclusive photojournalist. As you start using this camera, you discover that it has an unusual ability: every time you take a photo of a place, the camera reveals—

IMAGINARY WORLD EXPLORATION - 6 Minutes [Set Timer]

Find a quiet space to relax and focus. **Close your eyes** and let your imagination run wild. **Tip:** Engage all your senses to explore this environment. Touch, taste, smell etc and allow your emotions to guide you. **Extra:** After you explore this world with your senses, you could introduce characters and have a dialogue with them. Are they friends or foes?

IMAGINARY WORLD: THE WHISPERING MEADOW - Imagine a vast, open meadow with a gentle breeze that carries with it the whispers of memories. You stand in the midst of this serene landscape, surrounded by vibrant wildflowers.

JOURNAL YOUR EXPERIENCE - 2 Minutes [Set Timer]

_____
_____
_____
_____
_____
_____
_____
_____

WORKOUT COMPLETED [ ]

You can't depend on your eyes when your
imagination is out of focus.
Mark Twain

ANCHORING INTO YOUR CHARACTER COLOUR & MUSIC

Anchoring yourself into your character is vital. It's one of the most freeing feelings when you understand their *essence* because everything they do, how they do it and what their purpose is, becomes so clear to you and the audience. Every choice you make after you find your *anchor*, feels easy, because you're acting from who and what your character is at the core. You can call it an essence, an aura, vibe, energy etc. We all have it and feel it from everyone around us. There are many ways into your character but music and colour are my favourite. Music can inform the script, your character, even each scene. Colours, I think you will find, can work incredibly because we as humans respond to colours like frequencies. Colours evoke many feelings and if you pay attention closely, you can see everyone has their own 'colour' that defines their core. An essence that informs how they operate and move through the world.

THEIR COLOUR - 2 Minutes [Set Timer]
Think of **someone you know**, and **define them with a colour**. **Tip**: Trust yourself. Your initial colour is usually close. **Tip**: Start with basic colours then eventually become much more specific. **Example**: Corinna is an earthy green with rays of sunlight flowing through the green. **Extra**: Ask someone who knows *that person* as well, what they think this person's colour is and why. See how close your answers are or not.

YOUR CHARACTERS COLOUR
Read the given character description just as you would an audition, **assign a colour to that character.** Now take that colour you chose and **allow it to infuse into your entire body**, affecting your every move, your speaking, the way you see the world etc. **Take any book** you have, flip to a random page and **read the text as this Colour/Character**. **Tip**: Be specific, choose a colour that excites you and don't be afraid to get creative.

CHARACTER DESCRIPTION: [JORDAN] Mid-20s, Jordan has a unique obsession with collecting and immersing themselves in books, transforming their small apartment into a labyrinth of literary treasures. They are introverted but come alive with animated passion when discussing literature, often dreaming of writing their own novel. Jordan wears vintage glasses, a constant companion that further accentuates their scholarly demeanour. This role requires a deep love for books, introspection, and a subtle yet expressive range of emotions, embodying a sense of wonder and a rich inner world.

CHOOSE THEIR COLOUR - 4 Minutes [Set Timer]
THEIR COLOUR:

CHOOSE THEIR SONG - 4 Minutes [Set Timer]
THEIR SONG:

READ PASSAGE FROM BOOK - 2 Minutes [Set Timer]

FREEFORM DANCE - 2 minutes - [Set Timer]
Put on the selected music and **engage in freeform dancing, anchored in your colour/character,** Allow your body to move spontaneously and without inhibition. This can help you tap into your creative instincts and develop physical expressiveness *while staying in character.* **Tip**: Journal about the differences as opposed to how you normally dance.

JOURNAL YOUR EXPERIENCE - 1 Minute [Set Timer]
_____
_____
_____
_____

WORKOUT COMPLETED [ ]

The word theatre comes from the Greeks. It means the seeing place. It is the place people come to see the truth about life and the social situation.
Stella Adler

HISTORICAL RESEARCH

We are in the information era and have access to the world and its rich history at our fingertips. This exploration is not about 'learning facts'; it's a journey to the heart of human experience. The empathy and the understanding, especially on the things you disagree with, are incredibly valuable. If you look closely, you'll find the way people think, at different times in history, their attitudes, choices, and the way they move their bodies can teach you so much about us, right now. Fill your toolbox so it's overflowing with information and ideas to pull from so your imagination has so much to play with.

PHYSICAL WARMUP - 2 minutes - [Set Timer]
Freeform Dance: Put on some music and engage in freeform dancing. Allow your body to move spontaneously and without inhibition. This can help you tap into your creative instincts and develop physical expressiveness. **Tip**: Try music you've never listened to.

RESEARCH - 13 Minutes [Set Timer]
YouTube, streaming platforms, the internet or books, **research the given era/person/moment in time,** journal or make notes on your device, so when you want to find this information, it's organized and readily accessible. As you go, **write anything and everything _you_ find fascinating. Tip:** If the topic doesn't interest you, choose your own, or take a chance and still research it, but from a different perspective. Physicalities, voice, ideals, etc. Trust your body that when you see something interesting, you'll know. **Extra**: Speak it out and copy their movements. Our memory recall is massively affected by our bodies. Be specific and when you re-read your notes, you'll be amazed by how much your mind and body remember.

TOPIC:
The Lost Colony of Roanoke (1585): A significant yet mysterious event in early American history, this colony was one of the first English settlements in the New World. After initial establishment and interaction with native tribes, the colony's leader, John White, returned from a supply trip to England to find it completely deserted, with no trace of the settlers except the word "CROATOAN" carved into a post. The fate of the Roanoke colonists remains one of the greatest mysteries in American history.

_____
_____
_____
_____
_____
_____
_____
_____
_____
_____

WORKOUT COMPLETED [ ]

Our greatest weakness lies in giving up. The most certain way to succeed is always to try just one more time.
Thomas Edison

BELIEF

Beliefs are the convictions that something exists or is true, especially without proof. That is also the definition of what we do as actors. We play make-believe. Our beliefs shape our world, especially our beliefs about ourselves and it works for the characters you play. Understand your beliefs and how they influence your mind, body and spirit, then you will be able to better understand others, so you can embody them. Allow the beliefs of your character to colour your perception of your world and your interaction with everything in it. "Acting is the best magic trick in the world. We applaud performances not because it's real, but because you made us believe."

VOCAL WORK - 2 Minutes - [Set timer]

Lip Trills: Close your lips together lightly, like you're going to blow a raspberry. Then, blow air through your closed lips while making sounds. You should feel a tickling sensation. Pick a song and Lip Trill along with it. **Tip**: Stretch your range as much as you can and pick a song you've never listened to.

BELIEF WORKOUT

Get your journal or write in here. **Define your personal belief/view** on the given subject. **Grab any book you own,** flip to a random page and **read it out loud,** colouring the words and intention with your belief system. **Tip**: Write trigger words you can hook into in the future: **Optimism-** Always smiling, grateful, opportunity, sunshine yellow.

YOUR PERSONAL BELIEF

Following your Dreams - 7 Minutes [Set Timer]

_____
_____
_____
_____

READ WITH BELIEF - 2 Minutes [Set Timer]

CHARACTERS BELIEF

Following your Dreams

Dreams are a waste of time, a distraction from what's really important. People get so caught up in chasing these wild fantasies that they miss out on real opportunities right in front of them. Don't get lost in dreams. Face reality, work hard on what's tangible, and you'll finally live life.

READ WITH CHARACTERS BELIEF - 2 Minutes [Set Timer]

Forget your personal view and **fully embrace the character's belief**. Read out loud again.

JOURNAL YOUR EXPERIENCE - 2 Minutes [Set Timer]

_____
_____
_____

WORKOUT COMPLETED [ ]

PERFORMANCE STRATEGY
14 DAY REVIEW

TAKE A MOMENT OF REFLECTION AND BREAKDOWN WHERE YOU ARE RIGHT NOW IN YOUR CAREER AND AS AN ACTOR.
THE MORE SPECIFIC YOU ARE THE MORE CLEAR YOU CAN SEE WHERE YOU ARE NOW SO YOU CAN GET TO WHERE YOU WANT TO GO FASTER

★ ★ ★ ★ ★

J.K. Rowling: Before "Harry Potter" became a global phenomenon, Rowling faced rejections from multiple publishers. Her persistence led to one of the most successful book series in history.

DATE:

MY WHY
WHY ARE YOU DOING WHAT YOU ARE DOING
BE SPECIFIC

MY MAIN GOALS
IN-ORDER OF IMPORTANCE

1.

    Action Step(s):

2.

    Action Step(s):

3.

    Action Step(s):

FROM THE LAST 14 DAYS
5 STAR RATING

YOUR KEY POINTS AND TAKEAWAYS - WHY THAT AMOUNT OF STAR RATING, LIKES, DISLIKES, THE BIGGEST LESSON YOU LEARNED, GOOD OR BAD:

STRENGTHS:

WEAKNESSES:

IMPROVEMENT STRATEGY
HOW CAN YOU IMPROVE ON THESE AREAS FOR THE NEXT 14 DAYS:

GOAL FROM LAST :
DID YOU ACHIEVE IT?

WHY OR WHY NOT?

GOAL FOR THE NEXT 14 EXERCISES
THE MORE SPECIFIC YOU ARE THE GREATER THE RESULT

    Action Step(s):

Sometimes all you need is twenty seconds of insane courage and I promise you something great will come of it.
Benjamin Mee, We Bought a Zoo

MY WHY:

GOAL(s):

PHYSICAL WARMUP - 1 minute [Set Timer]
Freeform Dance: Put on some music and engage in freeform dancing. Allow your body to move spontaneously and without inhibition. This can help you tap into your creative instincts and develop physical expressiveness. **Tip**: Try music you've never listened to.

VOCAL WORK - 3 minutes - [Set Timer]
Lip Trills: Close your lips together lightly, like you're going to blow a raspberry. Then, blow air through your closed lips while making sounds. You should feel a tickling sensation. Pick a song and Lip Trill along with it. **Tip**: Stretch your range as much as you can and pick a song you've never listened to.

EMOTIONAL RECALL - 5 minutes [Set Timer]
Laughter in Solitude: Remember a moment when you found yourself laughing alone — the reason behind it, the sound of your laughter echoing in the space. **Tip**: Use the purity of this joy to bring lightness to a character or scene, letting it shine through even in moments of solitude.

ANIMAL WORK - FIREFLY

Research - 2 minutes [Set Timer]
Contemplate the firefly's gentle glow and its serene, rhythmic flight in the quiet of the night.

Animal Exercise - 3 minutes [Set Timer]

Embody the delicate lightness of the firefly, the soft pulsing glow translated into a rhythm in your movements. As you evolve into human form, maintain the subtle glow in your demeanour.

Discovery Journal - 1 Minute [Set Timer]
3 Main Characteristics: (Whatever stands out to YOU to embody the essence)

_____
_____
_____
_____
_____
_____

WORKOUT COMPLETED [ ]

Always tell the truth - it's the easiest
thing to remember.
David Mamet

SCRIPT ANALYSIS for RELATIONSHIPS & SPECIFICITY - 15 minutes [Set Timer]
Choose your character, circle everything in this script you have a relationship with. Including people, places, things, smells, time of day etc. **Write what your relationship with those items are and be specific.** The more specific and fun you have with your relationships, the more interesting your characters will be and the more fun the audience has. **Tip:** Everything isn't in the scene. Use your imagination to create details, <u>only if</u> it's contextually appropriate. **Extra:** Write your > **Objective, win or lose? Consequence of failing?** The *Who What Where When Why.*

Title: Fractured Reflections
INT. STARKLY LIT KITCHEN - MIDNIGHT
The kitchen is bathed in harsh, unflattering light. JENNA (emotionally raw and determined) stands across from her mother, HELEN (domineering and intense), sits at the kitchen table.

JENNA
Mom, this... this has to end.

HELEN
You're being dramatic. Stop pussy footin' around and just say it Je—

JENNA
It's about you. Your control, your constant criticism... It's crushing me.

HELEN
You've always been so fragile.

JENNA
Because of *you*. You've been breaking me down, piece by piece!

   Helen stares at her daughter. Not blinking.

HELEN
I've given you everything. Shaped you into someone capable, competent.

JENNA
You shaped me into your version of perfect. But I'm not you!

HELEN
You could never be me. You don't have the spine for it.

   Jenna let's it finally fall out her mouth...

JENNA
I'm leaving.

HELEN
(leaning in)
You think you can survive without my guidance? You'll fall apart.

JENNA
I'm leaving.

Jenna's eyes are filled with a chaotic mix of fear, anger, and resolve, then— She heads for the door

HELEN
You'll be back. You always come back.

Jenna's whole body trembles. She stops, hand on the doorknob.

JENNA
(whispering to herself)
Not this time.

She exits, slamming the door behind her. Helen remains seated, her face an emotionless mask, as the kitchen light flickers and casts unsettling shadows. This quiet is unsettling for her...

WORKOUT COMPLETED [ ]

To make a great film you need three things -
the script, the script, and the script.
Alfred Hitchcock

IMAGINATION

We have a lot of tools in our arsenal as actors but I believe **imagination is the most powerful.** "If you hook into the character's belief system and you believe it 100%, there is no way the audience won't." - Meryl Streep "Imagination is more important than knowledge for knowledge is limited. - Einstein. Everyone has an Imagination but it must be worked out to get stronger. Think of your imagination as a limitless playground. In this space, you can be anyone, go anywhere, and do anything. **Have the courage to allow yourself to play!**

Imaginary World Exploration - 6 Minutes [Set Timer]

Find a quiet space to relax and focus. **Close your eyes** and let your imagination run wild. **Tip:** Engage all your senses to explore this environment. Touch, taste, smell etc and allow your emotions to guide you as well. **Extra:** After you explore this world with your senses, you could introduce characters and have a dialogue with them. Are they friends or foes?

IMAGINARY WORLD: A SECRET SPOT - An imaginary place where a relative/friend/hero who has passed away is waiting to see you again. See the world first then that person. You can do anything with them. What do you talk about? Ask them questions, and discover the world together!

JOURNAL YOUR EXPERIENCE - 2 Minutes [Set Timer]

_____
_____
_____
_____
_____
_____
_____

Your Characters Filter - 5 Minutes [Set Timer]

Everyone including the characters you play see the world through their own specific perspective/filter. I like to use the word filter because you can take out a filter, clean it, change its style, colour, an optimist or a pessimist, comedian or a nihilist, etc. **Find a quiet space** to focus. **Close your eyes and let go of your personal thoughts and emotions** to make space for your characters. **Open your eyes and allow the filter provided to effect everything around you**. **Tip**: Explore wherever you are and interact with the objects. **Extra:** How does *this* character walk and move in their world?

FILTER: LIAR - You are the world's best liar and you know it.

JOURNAL YOUR EXPERIENCE - 2 Minutes [Set Timer]

_____
_____
_____
_____
_____
_____

WORKOUT COMPLETED [ ]

The job of the dramatist is to make the
audience wonder what happens next.
David Mamet

CHARACTER STUDY "PEOPLE WATCHING"

Actors are required to portray characters that are believable and relatable. You don't have to agree with them but you have to understand them. Walk like them, talk like them, see the world like them. So, in order to fill our toolbox, we have to **go out into the world and study**. Then practice them over and over so we can "walk in their shoes', comfortably and confidently. Study their movements, mannerisms, the "vibe" they give off, the clothes they wear etc. **Fill your toolbox with the rhythms and idiosyncrasies of human behaviour.**

OBSERVATION CHARACTER STUDY - 15 Minutes [Set Timer]

Find a busy place where you can **sit and observe.** Choose anyone you find interesting. **Write down what stands out about them**. *The way they sit, drink their coffee, walk, talk, interact with others etc.* **Tip**: **Mirror them immediately**. This will help memorize the feeling of that character so whenever you come back to these characters you're discovering, your body will remember. **Extra**: Before you go to sleep, read over the characters from today and reenact their movements.

_____
_____
_____
_____
_____
_____
_____
_____
_____
_____
_____
_____
_____
_____
_____
_____
_____
_____
_____
_____
_____
_____
_____

COLOURS: We as humans respond to colours like frequencies. If you pay attention closely, you can see everyone has their own 'colour' that defines their core. An essence that informs how they operate and move through the world.

WHAT COLOUR ARE THEY:

WORKOUT COMPLETED [ ]

Cinema should make you forget you are
sitting in a theatre.
Roman Polanski

VOICE & DICTION

I wish I had learned this at the beginning of my career. The confidence to communicate clearly and powerfully is a game-changer for you as an actor. **Think of your voice as a musical instrument that needs regular tuning. This workout is your daily tuning session,** ensuring that your instrument is always ready. "The word 'theatre' comes from the Greeks. It means the seeing place. It is the place people come to see the truth about life and the social situation." - Stella Adler. Embrace this workout as a key to unlocking and portraying *that* truth by letting your voice be the vehicle that transports your audience into the heart of your story.

READ PASSAGE - 30 Seconds [Set Timer]
Speak the passage and take note of its quality. **Tip**: Record Audio to compare afterward.

"As dawn breaks, the silent forest awakens. Birds sing in chorus, leaves rustle in the morning breeze, and the world stirs in harmony. The first rays of sunlight pierce through the canopy, illuminating the dance of life."

RELAXATION - 1 Minute [Set Timer]
Deep Breathing: Sit and Inhale deeply through your nose, filling your lungs, then exhale slowly through your mouth. Imagine stress leaving your body with each breath.

Nay Nay Nay - 1 Minute [Set Timer]
Pick a song and sing the word "Nay" repeatedly. Start with a comfortable pitch and gradually move the sound from your nose to your chest, ensuring each "Nay" is clear and resonant. Stretch your range as best you can to strengthen.

Sustained 'S' - 2 Minutes [Set Timer]
Inhale deeply and then exhale slowly, making a continuous 's' sound. Keep the sound as even and steady as you can. Always push a little longer than you think you can.

Vowel Pronunciation Drill - 2 Minutes [Set Timer]
Slowly go through each vowel sound **(A, E, I, O, U)**, holding and exaggerating each sound. **Combine them with consonants** (e.g., ba, be, bi, bo, bu). Pay attention to the clarity and sharpness of each sound. Repeat a few times before moving to the next.

Lip Trills - 3 minutes - [Set timer]
Close your lips together lightly, like you're going to blow a raspberry. Then, blow air through your closed lips while making sounds. You should feel a tickling sensation. Pick a song and Lip Trill the whole along with it. **Tip**: Stretch your range as much as you can and pick a song you've never listened to.

The Cork Exercise - 4 Minutes [Set Timer]
Place a cork between your teeth and try to read a passage aloud. This forces your articulation muscles to work harder. If you don't have a cork, bite down gently on your thumb. You can use the following text for this exercise:

READ PASSAGE AGAIN - 30 Seconds [Set Timer]
Speak the passage and take note of its quality. **Tip**: Record Audio to compare.

Discovery Journal - 1 Minute [Set Timer]

WORKOUT COMPLETED [ ]

Even nothing is something.
A practical handbook for the actor

SUBTEXT

Subtext is what lies beneath the surface of our words. It's the hidden layer of meaning, driven by the character's internal thoughts, emotions, desires, and motivations. Subtext is one of my favourite things as an actor because so much can be said with one simple line of dialogue. The power of "Hello" can be exciting if you told that person years ago "If I ever see you again, I'll kill you. Maybe it's the most beautiful person you've ever seen. Now, say "hello". *Subtext* shows the audience what your relationship with the characters/places/situations are, without having to explain it. We experience it every day and it is our job to create characters that interact as we do.

VOCAL WORK - 3 minutes - [Set Timer]
Lip Trills: Close your lips together lightly, like you're going to blow a raspberry. Then, blow air through your closed lips while making sounds. You should feel a tickling sensation. Pick a song and Lip Trill along with it. **Tip**: Stretch your range as much as you can and pick a song you've never listened to.

SUBTEXT PRACTICE
Use the line of dialogue provided and practice each of these subtexts **out loud.** Move on to the next, only when you believe yourself. Trust that you will know when *that* is. Before you begin, **pick a spot to look at and imagine** in detail, **who you are speaking with**. **Tip**: *Sometimes* we mean exactly what we are saying. Look for that too. **Extra**: Substitute someone you have a strong relationship with in real life, good or bad, and see it's affect.

Initial Line: "Have you seen the latest art exhibit that I designed at the museum?"
Your Response Line: "I've heard about it. They say it's quite a collection. Might be worth a visit, don't you think? Could be inspiring, or at least a good way to spend an afternoon."

SUBTEXTS - 6 Minutes [Set Timer]
[ ] Hiding jealousy: You're envious of the artist's talent.
[ ] Contemplative: You're deeply moved by art and its impact on society.
[ ] Indifferent: Art doesn't really excite you, but you go along with it.
[ ] Curious: You're genuinely interested in exploring new art forms.
[ ] Dismissive: You don't see the big deal about art exhibits.
[ ] Your Own Subtext

RELATIONSHIP SUBTEXTS - 6 Minutes [Set Timer]
[ ] Supportive Friend: You're encouraging them to pursue their art interests.
[ ] Disapproving Parent: You don't understand their fascination with art.
[ ] Inquisitive Colleague: You're curious about their perspective on art.
[ ] Secret Admirer: You're using this as an opportunity to spend time together.
[ ] Jaded Ex: You resent the shared memories associated with art.
[ ] Your Own Subtext

Discovery Journal
_____
_____
_____
_____

WORKOUT COMPLETED [ ]

We think too much and feel too little.
Charlie Chaplin

EMOTIONS
The 'moment before', **the emotional preparation, is the most important key to a great scene**. If you start any scene *without* an emotional preparation it feels like trying to drive a car in neutral. The preparation is the uphill climb of every rollercoaster; Once you grind all the way to the top, the chains let go and the rest of the ride takes care of itself. "No one wants to see a play or a movie and look at technical proficiency. You want to be moved, you want a human experience, you want to feel less alone" - Viola Davis. **Practice your emotions over and over** so when it's time, you aren't worried "Will I get there?" **You're imagination and emotions should be a tinderbox, so easy to light up. All it take is half a spark.**

EULOGY - 12 Minutes [Set Timer]
Find a quiet comfortable space. Choose someone in your life who is alive and important to you. Create an imaginary reason for why they have died. Now start from the point of the phone call— Imagine who calls, what they say and what you say. Eventually find yourself at the funeral, about to begin the eulogy. See the casket, is it open or closed?? What is that person wearing and any other details for yourself. Before you begin to speak, look into the audience and see who is there- Family, friends etc **Then begin the eulogy**. **Tip**: Be as specific as you can with everything. **Inside of specificity is where you will find the triggers to your heart.** Let your imagination take you wherever you want in this exercise. **Example**: Placing her favourite sheep stuffed animal in the casket, tucked under her arm like she always held it, then kissing her goodbye one last time.

DISCOVERY JOURNAL - 3 Minutes [Set Timer]
Make sure to **include the specific triggers** you experience because you can use these **TRIGGER MOMENTS** in the future instead of repeating the *entire* exercise.

_____
_____
_____
_____
_____
_____
_____
_____
_____
_____
_____
_____
_____
_____
_____
_____
_____
_____
_____
_____

WORKOUT COMPLETED [ ]

It's only words... unless they're true.
David Mamet

THE CORK EXERCISE - 4 Minutes [Set Timer]
Place a cork between your teeth and read a passage aloud. This forces your articulation muscles to work harder. If you don't have a cork, bite down gently on your thumb. You can use the following text for this exercise:

"Along the winding river, the gentle current carries fallen leaves, twirling them in a delicate ballet. The water's edge is a meeting place for wildlife, where herons stand poised and frogs croak in chorus. It's a world of serene beauty, where nature's rhythm is the only guide."

WRITE A LETTER - 10 Minutes [Set Timer]
Get a piece of paper or write this in your device. **Take a moment** to let this situation and relationship sink in. Then let your imagination run wild and **write them a letter.**

Your Character: Taylor, a seasoned paramedic who has faced numerous high-pressure situations in their career.
Other Character: Alex, a former colleague who has publicly blamed Taylor for a critical error during a life-saving operation, an error Taylor contests ever happened.

Relationship: Taylor and Alex worked closely on many emergency calls, building a bond of trust and mutual reliance in the high-stakes world of emergency medical services. The public accusation has not only tarnished Taylor's professional reputation but also deeply affected their personal sense of honour and duty.

Context of the Letter: Struggling with feelings of betrayal and a desire to clear their name, Taylor writes a letter to Alex. This letter is a confrontation of the accusation, an exploration of the facts of the case, and a plea for Alex to reconsider their version of events. It's a heartfelt attempt to address the damage caused to their professional relationship and to restore Taylor's integrity in the eyes of their peers.

Discovery Journal - 1 minute [Set Timer]

_____
_____
_____
_____
_____
_____
_____
_____
_____

WORKOUT COMPLETED [ ]

I am not what happened to me. I am what I choose to become.
Carl Jung, A Dangerous Method

VOCAL WORK - 3 minutes [Set timer]
Lip Trills: Close your lips together lightly, like you're going to blow a raspberry. Then, blow air through your closed lips while making sounds. You should feel a tickling sensation. Pick a song and Lip Trill along with it. **Tip**: Stretch your range as much as you can and pick a song you've never listened to.

VERBAL IMPROV - 10 Minutes [Set Timer]

Find a space where you are comfortable and free to express yourself. Take a moment to **let this situation, character and prompt, sink in**. Then let your imagination run wild: **Picture who you are talking to** then **begin with *the prompt*** and **continue to verbalize everything** this character would say. **Tip**: This is exploration! There is no "getting it right". BE BRAVE to explore and discover.

Character: Riley, a devoted and principled bank manager, is shocked to discover that their trusted friend and colleague, Jordan, who has always been charming but secretive, has been embezzling funds from elderly customers' accounts. Riley's grandmother was once a victim of a similar financial scam, making this betrayal deeply personal and infuriating.

Prompt: "Jordan, I can't believe you. How could you do something like this?"

Who are you talking to:

Describe them in two specific words:

Discovery Journal - 2 minutes [Set Timer]

_____
_____
_____
_____
_____
_____
_____

WORKOUT COMPLETED [ ]

You must decide what your ultimate goal is
then construct each individual action to bring
you a step closer to achieving that goal.
A practical handbook for the actor

SELF AWARENESS
The more you understand yourself, the more you are able to understand and develop your characters. Like you, your characters have thoughts, beliefs, traumas, passions etc. When you become aware of your own and start to see how those experiences and beliefs have shaped your life, how you operate and view the world, then you can develop your characters that are much more rich and vivid.

PHYSICAL WARMUP - 2 minutes [Set Timer]
Freeform Dance: Put on some music and engage in freeform dancing. Allow your body to move spontaneously and without inhibition. This can help you tap into your creative instincts and develop physical expressiveness. **Tip**: Try music you've never listened to.

CURRENT EMOTIONAL INVENTORY - 3 Minutes [Set Timer]
Write down and **record your current emotions**. Identify what you're feeling at this moment and why. **Tip**: Be as specific as you can, **don't disregard anything.** You can also **scan your body** to see how and where your current emotion is affecting you. Your posture, the way you walk, bouncing foot, sore neck etc

CURRENT EMOTIONAL STATE:

SELF DISCOVERY QUESTIONS - 10 Minutes [Set Timer]
I suggest a journal or writing it in your phone's notes so you don't run out of space here.

Reflecting on a moment of significant personal failure, what were the immediate emotions I felt, and how have my reflections on that event changed over time?

Name the person you most dislike in this world (Condense their name and description into something this simple > Sarah - You betrayed your own family)

WORKOUT COMPLETED [ ]

Remember why you started. Keep that fire burning within you, and let it drive you to greatness.
Charlize Theron

IMAGINATION

We have a lot of tools in our arsenal as actors but I believe imagination is the most powerful. "If you hook into the character's belief system and you believe it 100%, there is no way the audience won't." - Meryl Streep. Everyone has an Imagination but it must be worked out to get stronger. Think of your imagination as a limitless playground. In this space, you can be anyone, go anywhere, and do anything. **Have the courage to allow yourself to play!**

VOCAL WORK - 2 Minutes - [Set timer]
Lip Trills: Close your lips together lightly, like you're going to blow a raspberry. Then, blow air through your closed lips while making sounds. You should feel a tickling sensation. Pick a song and Lip Trill along with it. **Tip**: Stretch your range as much as you can and pick a song you've never listened to.

IMPROVISED STORYTELLING - 5 Minutes [Set Timer]
Speak out the scenario provided and continue the story! Focus on vivid details, character development and how the main character overcomes the main obstacle. **Tip**: Try not to stop speaking so you don't have time to "think". Allow your imagination to keep moving forward without interruption. **Tip:** Record these stories on your device, in case it's great but more importantly to see your progress as you go on.

STARTING POINT: You are Jordan, a quiet bookshop owner who is about to close up his shop when a young 10-year-old, child, enters and doesn't say a word when you greet them. They look oddly familiar... When you realize they are wearing the exact same clothes as you are, you look up and see the door close. You run out from behind the desk and give chase down the quiet cobblestone roads—

IMAGINARY WORLD EXPLORATION - 6 Minutes [Set Timer]

Find a quiet space to relax and focus. **Close your eyes** and let your imagination run wild. **Tip:** Engage all your senses to explore this environment. Touch, taste, smell etc and allow your emotions to guide you. **Extra:** After you explore this world with your senses, you could introduce characters and have a dialogue with them. Are they friends or foes?

IMAGINARY WORLD: You are where you are right now. But you can fly! You take flight and begin to discover your area for the first time from this vantage point.

JOURNAL YOUR EXPERIENCE - 2 Minutes [Set Timer]

_____
_____
_____
_____
_____
_____

WORKOUT COMPLETED [ ]

The most personal is the most creative.
Martin Scorsese

ANCHORING INTO YOUR CHARACTER COLOUR & MUSIC

Anchoring yourself into your character is vital. It's one of the most freeing feelings when you understand their *essence* because everything they do, how they do it and what their purpose is, becomes so clear to you and the audience. Every choice you make after you find your *anchor*, feels easy, because you're acting from who and what your character is at the core. You can call it an essence, an aura, vibe, energy etc. We all have it and feel it from everyone around us. There are many ways into your character but music and colour are my favourite. Music can inform the script, your character, and even each scene. Colours, I think you will find, can work incredibly because we as humans respond to colours like frequencies. Colours evoke many feelings and if you pay attention closely, you can see everyone has their own 'colour' that defines their core. An essence that informs how they operate and move through the world.

THEIR COLOUR - 2 Minutes [Set Timer]
Think of **someone you know**, and **define them with a colour**. **Tip**: Trust yourself. Your initial colour is usually close. **Tip**: Start with basic colours then eventually become much more specific. **Example**: Corinna is an earthy green with rays of sunlight flowing through the green. **Extra**: Ask someone who knows *that person* as well, what they think this person's colour is and why. See how close your answers are or not.

YOUR CHARACTERS COLOUR
Read the given character description just as you would an audition, **assign a colour to that character.** Now take that colour you chose and **allow it to infuse into your entire body**, affecting your every move, your speaking, the way you see the world etc. **Take any book** you have, flip to a random page and **read the text as this Colour/Character**. **Tip**: Be specific, choose a colour that excites you and don't be afraid to get creative.

CHARACTER DESCRIPTION: [SLOANE] Any ethnicity; Sloane is a reclusive but brilliant coder and app developer, known in tech circles for creating innovative and user-friendly applications. They prefer the solitude of their minimalist, tech-equipped home office, often working late into the night. Dressed in comfortable, smart-casual attire, Sloane is unassuming in appearance but commands respect in the digital world. Despite their introverted nature, Sloane's work impacts the daily lives of millions, reflecting a deep understanding of technology and user experience. Their character is a blend of technological prowess, quiet determination, and a subtle influence that extends far beyond their immediate presence.

CHOOSE THEIR COLOUR - 4 Minutes [Set Timer]
THEIR COLOUR:

CHOOSE THEIR SONG - 4 Minutes [Set Timer]
THEIR SONG:

READ PASSAGE FROM BOOK - 2 Minutes [Set Timer]

FREEFORM DANCE - 2 minutes - [Set Timer]
Put on the selected music and **engage in freeform dancing, anchored in your colour/character,** Allow your body to move spontaneously and without inhibition. This can help you tap into your creative instincts and develop physical expressiveness *while staying in character.* **Tip**: Journal about the differences as opposed to how you normally dance.

JOURNAL YOUR EXPERIENCE - 1 Minute [Set Timer]

WORKOUT COMPLETED [ ]

Every great film should seem new every time you see it.
Roger Ebert

HISTORICAL RESEARCH

We are in the information era and have access to the world and its rich history at our fingertips. This exploration is not about 'learning facts'; it's a journey to the heart of human experience. The empathy and the understanding, especially on the things you disagree with, are incredibly valuable. If you look closely, you'll find the way people think, at different times in history, their attitudes, choices, and the way they move their bodies can teach you so much about us, right now. Fill your toolbox so it's overflowing with information and ideas to pull from so your imagination has so much to play with.

PHYSICAL WARMUP - 2 minutes - [Set Timer]
Freeform Dance: Put on some music and engage in freeform dancing. Allow your body to move spontaneously and without inhibition. This can help you tap into your creative instincts and develop physical expressiveness. **Tip**: Try music you've never listened to.

RESEARCH - 13 Minutes [Set Timer]
YouTube, streaming platforms, the internet or books, **research the given era/person/moment in time,** journal or make notes on your device, so when you want to find this information, it's organized and readily accessible. As you go, **write anything and everything _you_ find fascinating. Tip:** If the topic doesn't interest you, choose your own, or take a chance and still research it, but from a different perspective. Physicalities, voice, ideals, etc. Trust your body that when you see something interesting, you'll know. **Extra**: Speak it out and copy their movements. Our memory recall is massively affected by our bodies. Be specific and when you re-read your notes, you'll be amazed by how much your mind and body remember.

TOPIC:
The Cuban Missile Crisis (1962) - The Perspective of Vasili Arkhipov: Vasili Arkhipov, a Soviet Navy officer during the Cuban Missile Crisis, offers an extraordinary and tense perspective on this critical moment in the Cold War. Arkhipov is credited with preventing a nuclear war during the height of the crisis. As second-in-command aboard the Soviet submarine B-59, he refused to authorize the captain's decision to launch a nuclear torpedo in response to aggressive U.S. Navy depth charging. This decision, made under extreme pressure, required immense courage and calm judgment.

WORKOUT COMPLETED [ ]

You should feel a flow of joy because you are alive. Your body will feel full of life. That is what you must give from the stage. Your life. No less. That is art: to give all you have.
Anton Chekhov

BELIEF

Beliefs are the convictions that something exists or is true, especially without proof. That is also the definition of what we do as actors. We play make-believe. Our beliefs shape our world, especially our beliefs about ourselves and it works for the characters you play. Understand your beliefs and how they influence your mind, body and spirit, then you will be able to better understand others, so you can embody them. Allow the beliefs of your character to colour your perception of your world and your interaction with everything in it. "Acting is the best magic trick in the world." We applaud performances not because it's real, but because you made us believe.

VOCAL WORK - 2 Minutes - [Set timer]

Lip Trills: Close your lips together lightly, like you're going to blow a raspberry. Then, blow air through your closed lips while making sounds. You should feel a tickling sensation. Pick a song and Lip Trill along with it. **Tip**: Stretch your range as much as you can and pick a song you've never listened to.

BELIEF WORKOUT

Get your journal or write in here. **Define your personal belief/view** on the given subject. **Grab any book you own,** flip to a random page and **read it out loud,** colouring the words and intention with your belief system. **Tip**: Write trigger words you can hook into in the future: **Optimism-** Always smiling, grateful, opportunity, sunshine yellow.

YOUR PERSONAL BELIEF

Star Signs - 7 Minutes [Set Timer]

_____
_____
_____

READ WITH BELIEF - 2 Minutes [Set Timer]

CHARACTERS BELIEF

Star Signs

It's not "star signs" it's astrology and I live for it! I think it's incredible and based on so much science. How were aligned and move with the universe. We are all connected. There are signs everywhere guiding you to your destiny. If you're open and look for it. Trust your soul and trust the universe.

READ WITH CHARACTERS BELIEF - 2 Minutes [Set Timer]

Forget your personal view and **fully embrace the character's belief. Read out loud again.**

JOURNAL YOUR EXPERIENCE - 2 Minutes [Set Timer]

_____
_____
_____
_____

WORKOUT COMPLETED [ ]

PERFORMANCE STRATEGY
14 DAY REVIEW

TAKE A MOMENT OF REFLECTION AND BREAKDOWN WHERE YOU ARE RIGHT NOW IN YOUR CAREER AND AS AN ACTOR.
THE MORE SPECIFIC YOU ARE THE MORE CLEAR YOU CAN SEE WHERE YOU ARE NOW SO YOU CAN GET TO WHERE YOU WANT TO GO FASTER

★ ★ ★ ★ ★

Marilyn Monroe: She spent much of her childhood in foster homes and initially struggled to find work as an actress. Monroe eventually became a major sex symbol and one of the most popular actresses of the 1950s and early 1960s.

DATE:

MY WHY
WHY ARE YOU DOING WHAT YOU ARE DOING
BE SPECIFIC

MY MAIN GOALS
IN-ORDER OF IMPORTANCE

1.

   Action Step(s):

2.

   Action Step(s):

3.

   Action Step(s):

FROM THE LAST 14 DAYS
5 STAR RATING

YOUR KEY POINTS AND TAKEAWAYS - WHY THAT AMOUNT OF STAR RATING, LIKES, DISLIKES, THE BIGGEST LESSON YOU LEARNED, GOOD OR BAD:

STRENGTHS:

WEAKNESSES:

IMPROVEMENT STRATEGY
HOW CAN YOU IMPROVE ON THESE AREAS FOR THE NEXT 14 DAYS:

GOAL FROM LAST :
DID YOU ACHIEVE IT?

WHY OR WHY NOT?

GOAL FOR THE NEXT 14 EXERCISES
THE MORE SPECIFIC YOU ARE THE GREATER THE RESULT

   Action Step(s):

Don't wait for people to tell you who you are.
Show them.
Laura Benanti

MY WHY:

GOAL(s):

PHYSICAL WARMUP - 1 minute [Set Timer]
Whirling Dervish: Spin safely and gently in place, arms outstretched, eyes closed. As you turn, imagine the air around you is thick with vivid colours, each one swirling with you.

VOCAL WORK - 3 minutes [Set Timer]
Echoic Imagery: Make a series of sounds that mimic natural phenomena, such as the whistle of the wind or the crash of ocean waves. Allow the sounds to grow and shrink to stretch your vocal muscles.

EMOTIONAL RECALL - 5 minutes [Set Timer]
Childhood Imagination: Dive deep into a childhood memory where your imagination was boundless. Relive the sense of wonder and the belief that anything is possible. **Tip:** Embrace the innocence and curiosity of your younger self to bring freshness and authenticity to your acting.

ANIMAL WORK - CHAMELEON

Research - 2 minutes [Set Timer]
Delve into the chameleon's world of colour change and subtle motion.

Animal Exercise 3 minutes [Set Timer]
Imitate the chameleon's slow, deliberate movements and then infuse these into a human character who is equally adept at blending into different social environments.

Discovery Journal - 1 Minute [Set Timer]
3 Main Characteristics: (Whatever stands out to YOU to embody the essence)

_____
_____
_____
_____
_____

WORKOUT COMPLETED [ ]

Find joy in the process. Acting is a privilege, so enjoy every moment and be grateful for the opportunity to tell stories.
Tom Hanks

SCRIPT ANALYSIS for RELATIONSHIPS & SPECIFICITY - 15 minutes [Set Timer]

Choose your character, circle everything in this script you have a relationship with. Including people, places, things, smells, time of day etc. **Write what your relationship with those items are and be specific**. The more specific and fun you have with your relationships, the more interesting your characters will be and the more fun the audience has. **Tip:** Everything isn't in the scene. Use your imagination to create details, <u>only if</u> it's contextually appropriate. **Extra:** Write your > ***Objective, win or lose? Consequence of failing?*** The **Who What Where When Why.**

Titled: **Unspoken Words**
INT. KITCHEN - EVENING
A cozy, well-lived-in kitchen. LAURA, early 40s, composed yet with a trace of weariness, is cooking. BRETT, mid-40s, thoughtful and slightly dishevelled, enters. The air is thick with the tension of a long, unsaid conversation.

LAURA
You're home late.
BRETT
(avoiding eye contact)
Traffic. The bridge was a nightmare.
BRETT
(leaning against the counter)
Smells good.
LAURA
It's your favorite. Figured we needed something... nice.
BRETT
Laura, I...
LAURA
Can we just... not tonight? Please?

Michael looks at her, a mixture of relief and frustration in his eyes.

BRETT
Okay. Not tonight.

He moves closer, watching her cook. They stand in silence, the unspoken hanging between them.

LAURA
How's work?
BRETT
It's... fine. The usual chaos.

Laura nods again, a small, sad smile on her lips.

LAURA
Remember when chaos was our thing?
BRETT
(chuckles)
Yeah. We were good at chaos.

Their eyes meet, sharing a moment of nostalgia and mutual understanding.

LAURA
Dinner will be ready soon. Can you set the table?
BRETT
Sure.

As Michael sets the table, Laura continues cooking. The normalcy of the task juxtaposes their complex emotions. They move around each other in a familiar dance.

BRETT
I miss us.
LAURA
I know. Me too.

They share a glance, full of love and regret, before turning back to their tasks. The scene ends with the camera lingering on their separate yet intertwined lives in the quiet kitchen.

WORKOUT COMPLETED [ ]

The more detailed you are in your work the more universal it is.
A practical handbook for the actor

IMAGINATION

We have a lot of tools in our arsenal as actors but **I believe imagination is the most powerful.** "If you hook into the character's belief system and you believe it 100%, there is no way the audience won't." - Meryl Streep "Imagination is more important than knowledge for knowledge is limited. - Einstein. Everyone has an Imagination but it must be worked out to get stronger. Think of your imagination as a limitless playground. In this space, you can be anyone, go anywhere, and do anything. **Have the courage to allow yourself to play!**

Solo Imaginary World Exploration - 6 Minutes [Set Timer]

Find a quiet space to relax and focus. **Close your eyes** and **let your imagination run wild. Tip:** Engage all your senses to explore this environment. Touch, taste, smell etc. Allow your emotions to guide you. **Extra:** After you establish this world in your imagination, you could introduce characters and have a dialogue with them. Are they friends or foes?

IMAGINARY WORLD: Fluorescent - This world. Just as it is but everything is fluorescent. Not just its colour but the way it makes you feel. Almost as if you're seeing colour for the first time.

JOURNAL YOUR EXPERIENCE - 2 Minutes [Set Timer]

_____
_____
_____
_____
_____

Your Characters Filter - 5 Minutes [Set Timer]

Everyone including the characters you play see the world through their own specific perspective/filter. I like to use the word filter because you can take out a filter, clean it, change its style, colour, an optimist or a pessimist, comedian or a nihilist, etc. **Find a quiet space** to focus. **Close your eyes and let go of your personal thoughts and emotions** to make space for your characters. **Open your eyes, and allow the filter provided to effect everything around you. Tip:** Explore wherever you are and interact with the objects. **Extra:** How does *this* character walk and move in their world?

FILTER: POISONOUS - You have the power of poisoning anything you touch and want to poison everything. But will lose your power if you are caught. Be subtle.

JOURNAL YOUR EXPERIENCE - 2 Minutes [Set Timer]

_____
_____
_____
_____
_____

WORKOUT COMPLETED [ ]

Have the courage to contribute more than
what's on the page.
Victor Zinck Jr

CHARACTER STUDY "PEOPLE WATCHING"

Actors are required to portray characters that are believable and relatable. You don't have to agree with them but you have to understand them. Walk like them, talk like them, see the world like them. So, in order to fill our toolbox, we have to **go out into the world and study**. Then practice them over and over so we can "walk in their shoes', comfortably and confidently. Study their movements, mannerisms, the "vibe" they give off, the clothes they wear etc. **Fill your toolbox with the rhythms and idiosyncrasies of human behaviour.**

OBSERVATION CHARACTER STUDY - 15 Minutes [Set Timer]

Find a busy place where you can **sit and observe.** Choose anyone you find interesting. **Write down what stands out about them.** *The way they sit, drink their coffee, walk, talk, interact with others etc.* **Tip**: **Mirror them immediately.** This will help memorize the feeling of that character so whenever you come back to these characters you're discovering, your body will remember. **Extra**: Before you go to sleep, read over the characters from today and reenact their movements.

_____
_____
_____
_____
_____
_____
_____
_____
_____
_____
_____
_____
_____
_____
_____
_____
_____
_____
_____
_____
_____
_____
_____
_____

COLOURS: We as humans respond to colours like frequencies. If you pay attention closely, you can see everyone has their own 'colour' that defines their core. An essence that informs how they operate and move through the world.

WHAT COLOUR ARE THEY:

WORKOUT COMPLETED [ ]

We don't stop playing because we grow old;
we grow old because we stop playing.
George Bernard Shaw

VOICE & DICTION

I wish I had learned this at the beginning of my career. The confidence to communicate clearly and powerfully is a game-changer for you as an actor. **Think of your voice as a musical instrument that needs regular tuning. This workout is your daily tuning session,** ensuring that your instrument is always ready. "The word 'theatre' comes from the Greeks. It means the seeing place. It is the place people come to see the truth about life and the social situation." - Stella Adler. Embrace this workout as a key to unlocking and portraying *that* truth by letting your voice be the vehicle that transports your audience into the heart of your story.

READ PASSAGE - 30 Seconds [Set Timer]
Speak the passage and take note of its quality. **Tip**: Record Audio to compare afterward.

> "As dawn breaks, the silent forest awakens. Birds sing in chorus, leaves rustle in the morning breeze, and the world stirs in harmony. The first rays of sunlight pierce through the canopy, illuminating the dance of life."

RELAXATION - 1 Minute [Set Timer]
Deep Breathing: Sit and Inhale deeply through your nose, filling your lungs, then exhale slowly through your mouth. Imagine stress leaving your body with each breath.

Nay Nay Nay - 1 Minute [Set Timer]
Pick a song and sing the word "Nay" repeatedly. Start with a comfortable pitch and gradually move the sound from your nose to your chest, ensuring each "Nay" is clear and resonant. Stretch your range as best you can to strengthen.

Sustained 'S' - 2 Minutes [Set Timer]
Inhale deeply and then exhale slowly, making a continuous 's' sound. Keep the sound as even and steady as you can. Always push a little longer than you think you can.

Vowel Pronunciation Drill - 2 Minutes [Set Timer]
Slowly go through each vowel sound **(A, E, I, O, U), holding and exaggerating each sound. Combine them with consonants** (e.g., ba, be, bi, bo, bu). Pay attention to the clarity and sharpness of each sound. Repeat a few times before moving to the next.

Lip Trills - 3 minutes - [Set timer]
Close your lips together lightly, like you're going to blow a raspberry. Then, blow air through your closed lips while making sounds. You should feel a tickling sensation. Pick a song and Lip Trill the whole along with it. **Tip**: Stretch your range as much as you can and pick a song you've never listened to.

The Cork Exercise - 4 Minutes [Set Timer]
Place a cork between your teeth and try to read a passage aloud. This forces your articulation muscles to work harder. If you don't have a cork, bite down gently on your thumb. You can use the following text for this exercise:

READ PASSAGE AGAIN - 30 Seconds [Set Timer]
Speak the passage and take note of its quality. **Tip**: Record Audio to compare.

Discovery Journal - 1 Minute [Set Timer]

WORKOUT COMPLETED [ ]

An action must be physically capable of being done, be fun to do, be specific, have its test in the other person, not be an errand, not presuppose any physical or emotional state.
A practical handbook for the actor

SUBTEXT

Subtext is what lies beneath the surface of our words. It's the hidden layer of meaning, driven by the character's internal thoughts, emotions, desires, and motivations. Subtext is one of my favourite things as an actor because so much can be said with one simple line of dialogue. The power of "Hello" can be exciting if you told that person years ago "If I ever see you again, I'll kill you. Maybe it's the most beautiful person you've ever seen. Now, say "hello". *Subtext* shows the audience what your relationship with the characters/places/situations are, without having to explain it. We experience it every day and it is our job to create characters that interact as we do.

VOCAL WORK - 3 minutes - [Set Timer]
Lip Trills: Close your lips together lightly, like you're going to blow a raspberry. Then, blow air through your closed lips while making sounds. You should feel a tickling sensation. Pick a song and Lip Trill along with it. **Tip**: Stretch your range as much as you can and pick a song you've never listened to.

SUBTEXT PRACTICE
Use the line of dialogue provided and practice each of these subtexts **out loud.** Move on to the next, only when you believe yourself. Trust that you will know when *that* is. Before you begin, **pick a spot to look at and imagine** in detail, **who you are speaking with**. **Tip**: *Sometimes* we mean exactly what we are saying. Look for that too. **Extra**: Substitute someone you have a strong relationship with in real life, good or bad, and see it's affect.

Initial Line: "Did you catch the news about the city council election results?"
Your Response Line: "Yes, I saw it. Quite a shake-up, isn't it? It's going to change the whole dynamic of the city. It's interesting to think about what lies ahead for us now. What's your take on it?"

SUBTEXTS - 6 Minutes [Set Timer]
[ ] Concealing a secret: You were involved in a scandal with a candidate.
[ ] Seething anger: You're furious about the results and what they imply.
[ ] Fearful: The results have you worried about the future.
[ ] Elated: The candidate you secretly supported won.
[ ] Plotters delight: You see an opportunity to benefit from the new changes.
[ ] Your Own Subtext

RELATIONSHIP SUBTEXTS - 6 Minutes [Set Timer]
[ ] Worried Spouse: You're concerned how the results will affect your family.
[ ] Rival Politician: You're masking your frustration at your opponent's victory.
[ ] Protective Parent: Anxious about what this means for your children's future.
[ ] Scheming Business Partner: Plotting to leverage the new political landscape.
[ ] Disillusioned Friend: Losing faith in your friend who diagrees with you.
[ ] Your Own Subtext

Discovery Journal
_____
_____
_____
_____

WORKOUT COMPLETED [ ]

The theatre can put forward simple
human value in hopes that the
audience may leave inspired to try
to live by such values.
A practical handbook for the actor

EMOTIONS

The 'moment before', **the emotional preparation, is the most important key to a great scene.** If you start any scene _without_ an emotional preparation it feels like trying to drive a car in neutral. The preparation is the uphill climb of every rollercoaster; Once you grind all the way to the top, the chains let go and the rest of the ride takes care of itself. "No one wants to see a play or a movie and look at technical proficiency. You want to be moved, you want a human experience, you want to feel less alone" - Viola Davis. **Practice your emotions over and over** so when it's time, you aren't worried "Will I get there?" **You're imagination and emotions should be a tinderbox, so easy to light up. All it take is half a spark.**

EULOGY - 12 Minutes [Set Timer]

Find a quiet comfortable space. Choose someone in your life who is alive and important to you. Create an imaginary reason for why they have died. Now start from the point of the phone call— Imagine who calls, what they say and what you say. Eventually find yourself at the funeral, about to begin the eulogy. See the casket, is it open or closed?? What is that person wearing and any other details for yourself. Before you begin to speak, look into the audience and see who is there- Family, friends etc **Then begin the eulogy.**
Tip: Be as specific as you can with everything. **Inside of specificity is where you will find the triggers to your heart.** Let your imagination take you wherever you want in this exercise. **Example**: Placing her favourite sheep stuffed animal in the casket, tucked under her arm like she always held it, then kissing her goodbye one last time.

DISCOVERY JOURNAL - 3 Minutes [Set Timer]

Make sure to **include the specific triggers** you experience because you can use these **TRIGGER MOMENTS** in the future instead of repeating the _entire_ exercise.

_____
_____
_____
_____
_____
_____
_____
_____
_____
_____
_____
_____
_____
_____
_____
_____
_____
_____
_____
_____

WORKOUT COMPLETED [ ]

It will never be perfect, but perfect is overrated. Perfect is boring.
Tina Fey

THE CORK EXERCISE - 4 Minutes [Set Timer]
Place a cork between your teeth and read a passage aloud. This forces your articulation muscles to work harder. If you don't have a cork, bite down gently on your thumb. You can use the following text for this exercise:

> "In the heart of the bustling marketplace, vibrant colours and lively sounds envelop the senses. Vendors call out, their voices weaving through the aroma of exotic spices and fresh produce. Handcrafted goods display the richness of tradition, each piece telling its own story of skill and heritage."

WRITE A LETTER - 10 Minutes [Set Timer]
Get a piece of paper or write this in your device. **Take a moment** to let this situation and relationship sink in. Then let your imagination run wild and **write them a letter.**

Your Character: Chris, a high school teacher who has always prioritized the well-being and success of their students.

Other Character: Jordan, a former student who, years later, has publicly accused Chris of stifling their creativity and discouraging their aspirations, which Jordan claims led to years of self-doubt and missed opportunities.

Relationship: Chris remembers Jordan as a talented and imaginative student and always tried to provide constructive guidance, believing it would help Jordan achieve their potential. However, Jordan's accusations have come as a shock, casting a shadow over Chris's self-perception and dedication as an educator.

Context of the Letter: Faced with these unexpected and hurtful allegations, Chris writes a letter to Jordan. The letter is an attempt to reconcile Jordan's perception with Chris's intentions as a teacher. It's a blend of self-reflection, a defence of their teaching philosophy, and a genuine wish to understand and possibly help resolve the lingering issues Jordan is experiencing.

Discovery Journal - 1 minute [Set Timer]

_____
_____
_____
_____
_____
_____
_____

WORKOUT COMPLETED [ ]

If you're not invited to the party,
throw your own!
Diahann Caroll

VOCAL WORK - 3 minutes [Set timer]

Lip Trills: Close your lips together lightly, like you're going to blow a raspberry. Then, blow air through your closed lips while making sounds. You should feel a tickling sensation. Pick a song and Lip Trill along with it. **Tip**: Stretch your range as much as you can and pick a song you've never listened to.

VERBAL IMPROV - 10 Minutes [Set Timer]

Find a space where you are comfortable and free to express yourself. Take a moment to **let this situation, character and prompt, sink in**. Then let your imagination run wild: **Picture who you are talking to** then **begin with *the prompt*** and **continue to verbalize everything** this character would say. **Tip**: This is exploration! There is no "getting it right". BE BRAVE to explore and discover.

Character: Casey, a non-profit worker known for their empathy and commitment to community service, discovers that their coworker, Taylor, typically enthusiastic and supportive, has been using the non-profit's resources for personal gain. Casey's personal values and commitment to the community's welfare compel them to act.

Prompt: "Taylor, I've noticed you're using our resources for personal purposes. Let's talk about what's been happening."

Who are you talking to:

Describe them in two specific words:

Discovery Journal - 2 minutes [Set Timer]

_____
_____
_____
_____
_____
_____
_____
_____

WORKOUT COMPLETED [ ]

Filmmaking is a chance to live many lifetimes.
Robert Altman

SELF AWARENESS

The more you understand yourself, the more you are able to understand and develop your characters. Like you, your characters have thoughts, beliefs, traumas, passions etc. When you become aware of your own and start to see how those experiences and beliefs have shaped your life, how you operate and view the world, then you can develop your characters that are much more rich and vivid.

PHYSICAL WARMUP - 2 minutes [Set Timer]

Freeform Dance: Put on some music and engage in freeform dancing. Allow your body to move spontaneously and without inhibition. This can help you tap into your creative instincts and develop physical expressiveness. **Tip**: Try music you've never listened to.

CURRENT EMOTIONAL INVENTORY - 3 Minutes [Set Timer]

Write down and **record your current emotions**. Identify what you're feeling at this moment and why. **Tip**: Be as specific as you can, **don't disregard anything.** You can also **scan your body** to see how and where your current emotion is affecting you. Your posture, the way you walk, bouncing foot, sore neck etc

CURRENT EMOTIONAL STATE:

SELF DISCOVERY QUESTIONS - 10 Minutes [Set Timer]

I suggest a journal or writing it in your phone's notes so you don't run out of space here.

What is a memory from my childhood that still strongly influences my behaviour or emotional responses today, and why does it have such a lasting impact?

Name your favourite person in this world and why. (Condense their name and description into something this simple > Daniel - Blueberry) It's incredibly specific to me and evokes a strong feeling when I say it.

WORKOUT COMPLETED [ ]

No one ever made a difference by
being like everyone else.
P.T. Barnum

IMAGINATION

We have a lot of tools in our arsenal as actors but I believe imagination is the most powerful. "If you hook into the character's belief system and you believe it 100%, there is no way the audience won't." - Meryl Streep. Everyone has an Imagination but it must be worked out to get stronger. Think of your imagination as a limitless playground. In this space, you can be anyone, go anywhere, and do anything. **Have the courage to allow yourself to play!**

VOCAL WORK - 2 Minutes - [Set timer]
Lip Trills: Close your lips together lightly, like you're going to blow a raspberry. Then, blow air through your closed lips while making sounds. You should feel a tickling sensation. Pick a song and Lip Trill along with it. **Tip**: Stretch your range as much as you can and pick a song you've never listened to.

IMPROVISED STORYTELLING - 5 Minutes [Set Timer]
Speak out the scenario provided and continue the story! Focus on vivid details, character development and how the main character overcomes the main obstacle. **Tip**: Try not to stop speaking so you don't have time to "think". Allow your imagination to keep moving forward without interruption. **Tip:** Record these stories on your device, in case it's great but more importantly to see your progress as you go on.

STARTING POINT: Starting Point: You are Morgan, a professional diver who, while exploring an uncharted section of a coral reef, discovers an ancient sunken ship not recorded in any historical texts. Inside the ship, you find a perfectly preserved cabin and as you swim into it, the door closes behind you and the cabin's water, floods out in an instant, leaving you lying on the ground, confused and in awe.

IMAGINARY WORLD EXPLORATION - 6 Minutes [Set Timer]

Find a quiet space to relax and focus. **Close your eyes** and let your imagination run wild. **Tip:** Engage all your senses to explore this environment. Touch, taste, smell etc and allow your emotions to guide you. **Extra:** After you explore this world with your senses, you could introduce characters and have a dialogue with them. Are they friends or foes?

IMAGINARY WORLD: CRYSTAL CLEAR LAKE - A serene world where a pristine, shimmering lake reflects the azure sky and lush, green surroundings. The tranquil waters invite you to dip your toes or simply sit by the shore, providing a sense of peace and connection with nature.

JOURNAL YOUR EXPERIENCE - 2 Minutes [Set Timer]

___

WORKOUT COMPLETED [ ]

Somewhere in our DNA we know that stories are out there to help us understand what we're doing here on this planet.
Theresa Rebeck

ANCHORING INTO YOUR CHARACTER COLOUR & MUSIC

Anchoring yourself into your character is vital. It's one of the most freeing feelings when you understand their *essence* because everything they do, how they do it and what their purpose is, becomes so clear to you and the audience. Every choice you make after you find your *anchor*, feels easy, because you're acting from who and what your character is at the core. You can call it an essence, an aura, vibe, energy etc. We all have it and feel it from everyone around us. There are many ways into your character but music and colour are my favourite. Music can inform the script, your character, even each scene. Colours, I think you will find, can work incredibly because we as humans respond to colours like frequencies. Colours evoke many feelings and if you pay attention closely, you can see everyone has their own 'colour' that defines their core. An essence that informs how they operate and move through the world.

THEIR COLOUR - 2 Minutes [Set Timer]
Think of **someone you know**, and **define them with a colour**. **Tip**: Trust yourself. Your initial colour is usually close. **Tip**: Start with basic colours then eventually become much more specific. **Example**: Corinna is an earthy green with rays of sunlight flowing through the green. **Extra**: Ask someone who knows *that person* as well, what they think this person's colour is and why. See how close your answers are or not.

YOUR CHARACTERS COLOUR
Read the given character description just as you would an audition, **assign a colour to that character.** Now take that colour you chose and **allow it to infuse into your entire body**, affecting your every move, your speaking, the way you see the world etc. **Take any book** you have, flip to a random page and **read the text as this Colour/Character**. **Tip**: Be specific, choose a colour that excites you and don't be afraid to get creative.

CHARACTER DESCRIPTION: [BAILEY] Bailey is a young, talented skateboarder making waves in the urban skateboarding scene. Often with a baseball cap and headphones, Bailey is known for their effortless style and daring tricks. They spend most of their time at local skate parks or exploring the city, showcasing a blend of athleticism and creative expression. Despite occasional run-ins with authority figures for skating in prohibited areas, Bailey remains dedicated to their sport, embodying the rebellious and free-spirited nature of skateboarding culture. Their character is a vibrant mix of youthful energy, resilience, and a passion for pushing the limits of what's possible on a skateboard.

CHOOSE THEIR COLOUR - 4 Minutes [Set Timer]
THEIR COLOUR:

CHOOSE THEIR SONG - 4 Minutes [Set Timer]
THEIR SONG:

READ PASSAGE FROM BOOK - 2 Minutes [Set Timer]

FREEFORM DANCE - 2 minutes - [Set Timer]
Put on the selected music and **engage in freeform dancing, anchored in your colour/character,** Allow your body to move spontaneously and without inhibition. This can help you tap into your creative instincts and develop physical expressiveness *while staying in character.* **Tip**: Journal about the differences as opposed to how you normally dance.

JOURNAL YOUR EXPERIENCE - 1 Minute [Set Timer]

WORKOUT COMPLETED [ ]

Victories aren't born on the field. You create them during practice – day in and day out.
Silvia Pencak

HISTORICAL RESEARCH

We are in the information era and have access to the world and its rich history at our fingertips. This exploration is not about 'learning facts'; it's a journey to the heart of human experience. The empathy and the understanding, especially on the things you disagree with, are incredibly valuable. If you look closely, you'll find the way people think, at different times in history, their attitudes, choices, and the way they move their bodies can teach you so much about us, right now. Fill your toolbox so it's overflowing with information and ideas to pull from so your imagination has so much to play with.

PHYSICAL WARMUP - 2 minutes - [Set Timer]
Freeform Dance: Put on some music and engage in freeform dancing. Allow your body to move spontaneously and without inhibition. This can help you tap into your creative instincts and develop physical expressiveness. **Tip**: Try music you've never listened to.

RESEARCH - 13 Minutes [Set Timer]
YouTube, streaming platforms, the internet or books, **research the given era/person/moment in time,** journal or make notes on your device, so when you want to find this information, it's organized and readily accessible. As you go, **write anything and everything _you_ find fascinating. Tip:** If the topic doesn't interest you, choose your own, or take a chance and still research it, but from a different perspective. Physicalities, voice, ideals, etc. Trust your body that when you see something interesting, you'll know. **Extra**: Speak it out and copy their movements. Our memory recall is massively affected by our bodies. Be specific and when you re-read your notes, you'll be amazed by how much your mind and body remember.

TOPIC:
The Peloponnesian War (431–404 BC) - The Perspective of Alcibiades: Alcibiades, an Athenian statesman, orator, and general, offers a compelling perspective on the Peloponnesian War, a pivotal conflict in ancient Greek history. He was a charismatic and controversial figure known for his shifting allegiances between Athens, Sparta, and Persia. While direct footage of Alcibiades doesn't exist, his life and actions are well-documented in historical texts, including those by Thucydides and Plutarch. Actors can delve into these accounts to understand his complex personality, his strategic and political maneuvers, and his impact on the course of the war.

_____
_____
_____
_____
_____
_____
_____
_____
_____
_____
_____
_____
_____
_____

WORKOUT COMPLETED [ ]

Don't wait for opportunities, create them.
Viola Davis

BELIEF

Beliefs are the convictions that something exists or is true, especially without proof. That is also the definition of what we do as actors. We play make-believe. Our beliefs shape our world, especially our beliefs about ourselves and it works for the characters you play. Understand your beliefs and how they influence your mind, body and spirit, then you will be able to better understand others, so you can embody them. Allow the beliefs of your character to colour your perception of your world and your interaction with everything in it. "Acting is the best magic trick in the world. We applaud performances not because it's real, but because you made us believe."

VOCAL WORK - 2 Minutes - [Set timer]

Lip Trills: Close your lips together lightly, like you're going to blow a raspberry. Then, blow air through your closed lips while making sounds. You should feel a tickling sensation. Pick a song and Lip Trill along with it. **Tip**: Stretch your range as much as you can and pick a song you've never listened to.

BELIEF WORKOUT

Get your journal or write in here. **Define your personal belief/view** on the given subject. **Grab any book you own,** flip to a random page and **read it out loud,** colouring the words and intention with your belief system. **Tip:** Write trigger words you can hook into in the future: **Optimism-** Always smiling, grateful, opportunity, sunshine yellow.

YOUR PERSONAL BELIEF

Crowded Spaces - 7 Minutes [Set Timer]

_____
_____
_____
_____

READ WITH BELIEF - 2 Minutes [Set Timer]

CHARACTERS BELIEF

Crowded Spaces
I prefer it. I love all the different personalities and lives flying around me. I hate being alone. Drives me crazy being in the quiet and no one is around. Very sad actually. I catch myself being extremely fidgety when I'm alone.

READ WITH CHARACTERS BELIEF - 2 Minutes [Set Timer]

Forget your personal view and **fully embrace the character's belief. Read out loud again.**

JOURNAL YOUR EXPERIENCE - 2 Minutes [Set Timer]

_____
_____
_____

WORKOUT COMPLETED [ ]

PERFORMANCE STRATEGY
14 DAY REVIEW

TAKE A MOMENT OF REFLECTION AND BREAKDOWN WHERE YOU ARE RIGHT NOW IN YOUR CAREER AND AS AN ACTOR. THE MORE SPECIFIC YOU ARE THE MORE CLEAR YOU CAN SEE WHERE YOU ARE NOW SO YOU CAN GET TO WHERE YOU WANT TO GO FASTER

★ ★ ★ ★ ★

Richard Branson: Despite being dyslexic and a high school dropout, Branson founded the Virgin Group, an expansive business empire encompassing hundreds of diverse companies across multiple industries.

DATE:

MY WHY
WHY ARE YOU DOING WHAT YOU ARE DOING
BE SPECIFIC

MY MAIN GOALS
IN-ORDER OF IMPORTANCE

1.

   Action Step(s):

2.

   Action Step(s):

3.

   Action Step(s):

FROM THE LAST 14 DAYS
5 STAR RATING

☆☆☆☆☆

YOUR KEY POINTS AND TAKEAWAYS - WHY THAT AMOUNT OF STAR RATING, LIKES, DISLIKES, THE BIGGEST LESSON YOU LEARNED, GOOD OR BAD:

STRENGTHS:

WEAKNESSES:

IMPROVEMENT STRATEGY
HOW CAN YOU IMPROVE ON THESE AREAS FOR THE NEXT 14 DAYS:

GOAL FROM LAST :
DID YOU ACHIEVE IT?

WHY OR WHY NOT?

GOAL FOR THE NEXT 14 EXERCISES
THE MORE SPECIFIC YOU ARE THE GREATER THE RESULT

   Action Step(s):

Your uniqueness is your superpower. Embrace it
and let it shine in your work.
Lupita Nyong'o

MY WHY:

GOAL(s):

PHYSICAL WARMUP - 1 minute [Set Timer]
Freeform Dance: Allow yourself to engage with the music freely, responding instinctively to the rhythm and melody. **Tip**: Close your eyes if it helps you disconnect from your environment and fully immerse in the music.

VOCAL WORK - 3 minutes [Set Timer]
Lip Trills: Practice lip trills by blowing air through your lips while producing a sustained pitch. **Tip**: Start with a comfortable note and then move up and down your range to gently warm up your vocal cords.

EMOTIONAL RECALL - 5 minutes [Set Timer]
Romantic Nostalgia: Dive deep into a personal memory that stirs feelings of love or longing. **Tip**: Allow the emotions to manifest physically, whether it's through facial expressions, gestures, or even tears.

ANIMAL WORK - HORSE

Research - 2 minutes [Set Timer]
Research or recall the powerful yet graceful movements of a horse.

Animal Exercise - 3 minutes [Set Timer]
Emulate the horse's movements, from calm grazing to galloping. **Tip**: When transitioning to human behaviour, maintain the animal's noble and strong yet calm demeanour in your presence and movements.

Discovery Journal - 1 Minute [Set Timer]
3 Main Characteristics: (Whatever stands out to YOU to embody the essence)

_____
_____
_____
_____
_____
_____
_____

WORKOUT COMPLETED [ ]

The whole art of filmmaking is to achieve what is in your head. You ask people to believe that what they are seeing is real.
Alfred Hitchcock

SCRIPT ANALYSIS for **RELATIONSHIPS & SPECIFICITY** - 15 minutes [Set Timer]
Choose your character, circle everything in this script you have a relationship with. Including people, places, things, smells, time of day etc. **Write what your relationship with those items are** and **be specific**. The more specific and fun you have with your relationships, the more interesting your characters will be and the more fun the audience has. **Tip:** Everything isn't in the scene. Use your imagination to create details, only if it's contextually appropriate. **Extra:** Write your > ***Objective, win or lose? Consequence of failing?*** The **Who What Where When Why.**

Title: In the Shadows of Empires
EXT. ABANDONED WAREHOUSE DISTRICT - NIGHT

A desolate urban landscape, with the ruins of industrial glory. MARC, 18, tough and brooding, stands in the shadows, looking up at a crumbling building. LUCILLA, 17, fierce and determined, appears from the darkness, her eyes reflecting a fire within.

MARC
You shouldn't have come. It's dangerous.

LUCILLA
I walk where I please. Even emperors can't dictate my path.

MARC
Yet, even emperors fear the unknown, Lucilla.

LUCILLA
Let them fear. We are not their pawns.

They share a moment of understanding, two souls united against a world of power and corruption.

MARC
Your brother, he watches you. He knows.

LUCILLA
My brother is a fool blinded by his own shadow.

MARC
And fools with power are dangerous. We must be cautious.

LUCILLA
I grow tired of hiding, of whispered words and cloaked meetings.

MARC
Patience, Lucilla. The day will come when we can stand openly against them.

LUCILLA
I dream of that day. When love and honour overthrow deceit and tyranny.

MARC
It will come. For now, we must survive.

They stand close, the weight of their struggle tangible in the air.

LUCILLA
Promise me, Marc. That we will see that day.

MARC
I promise. In this life or the next, we will be free.

They exchange a look of fierce determination before parting ways, disappearing into the night, each a gladiator in their own right, battling for a future where their love can reign free.

WORKOUT COMPLETED [ ]

The only safe thing is to take a chance.
Mike Nichols

IMAGINATION

We have a lot of tools in our arsenal as actors but **I believe imagination is the most powerful.** "If you hook into the character's belief system and you believe it 100%, there is no way the audience won't." - Meryl Streep "Imagination is more important than knowledge for knowledge is limited. - Einstein. Everyone has an Imagination but it must be worked out to get stronger. Think of your imagination as a limitless playground. In this space, you can be anyone, go anywhere, and do anything. **Have the courage to allow yourself to play!**

Solo Imaginary World Exploration - 6 Minutes [Set Timer]

Find a quiet space to relax and focus. **Close your eyes** and **let your imagination run wild. Tip:** Engage all your senses to explore this environment. Touch, taste, smell etc. Allow your emotions to guide you. **Extra:** After you establish this world in your imagination, you could introduce characters and have a dialogue with them. Are they friends or foes?

IMAGINARY WORLD: Ice Fortress in the Arctic: Discover a fortress of ice and snow, uncovering hidden chambers and ancient civilizations.

JOURNAL YOUR EXPERIENCE - 2 Minutes [Set Timer]

_____
_____
_____
_____
_____
_____

Your Characters Filter - 5 Minutes [Set Timer]

Everyone including the characters you play see the world through their own specific perspective/filter. I like to use the word filter because you can take out a filter, clean it, change its style, colour, an optimist or a pessimist, comedian or a nihilist, etc. **Find a quiet space** to focus. **Close your eyes and let go of your personal thoughts and emotions** to make space for your characters. **Open your eyes, and allow the filter provided to effect everything around you. Tip:** Explore wherever you are and interact with the objects. **Extra:** How does *this* character walk and move in their world?

FILTER: Tired Heart - Weary from a life of struggle, everything is grey and hopeless.

JOURNAL YOUR EXPERIENCE - 2 Minutes [Set Timer]

_____
_____
_____
_____
_____
_____

WORKOUT COMPLETED [ ]

The Wright Brothers flew right through
the smoke screen of impossibility.
Charles Kettering

CHARACTER STUDY "PEOPLE WATCHING"

Actors are required to portray characters that are believable and relatable. You don't have to agree with them but you have to understand them. Walk like them, talk like them, see the world like them. So, in order to fill our toolbox, we have to **go out into the world and study**. Then practice them over and over so we can "walk in their shoes', comfortably and confidently. Study their movements, mannerisms, the "vibe" they give off, the clothes they wear etc. **Fill your toolbox with the rhythms and idiosyncrasies of human behaviour.**

OBSERVATION CHARACTER STUDY - 15 Minutes [Set Timer]

Find a busy place where you can **sit and observe.** Choose anyone you find interesting. **Write down what stands out about them.** *The way they sit, drink their coffee, walk, talk, interact with others etc.* **Tip: Mirror them immediately.** This will help memorize the feeling of that character so whenever you come back to these characters you're discovering, your body will remember. **Extra:** Before you go to sleep, read over the characters from today and reenact their movements.

___

COLOURS: We as humans respond to colours like frequencies. If you pay attention closely, you can see everyone has their own 'colour' that defines their core. An essence that informs how they operate and move through the world.

WHAT COLOUR ARE THEY:

___

WORKOUT COMPLETED [ ]

If you act brave, you can seem brave, and if you do it enough, you can talk yourself into believing you're brave.
Kelli O'Hara

VOICE & DICTION

I wish I had learned this at the beginning of my career. The confidence to communicate clearly and powerfully is a game-changer for you as an actor. **Think of your voice as a musical instrument that needs regular tuning. This workout is your daily tuning session,** ensuring that your instrument is always ready. "The word 'theatre' comes from the Greeks. It means the seeing place. It is the place people come to see the truth about life and the social situation." - Stella Adler. Embrace this workout as a key to unlocking and portraying *that* truth by letting your voice be the vehicle that transports your audience into the heart of your story.

READ PASSAGE - 30 Seconds [Set Timer]
Speak the passage and take note of its quality. **Tip**: Record Audio to compare afterward.

"As dawn breaks, the silent forest awakens. Birds sing in chorus, leaves rustle in the morning breeze, and the world stirs in harmony. The first rays of sunlight pierce through the canopy, illuminating the dance of life."

RELAXATION - 1 Minute [Set Timer]
Deep Breathing: Sit and Inhale deeply through your nose, filling your lungs, then exhale slowly through your mouth. Imagine stress leaving your body with each breath.

Nay Nay Nay - 1 Minute [Set Timer]
Pick a song and sing the word "Nay" repeatedly. Start with a comfortable pitch and gradually move the sound from your nose to your chest, ensuring each "Nay" is clear and resonant. Stretch your range as best you can to strengthen.

Sustained 'S' - 2 Minutes [Set Timer]
Inhale deeply and then exhale slowly, making a continuous 's' sound. Keep the sound as even and steady as you can. Always push a little longer than you think you can.

Vowel Pronunciation Drill - 2 Minutes [Set Timer]
Slowly go through each vowel sound **(A, E, I, O, U), holding and exaggerating each sound. Combine them with consonants** (e.g., ba, be, bi, bo, bu). Pay attention to the clarity and sharpness of each sound. Repeat a few times before moving to the next.

Lip Trills - 3 minutes - [Set timer]
Close your lips together lightly, like you're going to blow a raspberry. Then, blow air through your closed lips while making sounds. You should feel a tickling sensation. Pick a song and Lip Trill the whole along with it. **Tip**: Stretch your range as much as you can and pick a song you've never listened to.

The Cork Exercise - 4 Minutes [Set Timer]
Place a cork between your teeth and try to read a passage aloud. This forces your articulation muscles to work harder. If you don't have a cork, bite down gently on your thumb. You can use the following text for this exercise:

READ PASSAGE AGAIN - 30 Seconds [Set Timer]
Speak the passage and take note of its quality. **Tip**: Record Audio to compare.

Discovery Journal - 1 Minute [Set Timer]

_____
_____
_____

WORKOUT COMPLETED [ ]

Some people dream of success, while other people get up every morning and make it happen.
Wayne Huizenga

SUBTEXT

Subtext is what lies beneath the surface of our words. It's the hidden layer of meaning, driven by the character's internal thoughts, emotions, desires, and motivations. Subtext is one of my favourite things as an actor because so much can be said with one simple line of dialogue. The power of "Hello" can be exciting if you told that person years ago "If I ever see you again, I'll kill you. Maybe it's the most beautiful person you've ever seen. Now, say "hello". *Subtext* shows the audience what your relationship with the characters/places/situations are, without having to explain it. We experience it every day and it is our job to create characters that interact as we do.

VOCAL WORK - 3 minutes - [Set Timer]
Lip Trills: Close your lips together lightly, like you're going to blow a raspberry. Then, blow air through your closed lips while making sounds. You should feel a tickling sensation. Pick a song and Lip Trill along with it. **Tip**: Stretch your range as much as you can and pick a song you've never listened to.

SUBTEXT PRACTICE
Use the line of dialogue provided and practice each of these subtexts **out loud.** Move on to the next, only when you believe yourself. Trust that you will know when *that* is. Before you begin, **pick a spot to look at and imagine** in detail, **who you are speaking with**. **Tip**: *Sometimes* we mean exactly what we are saying. Look for that too. **Extra**: Substitute someone you have a strong relationship with in real life, good or bad, and see it's affect.

Initial Line: "Have you seen the new mural in the city square?"
Your Response Line: "Yeah, I've seen it. It's quite bold, isn't it? It's stirring up all sorts of opinions. It's not just art; it's a statement. What's your take on it?"

SUBTEXTS - 6 Minutes [Set Timer]
[ ] Personal connection: You secretly know the artist and their true intentions.
[ ] Outrage: You find the mural offensive and wish it hadn't been approved.
[ ] Pride: You see it as a progressive symbol and are proud of your city.
[ ] Confusion: You don't understand what all the fuss is about.
[ ] Curiosity: You're intrigued by the public's diverse reactions to the mural.
[ ] Your Own Subtext

RELATIONSHIP SUBTEXTS - 6 Minutes [Set Timer]
[ ] Supportive Partner: Your spouse is the artist, and you're their biggest fan.
[ ] Critical Parent: Your child painted it, and you don't approve of their choices.
[ ] Inspired Friend: Motivated by your friend's courage to create such a piece.
[ ] Jealous Colleague: You're an artist too and feel overshadowed by their success.
[ ] Unbiased Observer: Noo personal stake but find the situation interesting.
[ ] Your Own Subtext

Discovery Journal
___
___
___
___

WORKOUT COMPLETED [ ]

If there's a story that you want to read, but it hasn't been written yet, then you must write it.
Toni Morrison

EMOTIONS

The 'moment before', **the emotional preparation, is the most important key to a great scene.** If you start any scene *without* an emotional preparation it feels like trying to drive a car in neutral. The preparation is the uphill climb of every rollercoaster; Once you grind all the way to the top, the chains let go and the rest of the ride takes care of itself. "No one wants to see a play or a movie and look at technical proficiency. You want to be moved, you want a human experience, you want to feel less alone" - Viola Davis. **Practice your emotions over and over** so when it's time, you aren't worried "Will I get there?" **You're imagination and emotions should be a tinderbox, so easy to light up. All it take is half a spark.**

EULOGY - 12 Minutes [Set Timer]

Find a quiet comfortable space. Choose someone in your life who is alive and important to you. Create an imaginary reason for why they have died. Now start from the point of the phone call— Imagine who calls, what they say and what you say. Eventually find yourself at the funeral, about to begin the eulogy. See the casket, is it open or closed?? What is that person wearing and any other details for yourself. Before you begin to speak, look into the audience and see who is there- Family, friends etc **Then begin the eulogy.** **Tip**: Be as specific as you can with everything. **Inside of specificity is where you will find the triggers to your heart.** Let your imagination take you wherever you want in this exercise. **Example**: Placing her favourite sheep stuffed animal in the casket, tucked under her arm like she always held it, then kissing her goodbye one last time.

DISCOVERY JOURNAL - 3 Minutes [Set Timer]

Make sure to **include the specific triggers** you experience because you can use these **TRIGGER MOMENTS** in the future instead of repeating the *entire* exercise.

_____
_____
_____
_____
_____
_____
_____
_____
_____
_____
_____
_____
_____
_____
_____
_____
_____
_____
_____
_____

WORKOUT COMPLETED [ ]

Acting is making it seem like its
happening now.
Anne Jackson

THE CORK EXERCISE - 4 Minutes [Set Timer]
Place a cork between your teeth and read a passage aloud. This forces your articulation muscles to work harder. If you don't have a cork, bite down gently on your thumb. You can use the following text for this exercise:

> "Under the starlit sky, the desert comes alive with a symphony of sounds. The wind whispers secrets through the sand dunes, creating intricate patterns under the moon's glow. Cacti stand as silent sentinels, witnessing the timeless dance of the nocturnal creatures."

WRITE A LETTER - 10 Minutes [Set Timer]
Get a piece of paper or write this in your device. **Take a moment** to let this situation and relationship sink in. Then let your imagination run wild and **write them a letter.**

Your Character: Alex, a dedicated social worker who has spent years advocating for children in difficult family situations.

Other Character: Sam, a parent whose child Alex had to recommend be removed from their home due to safety concerns, has since made significant improvements in their life and circumstances.

Relationship: Alex's professional interaction with Sam was initially fraught with tension and conflict, due to the nature of the child welfare case. Despite the challenges, Alex always hoped for a positive change in Sam's situation.

Context of the Letter: Learning that Sam has turned their life around and is seeking to reunite with their child, Alex is moved to write a letter to Sam. This letter is an acknowledgment of Sam's efforts, a reflection on the difficult decisions made in the past, and an expression of support for Sam's journey towards becoming a better parent. It's a delicate balance of professional boundaries and personal empathy for a parent who has struggled but is striving for redemption.

Discovery Journal - 1 minute [Set Timer]
_____
_____
_____
_____

WORKOUT COMPLETED [ ]

One of the hardest things in life is having words in your heart that you don't utter.
James Earl Jones

VOCAL WORK - 3 minutes [Set timer]

Lip Trills: Close your lips together lightly, like you're going to blow a raspberry. Then, blow air through your closed lips while making sounds. You should feel a tickling sensation. Pick a song and Lip Trill along with it. **Tip**: Stretch your range as much as you can and pick a song you've never listened to.

VERBAL IMPROV - 10 Minutes [Set Timer]

Find a space where you are comfortable and free to express yourself. Take a moment to **let this situation, character and prompt, sink in**. Then let your imagination run wild: **Picture who you are talking to** then **begin with *the prompt*** and **continue to verbalize everything** this character would say. **Tip**: This is exploration! There is no "getting it right". BE BRAVE to explore and discover.

Character: Harper, an environmental engineer known for their innovative solutions and dedication to sustainability, learns that their mentor, Alex, who they've always seen as a role model, has been accepting bribes to approve environmentally harmful projects. Harper's respect for the environment makes this a critical issue.

Prompt: "Alex, I've learned about the bribes and your project approvals. We need to discuss the consequences of your actions."

Who are you talking to:

Describe them in two specific words:

Discovery Journal - 2 minutes [Set Timer]

_____
_____
_____
_____
_____
_____
_____
_____
_____

WORKOUT COMPLETED [ ]

Acting is living truthfully under the
imaginary given circumstances.
A practical handbook for the actor

SELF AWARENESS

The more you understand yourself, the more you are able to understand and develop your characters. Like you, your characters have thoughts, beliefs, traumas, passions etc. When you become aware of your own and start to see how those experiences and beliefs have shaped your life, how you operate and view the world, then you can develop your characters that are much more rich and vivid.

PHYSICAL WARMUP - 2 minutes [Set Timer]
Freeform Dance: Put on some music and engage in freeform dancing. Allow your body to move spontaneously and without inhibition. This can help you tap into your creative instincts and develop physical expressiveness. **Tip**: Try music you've never listened to.

CURRENT EMOTIONAL INVENTORY - 3 Minutes [Set Timer]
Write down and **record your current emotions**. Identify what you're feeling at this moment and why. **Tip**: Be as specific as you can, **don't disregard anything.** You can also **scan your body** to see how and where your current emotion is affecting you. Your posture, the way you walk, bouncing foot, sore neck etc

CURRENT EMOTIONAL STATE:

SELF DISCOVERY QUESTIONS - 10 Minutes [Set Timer]
I suggest a journal or writing it in your phone's notes so you don't run out of space here.

When have I felt most vulnerable in a social situation, and what triggered that vulnerability?

What is my favourite smell and why?

WORKOUT COMPLETED [ ]

It's important to say that the more challenging a scene is, in a way, the more fun it is because the more of my job I get to do.
Daniel Radcliffe

IMAGINATION

We have a lot of tools in our arsenal as actors but I believe imagination is the most powerful. "If you hook into the character's belief system and you believe it 100%, there is no way the audience won't." - Meryl Streep. Everyone has an Imagination but it must be worked out to get stronger. Think of your imagination as a limitless playground. In this space, you can be anyone, go anywhere, and do anything. **Have the courage to allow yourself to play!**

VOCAL WORK - 2 Minutes - [Set timer]

Lip Trills: Close your lips together lightly, like you're going to blow a raspberry. Then, blow air through your closed lips while making sounds. You should feel a tickling sensation. Pick a song and Lip Trill along with it. **Tip**: Stretch your range as much as you can and pick a song you've never listened to.

IMPROVISED STORYTELLING - 5 Minutes [Set Timer]

Speak out the scenario provided and continue the story! Focus on vivid details, character development and how the main character overcomes the main obstacle. **Tip**: Try not to stop speaking so you don't have time to "think". Allow your imagination to keep moving forward without interruption. **Tip:** Record these stories on your device, in case it's great but more importantly to see your progress as you go on.

STARTING POINT: It's 10:02 p.m. Present Day. You go to sleep, safe in your bed, but with an odd feeling... As your heavy eyes shut, they suddenly open again staring at the clock. 3:33 a.m. Wide awake, you get out of bed and when you look in the mirror you see a 75-year-old! After you calm down you realize... It's you. Your body is 75 but you have the energy of your younger self. You run out of the bathroom as quickly as you can and grab your phone to call—

IMAGINARY WORLD EXPLORATION - 6 Minutes [Set Timer]

Find a quiet space to relax and focus. **Close your eyes** and let your imagination run wild. **Tip:** Engage all your senses to explore this environment. Touch, taste, smell etc and allow your emotions to guide you. **Extra:** After you explore this world with your senses, you could introduce characters' and have a dialogue with them. Are they friends or foes?

IMAGINARY WORLD: CANDLELIT CAVERN - An underground cavern aglow with the warm, flickering light of countless candles. The walls are adorned with glistening crystals, and the air is infused with a soothing, earthy fragrance. As you explore this tranquil refuge, the soft candlelight guides your way, creating a serene and contemplative atmosphere.

JOURNAL YOUR EXPERIENCE - 2 Minutes [Set Timer]

_____
_____
_____
_____
_____
_____
_____

WORKOUT COMPLETED [ ]

You have got to discover you, what
you do, and trust it.
Barbra Streisand

ANCHORING INTO YOUR CHARACTER COLOUR & MUSIC

Anchoring yourself into your character is vital. It's one of the most freeing feelings when you understand their *essence* because everything they do, how they do it and what their purpose is, becomes so clear to you and the audience. Every choice you make after you find your *anchor*, feels easy, because you're acting from who and what your character is at the core. You can call it an essence, an aura, vibe, energy etc. We all have it and feel it from everyone around us. There are many ways into your character but music and colour are my favourite. Music can inform the script, your character, even each scene. Colours, I think you will find, can work incredibly because we as humans respond to colours like frequencies. Colours evoke many feelings and if you pay attention closely, you can see everyone has their own 'colour' that defines their core. An essence that informs how they operate and move through the world.

THEIR COLOUR - 2 Minutes [Set Timer]
Think of **someone you know**, and **define them with a colour**. **Tip**: Trust yourself. Your initial colour is usually close. **Tip**: Start with basic colours then eventually become much more specific. **Example**: Corinna is an earthy green with rays of sunlight flowing through the green. **Extra**: Ask someone who knows *that person* as well, what they think this person's colour is and why. See how close your answers are or not.

YOUR CHARACTERS COLOUR
Read the given character description just as you would an audition, **assign a colour to that character.** Now take that colour you chose and **allow it to infuse into your entire body**, affecting your every move, your speaking, the way you see the world etc. **Take any book** you have, flip to a random page and **read the text as this Colour/Character**. **Tip**: Be specific, choose a colour that excites you and don't be afraid to get creative.

CHARACTER DESCRIPTION: [MORGAN] Morgan is a young, up-and-coming chef who runs a small popular fusion cuisine restaurant in the heart of the city. Known for their innovative flavour combinations, Morgan dresses in a sleek chef's uniform with a flair for the dramatic. Their kitchen is their sanctuary, a place of creativity and experimentation. Despite the pressures of the culinary world and the constant challenge to stay relevant, Morgan remains driven by a love for culinary arts and a desire to push the boundaries of traditional cooking. Their character combines culinary genius with a touch of artistic eccentricity.

CHOOSE THEIR COLOUR - 4 Minutes [Set Timer]
THEIR COLOUR:

CHOOSE THEIR SONG - 4 Minutes [Set Timer]
THEIR SONG:

READ PASSAGE FROM BOOK - 2 Minutes [Set Timer]

FREEFORM DANCE - 2 minutes - [Set Timer]
Put on the selected music and **engage in freeform dancing, anchored in your colour/character,** Allow your body to move spontaneously and without inhibition. This can help you tap into your creative instincts and develop physical expressiveness *while staying in character.* **Tip**: Journal about the differences as opposed to how you normally dance.

JOURNAL YOUR EXPERIENCE - 1 Minute [Set Timer]

WORKOUT COMPLETED [ ]

You are enough. You are so enough. It's unbelievable how enough you are.
Sierra Boggess

HISTORICAL RESEARCH

We are in the information era and have access to the world and its rich history at our fingertips. This exploration is not about 'learning facts'; it's a journey to the heart of human experience. The empathy and the understanding, especially on the things you disagree with, are incredibly valuable. If you look closely, you'll find the way people think, at different times in history, their attitudes, choices, and the way they move their bodies can teach you so much about us, right now. Fill your toolbox so it's overflowing with information and ideas to pull from so your imagination has so much to play with.

PHYSICAL WARMUP - 2 minutes - [Set Timer]
Freeform Dance: Put on some music and engage in freeform dancing. Allow your body to move spontaneously and without inhibition. This can help you tap into your creative instincts and develop physical expressiveness. **Tip**: Try music you've never listened to.

RESEARCH - 13 Minutes [Set Timer]
YouTube, streaming platforms, the internet or books, **research the given era/person/moment in time,** journal or make notes on your device, so when you want to find this information, it's organized and readily accessible. As you go, **write anything and everything _you_ find fascinating. Tip:** If the topic doesn't interest you, choose your own, or take a chance and still research it, but from a different perspective. Physicalities, voice, ideals, etc. Trust your body that when you see something interesting, you'll know. **Extra**: Speak it out and copy their movements. Our memory recall is massively affected by our bodies. Be specific and when you re-read your notes, you'll be amazed by how much your mind and body remember.

TOPIC:
The Civil Rights Movement (1950s-1960s) - The Perspective of Ruby Bridges: Ruby Bridges, as a six-year-old girl, became an iconic figure in the Civil Rights Movement when she integrated an all-white elementary school in New Orleans in 1960. Footage and photographs from this time, including her being escorted by federal marshals amidst protests, offer a unique perspective on this historical period. Actors can study these materials to understand the immense courage and resilience shown by a child in the face of overwhelming racial hostility. Ruby Bridges' story provides a powerful lens into the human impact of segregation and the fight for educational equality in the United States.

WORKOUT COMPLETED [ ]

If you get a chance to act in a room that somebody else has paid rent for, then you're given a free chance to practice your craft.
Phillip Seymour Hoffman

BELIEF

Beliefs are the convictions that something exists or is true, especially without proof. That is also the definition of what we do as actors. We play make-believe. Our beliefs shape our world, especially our beliefs about ourselves and it works for the characters you play. Understand your beliefs and how they influence your mind, body and spirit, then you will be able to better understand others, so you can embody them. Allow the beliefs of your character to colour your perception of your world and your interaction with everything in it. "Acting is the best magic trick in the world. We applaud performances not because it's real, but because you made us believe."

VOCAL WORK - 2 Minutes - [Set timer]

Lip Trills: Close your lips together lightly, like you're going to blow a raspberry. Then, blow air through your closed lips while making sounds. You should feel a tickling sensation. Pick a song and Lip Trill along with it. **Tip**: Stretch your range as much as you can and pick a song you've never listened to.

BELIEF WORKOUT

Get your journal or write in here. **Define your personal belief/view** on the given subject. **Grab any book you own,** flip to a random page and **read it out loud,** colouring the words and intention with your belief system. **Tip:** Write trigger words you can hook into in the future: **Optimism-** Always smiling, grateful, opportunity, sunshine yellow.

YOUR PERSONAL BELIEF

Hygiene - 7 Minutes [Set Timer]

_____
_____
_____
_____

READ WITH BELIEF - 2 Minutes [Set Timer]

CHARACTERS BELIEF

Hygiene

So important to me. I actually, might be a germaphobe. I'm not crazy, I just love things clean. It's incredibly important to me. When people don't wash the dishes properly, or don't wash their hands as soon as they get home.], I find it repulsive. And it's so easy to do. If you don't brush your teeth, don't even think of kissing me.

READ WITH CHARACTERS BELIEF - 2 Minutes [Set Timer]

Forget your personal view and **fully embrace the character's belief. Read out loud again.**

JOURNAL YOUR EXPERIENCE - 2 Minutes [Set Timer]

_____
_____
_____
_____

WORKOUT COMPLETED [ ]

PERFORMANCE STRATEGY
14 DAY REVIEW

TAKE A MOMENT OF REFLECTION AND BREAKDOWN WHERE YOU ARE RIGHT NOW IN YOUR CAREER AND AS AN ACTOR.
THE MORE SPECIFIC YOU ARE THE MORE CLEAR YOU CAN SEE WHERE YOU ARE NOW SO YOU CAN GET TO WHERE YOU WANT TO GO FASTER

★ ★ ★ ★ ★

Albert Einstein: Didn't speak until the age of four, didn't start reading until the age of 7, but Einstein went on to redefine the realm of physics, earning the Nobel Prize for his groundbreaking contributions. His theories, particularly that of relativity, dramatically transformed our understanding of space, time, and the very fabric of the universe.
A testament to human potential and perseverance.

DATE:

MY WHY
WHY ARE YOU DOING WHAT YOU ARE DOING
BE SPECIFIC

MY MAIN GOALS
IN-ORDER OF IMPORTANCE

1.

    Action Step(s):

2.

    Action Step(s):

3.

    Action Step(s):

FROM THE LAST 14 DAYS   ☆☆☆☆☆
5 STAR RATING

YOUR KEY POINTS AND TAKEAWAYS - WHY THAT AMOUNT OF STAR RATING, LIKES, DISLIKES, THE BIGGEST LESSON YOU LEARNED, GOOD OR BAD:

STRENGTHS:

WEAKNESSES:

IMPROVEMENT STRATEGY
HOW CAN YOU IMPROVE ON THESE AREAS FOR THE NEXT 14 DAYS:

GOAL FROM LAST :
DID YOU ACHIEVE IT?

WHY OR WHY NOT?

GOAL FOR THE NEXT 14 EXERCISES
THE MORE SPECIFIC YOU ARE THE GREATER THE RESULT

    Action Step(s):

You're not going there to get a job. You're going there to present what you do.
Bryan Cranston

MY WHY:

GOAL(s):

PHYSICAL WARMUP - 1 minute [Set Timer]
Elemental Dance: Move through the space, embodying each of the elements: begin with the fluidity of water, advance into the fieriness of fire, stabilize into the solidity of earth, and finish with the lightness of air. **Tip**: Let the characteristics of each element guide the quality of your movements and transitions.

VOCAL WORK - 3 minutes [Set Timer]
Consonant Play: Articulate sharp, clear consonants ('t', 'k', 'p', 's', 'r') progressively faster, focusing on precision and diction. **Tip**: Pay attention to your mouth and how it moves with each sound; feel each consonant's texture.

EMOTIONAL RECALL - 5 minutes [Set Timer]
Bittersweet Memory: Engage with a memory that holds both joy and sorrow. Express these layered emotions through your body language and facial expressions. **Tip**: Allow yourself to experience the flux of contrasting emotions, letting them coexist and inform your movements.

ANIMAL WORK - CAT

Research - 2 minutes [Set Timer]
Observe the nuanced movements of a house cat — its alertness and moments of relaxation.

Animal Exercise 3 minutes [Set Timer]
Emulate the cat's prowl and stretch, alternating between relaxed and tense states. Afterward, transition to observing humans with the same level of scrutiny a cat might, interpreting their movements and intentions. **Tip**: Reflect on the juxtaposition of a cat's instinctive movements with human social behaviours.

Discovery Journal - 1 Minute [Set Timer]
3 Main Characteristics: (Whatever stands out to YOU to embody the essence)

_____
_____
_____
_____
_____
_____
_____

WORKOUT COMPLETED [ ]

I'm curious about other people. That's the essence of my acting. I'm interested in what it would be like to be you.
Meryl Streep

SCRIPT ANALYSIS for **RELATIONSHIPS & SPECIFICITY** - 15 minutes [Set Timer]
Choose your character, circle everything in this script you have a relationship with. Including people, places, things, smells, time of day etc. **Write what your relationship with those items are and be specific.** The more specific and fun you have with your relationships, the more interesting your characters will be and the more fun the audience has. **Tip:** Everything isn't in the scene. Use your imagination to create details, <u>only if</u> it's contextually appropriate. **Extra:** Write your > **Objective, win or lose? Consequence of failing?** *The Who What Where When Why.*

Title: **Echoes of the Forgotten**
EXT. RUSTIC LAKESIDE - EVENING

A hauntingly beautiful lakeside with the sun setting. **JAKE**, rugged and contemplative, sits on an old dock, his feet dangling in the water. **EMMA**, quiet strength, approaches...

JAKE
Didn't expect anyone else here. It's my secret spot.

EMMA
Looks like it's not so secret anymore. It's beautiful though.

JAKE
It's the only place I can think straight.

EMMA
(sitting beside him)
What's on your mind?

JAKE
Just the regular, you know? Who am I, what am I doing for the rest of my life.

EMMA
Oh, that's it?

JAKE
Yup.

EMMA
It's okay not to have all the answers.

He looks at her... They watch the water, the sound of gentle waves as their feet dip in the water.

JAKE
What about you? What brings you here?

EMMA
Needed to escape for a bit. Sometimes the noise of the world gets—

JAKE
Loud...

EMMA
Loud. We all have our battles, I guess.

JAKE
Yeah. Not much of a fighter. I know I look tough but, big softy.

EMMA
You're funny. Or maybe... learn when to let go and trust you'll know the answer when you see it.

Their eyes meet... for more than a moment.

JAKE
Very wise.

EMMA
I can see that in you too... For being able to see that in me.

They continue to sit side by side with the tranquillity of the lakeside, finding solace in each other's company while letting go of life's pressures for a moment.

WORKOUT COMPLETED [ ]

My thought process has always been, I'm excited to show you what my version of this story would look like. You're going to be able to get a little condensed show. That took the pressure off getting the job.
Tituss Burgess

IMAGINATION

We have a lot of tools in our arsenal as actors but **I believe imagination is the most powerful.** "If you hook into the character's belief system and you believe it 100%, there is no way the audience won't." - Meryl Streep "Imagination is more important than knowledge for knowledge is limited. - Einstein. Everyone has an Imagination but it must be worked out to get stronger. Think of your imagination as a limitless playground. In this space, you can be anyone, go anywhere, and do anything. **Have the courage to allow yourself to play!**

Solo Imaginary World Exploration - 6 Minutes [Set Timer]

Find a quiet space to relax and focus. **Close your eyes** and **let your imagination run wild. Tip:** Engage all your senses to explore this environment. Touch, taste, smell etc. Allow your emotions to guide you. **Extra:** After you establish this world in your imagination, you could introduce characters and have a dialogue with them. Are they friends or foes?

IMAGINARY WORLD: City of Shadows and Fog: Navigate a foggy city where shadows come to life and reality blends with illusion.

JOURNAL YOUR EXPERIENCE - 2 Minutes [Set Timer]

_____
_____
_____
_____
_____
_____
_____

Your Characters Filter - 5 Minutes [Set Timer]

Everyone including the characters you play see the world through their own specific perspective/filter. I like to use the word filter because you can take out a filter, clean it, change its style, colour, an optimist or a pessimist, comedian or a nihilist, etc. **Find a quiet space** to focus. **Close your eyes and let go of your personal thoughts and emotions** to make space for your characters. **Open your eyes, and allow the filter provided to effect everything around you. Tip**: Explore wherever you are and interact with the objects. **Extra:** How does *this* character walk and move in their world?

FILTER: Old Soul: Feels a deep connection to the past and a sense of déjà vu in many experiences.

JOURNAL YOUR EXPERIENCE - 2 Minutes [Set Timer]

_____
_____
_____
_____
_____
_____

WORKOUT COMPLETED [ ]

If you live in the past that's depression, and if you live in the future that's anxiety. So you have no choice but to live in the present.
Sarah Silverman

CHARACTER STUDY "PEOPLE WATCHING"

Actors are required to portray characters that are believable and relatable. You don't have to agree with them but you have to understand them. Walk like them, talk like them, see the world like them. So, in order to fill our toolbox, we have to **go out into the world and study**. Then practice them over and over so we can "walk in their shoes', comfortably and confidently. Study their movements, mannerisms, the "vibe" they give off, the clothes they wear etc. **Fill your toolbox with the rhythms and idiosyncrasies of human behaviour.**

OBSERVATION CHARACTER STUDY - 15 Minutes [Set Timer]

Find a busy place where you can **sit and observe.** Choose anyone you find interesting. **Write down what stands out about them.** *The way they sit, drink their coffee, walk, talk, interact with others etc.* **Tip: Mirror them immediately.** This will help memorize the feeling of that character so whenever you come back to these characters you're discovering, your body will remember. **Extra**: Before you go to sleep, read over the characters from today and reenact their movements.

_____
_____
_____
_____
_____
_____
_____
_____
_____
_____
_____
_____
_____
_____
_____
_____
_____
_____
_____
_____
_____

COLOURS: We as humans respond to colours like frequencies. If you pay attention closely, you can see everyone has their own 'colour' that defines their core. An essence that informs how they operate and move through the world.

WHAT COLOUR ARE THEY:

WORKOUT COMPLETED [ ]

Finding and sticking to a good action is extremely important. It is your most powerful tool as an actor.
A practical handbook for the actor

VOICE & DICTION

I wish I had learned this at the beginning of my career. The confidence to communicate clearly and powerfully is a game-changer for you as an actor. **Think of your voice as a musical instrument that needs regular tuning. This workout is your daily tuning session,** ensuring that your instrument is always ready. "The word 'theatre' comes from the Greeks. It means the seeing place. It is the place people come to see the truth about life and the social situation." - Stella Adler. Embrace this workout as a key to unlocking and portraying *that* truth by letting your voice be the vehicle that transports your audience into the heart of your story.

READ PASSAGE - 30 Seconds [Set Timer]
Speak the passage and take note of its quality. **Tip**: Record Audio to compare afterward.

> "In the heart of the mountains, echoes bounce off ancient stone. Winds howl, rivers rush, and the majesty of nature resounds in every corner. The peaks stand tall, guardians of age-old secrets and silent stories."

RELAXATION - 1 Minute [Set Timer]
Deep Breathing: Sit and Inhale deeply through your nose, filling your lungs, then exhale slowly through your mouth. Imagine stress leaving your body with each breath.

Nay Nay Nay - 1 Minute [Set Timer]
Pick a song and sing the word "Nay" repeatedly. Start with a comfortable pitch and gradually move the sound from your nose to your chest, ensuring each "Nay" is clear and resonant. Stretch your range as best you can to strengthen.

Sustained 'S' - 2 Minutes [Set Timer]
Inhale deeply and then exhale slowly, making a continuous 's' sound. Keep the sound as even and steady as you can. Always push a little longer than you think you can.

Vowel Pronunciation Drill - 2 Minutes [Set Timer]
Slowly go through each vowel sound **(A, E, I, O, U), holding and exaggerating each sound. Combine them with consonants** (e.g., ba, be, bi, bo, bu). Pay attention to the clarity and sharpness of each sound. Repeat a few times before moving to the next.

Lip Trills - 3 minutes - [Set timer]
Close your lips together lightly, like you're going to blow a raspberry. Then, blow air through your closed lips while making sounds. You should feel a tickling sensation. Pick a song and Lip Trill the whole along with it. **Tip**: Stretch your range as much as you can and pick a song you've never listened to.

The Cork Exercise - 4 Minutes [Set Timer]
Place a cork between your teeth and try to read a passage aloud. This forces your articulation muscles to work harder. If you don't have a cork, bite down gently on your thumb. You can use the following text for this exercise:

READ PASSAGE AGAIN - 30 Seconds [Set Timer]
Speak the passage and take note of its quality. **Tip**: Record Audio to compare.

Discovery Journal - 1 Minute [Set Timer]

_____
_____
_____

WORKOUT COMPLETED [ ]

The enemy of art is the
absence of limitations.
Orson Welles

SUBTEXT

Subtext is what lies beneath the surface of our words. It's the hidden layer of meaning, driven by the character's internal thoughts, emotions, desires, and motivations. Subtext is one of my favourite things as an actor because so much can be said with one simple line of dialogue. The power of "Hello" can be exciting if you told that person years ago "If I ever see you again, I'll kill you. Maybe it's the most beautiful person you've ever seen. Now, say "hello". *Subtext* shows the audience what your relationship with the characters/places/situations are, without having to explain it. We experience it every day and it is our job to create characters that interact as we do.

VOCAL WORK - 3 minutes - [Set Timer]
Lip Trills: Close your lips together lightly, like you're going to blow a raspberry. Then, blow air through your closed lips while making sounds. You should feel a tickling sensation. Pick a song and Lip Trill along with it. **Tip**: Stretch your range as much as you can and pick a song you've never listened to.

SUBTEXT PRACTICE
Use the line of dialogue provided and practice each of these subtexts **out loud.** Move on to the next, only when you believe yourself. Trust that you will know when *that* is. Before you begin, **pick a spot to look at and imagine** in detail, **who you are speaking with**. **Tip**: *Sometimes* we mean exactly what we are saying. Look for that too. **Extra**: Substitute someone you have a strong relationship with in real life, good or bad, and see it's affect.

Initial Line: "Did you hear about the resignation of our CEO?"
Your Response Line: "Uh, huh. I heard about it this morning. It's quite a surprise, isn't it? Just when we thought things were finally calm. Makes you wonder what's really going on behind closed doors. What do you think prompted it?"

SUBTEXTS - 6 Minutes [Set Timer]
[ ] Insider knowledge: You know the real reason behind the resignation but can't disclose it.
[ ] Relief: You never liked their management style and are glad to see them go.
[ ] Concern: You're worried about how this will affect your job and the company's future.
[ ] Ambition: You see this as an opportunity to advance your own career.
[ ] Indifference: You're unfazed by office politics and just focus on your work.
[ ] Your Own Subtext

RELATIONSHIP SUBTEXTS - 6 Minutes [Set Timer]
[ ] Loyal Employee: Devoted to the CEO and feel betrayed by their departure.
[ ] Competitive Co-worker: You've always wanted their position and now see your chance.
[ ] Concerned Partner: Your spouse works at the company. You fear for their job security.
[ ] Skeptical Friend: You've always suspected something shady about the company.
[ ] Disinterested Sibling: Your sibling talks about the company non-stop, but you don't care.
[ ] Your Own Subtext

Discovery Journal

_____
_____
_____
_____
_____

WORKOUT COMPLETED [ ]

An actor is at most a poet and at least an
entertainer.
Marlon Brando

EMOTIONS

The 'moment before', **the emotional preparation, is the most important key to a great scene.** If you start any scene *without* an emotional preparation it feels like trying to drive a car in neutral. The preparation is the uphill climb of every rollercoaster; Once you grind all the way to the top, the chains let go and the rest of the ride takes care of itself. "No one wants to see a play or a movie and look at technical proficiency. You want to be moved, you want a human experience, you want to feel less alone" - Viola Davis. **Practice your emotions over and over** so when it's time, you aren't worried "Will I get there?" **You're imagination and emotions should be a tinderbox, so easy to light up. All it take is half a spark.**

EULOGY - 12 Minutes [Set Timer]

Find a quiet comfortable space. Choose someone in your life who is alive and important to you. Create an imaginary reason for why they have died. Now start from the point of the phone call— Imagine who calls, what they say and what you say. Eventually find yourself at the funeral, about to begin the eulogy. See the casket, is it open or closed?? What is that person wearing and any other details for yourself. Before you begin to speak, look into the audience and see who is there- Family, friends etc **Then begin the eulogy. Tip**: Be as specific as you can with everything. **Inside of specificity is where you will find the triggers to your heart.** Let your imagination take you wherever you want in this exercise. **Example**: Placing her favourite sheep stuffed animal in the casket, tucked under her arm like she always held it, then kissing her goodbye one last time.

DISCOVERY JOURNAL - 3 Minutes [Set Timer]

Make sure to **include the specific triggers** you experience because you can use these **TRIGGER MOMENTS** in the future instead of repeating the *entire* exercise.

_____
_____
_____
_____
_____
_____
_____
_____
_____
_____
_____
_____
_____
_____
_____
_____
_____
_____
_____
_____

WORKOUT COMPLETED [ ]

The best way to get past any barrier is to come at it from a different direction, which is one reason it is useful to work with a teacher or coach.
Anders Ericsson

THE CORK EXERCISE - 4 Minutes [Set Timer]
Place a cork between your teeth and read a passage aloud. This forces your articulation muscles to work harder. If you don't have a cork, bite down gently on your thumb. You can use the following text for this exercise:

"As evening descends on the countryside, the horizon glows with hues of pink and orange. Farm animals settle down for the night, and the scent of blooming flowers wafts through the air. The setting sun paints the sky, promising a peaceful night."

WRITE A LETTER - 10 Minutes [Set Timer]
Get a piece of paper or write this in your device. **Take a moment** to let this situation and relationship sink in. Then let your imagination run wild and **write them a letter.**

Your Character: Taylor, a seasoned war correspondent who has witnessed and reported on numerous conflicts.
Other Character: Jordan, a fellow journalist and close friend, who fabricated a story that endangered lives, including Taylor's, and damaged the credibility of all journalists in the region.

Relationship: Taylor and Jordan's bond was formed in the field, under the shared pressures and ethical challenges of war reporting. Their friendship was built on trust, respect, and a commitment to truth—values that Jordan's actions have now profoundly violated.

Context of the Letter: In the aftermath of the scandal and facing the dangers caused by Jordan's deception, Taylor writes a letter to Jordan. This letter is a blend of anger, disillusionment, and a plea for an explanation. It's a way for Taylor to address the breach of journalistic ethics, the personal betrayal, and the damage done to their profession and friendship.

Discovery Journal - 1 minute [Set Timer]
_____
_____
_____
_____
_____
_____
_____

WORKOUT COMPLETED [ ]

I believe in imagination. I did Kramer vs. Kramer before I had children. But the mother I would be was already inside me.
Meryl Streep

VOCAL WORK - 3 minutes - [Set Timer]

Lip Trills: Close your lips together lightly, like you're going to blow a raspberry. Then, blow air through your closed lips while making sounds. You should feel a tickling sensation. Pick a song and Lip Trill along with it. **Tip**: Stretch your range as much as you can and pick a song you've never listened to.

VERBAL IMPROV - 10 Minutes [Set Timer]

Find a space where you are comfortable and free to express yourself. Take a moment to **let this situation, character and prompt, sink in**. Then let your imagination run wild: **Picture who you are talking to** then **begin with *the prompt*** and **continue to verbalize everything** this character would say. **Tip**: This is exploration! There is no "getting it right". BE BRAVE to explore and discover.

Character: Sam, a local journalist known for their investigative skills and dedication to truth, finds out that their editor, Morgan, often perceived as supportive and ethical, has been censoring important news stories to favour certain political agendas. Sam's commitment to journalistic integrity makes them confront this issue head-on.

Prompt: "Morgan, it's clear you've been censoring our stories. Let's talk about why."

Who are you talking to:

Describe them in two specific words:

Discovery Journal - 2 minutes [Set Timer]

_____
_____
_____
_____
_____
_____
_____
_____
_____

WORKOUT COMPLETED [ ]

Do not let what you cannot do
interfere with what you can do.
John Wooden

SELF AWARENESS

The more you understand yourself, the more you are able to understand and develop your characters. Like you, your characters have thoughts, beliefs, traumas, passions etc. When you become aware of your own and start to see how those experiences and beliefs have shaped your life, how you operate and view the world, then you can develop your characters that are much more rich and vivid.

PHYSICAL WARMUP - 2 minutes [Set Timer]
Freeform Dance: Put on some music and engage in freeform dancing. Allow your body to move spontaneously and without inhibition. This can help you tap into your creative instincts and develop physical expressiveness. **Tip**: Try music you've never listened to.

CURRENT EMOTIONAL INVENTORY - 3 Minutes [Set Timer]
Write down and **record your current emotions**. Identify what you're feeling at this moment and why. **Tip**: Be as specific as you can, **don't disregard anything.** You can also **scan your body** to see how and where your current emotion is affecting you. Your posture, the way you walk, bouncing foot, sore neck etc

CURRENT EMOTIONAL STATE:

SELF DISCOVERY QUESTIONS - 10 Minutes [Set Timer]
I suggest a journal or writing it in your phone's notes so you don't run out of space here.

What would I like to be remembered for? (**Extra**: Condense and describe that into a strong, single image. **Example**: I'm standing on the stage accepting my Oscar for my dream role working with my favourite director and I see my family, my two children and my mom, with tears in her eyes clapping louder than everyone, sitting in the front row.

WORKOUT COMPLETED [ ]

Conflict is what creates drama. The more conflict actors find, the more interesting the performance.
Michael Shurtleff

IMAGINATION

We have a lot of tools in our arsenal as actors but I believe imagination is the most powerful. "If you hook into the character's belief system and you believe it 100%, there is no way the audience won't." - Meryl Streep. Everyone has an Imagination but it must be worked out to get stronger. Think of your imagination as a limitless playground. In this space, you can be anyone, go anywhere, and do anything. **Have the courage to allow yourself to play!**

VOCAL WORK - 2 Minutes - [Set timer]

Lip Trills: Close your lips together lightly, like you're going to blow a raspberry. Then, blow air through your closed lips while making sounds. You should feel a tickling sensation. Pick a song and Lip Trill along with it. **Tip**: Stretch your range as much as you can and pick a song you've never listened to.

IMPROVISED STORYTELLING - 5 Minutes [Set Timer]

Speak out the scenario provided and continue the story! Focus on vivid details, character development and how the main character overcomes the main obstacle. **Tip**: Try not to stop speaking so you don't have time to "think". Allow your imagination to keep moving forward without interruption. **Tip:** Record these stories on your device, in case it's great but more importantly to see your progress as you go on.

STARTING POINT: You are Riley, an antique restorer, who uncovers a beautifully crafted, ancient clock hidden within a recently acquired antique chest. Carved in the chest is 1111. You grab the clock and as soon as you set its hands to 11:11, the dials begin to spin out of control and you drop it. But the clock has created a black hole and begins sucking the objects around you into it. You struggle and struggle to get away but its pull is too strong for you to fight and—

IMAGINARY WORLD EXPLORATION - 6 Minutes [Set Timer]

Find a quiet space to relax and focus. **Close your eyes** and let your imagination run wild. **Tip:** Engage all your senses to explore this environment. Touch, taste, smell etc and allow your emotions to guide you. **Extra:** After you explore this world with your senses, you could introduce characters and have a dialogue with them. Are they friends or foes?

IMAGINARY WORLD: SILVER MOONBEAM FOREST - A moonlit forest where silvery beams illuminate the path ahead. You've never been here but you walk with a sense of "I'm home". Your favourite animal runs passed you—

JOURNAL YOUR EXPERIENCE - 2 Minutes [Set Timer]

_____
_____
_____
_____
_____
_____

WORKOUT COMPLETED [ ]

An ounce of behaviour is worth a
pound of words.
Sanford Meisner

ANCHORING INTO YOUR CHARACTER COLOUR & MUSIC

Anchoring yourself into your character is vital. It's one of the most freeing feelings when you understand their *essence* because everything they do, how they do it and what their purpose is, becomes so clear to you and the audience. Every choice you make after you find your *anchor*, feels easy, because you're acting from who and what your character is at the core. You can call it an essence, an aura, vibe, energy etc. We all have it and feel it from everyone around us. There are many ways into your character but music and colour are my favourite. Music can inform the script, your character, even each scene. Colours, I think you will find, can work incredibly because we as humans respond to colours like frequencies. Colours evoke many feelings and if you pay attention closely, you can see everyone has their own 'colour' that defines their core. An essence that informs how they operate and move through the world.

THEIR COLOUR - 2 Minutes [Set Timer]
Think of **someone you know**, and **define them with a colour**. **Tip**: Trust yourself. Your initial colour is usually close. **Tip**: Start with basic colours then eventually become much more specific. **Example**: Corinna is an earthy green with rays of sunlight flowing through the green. **Extra**: Ask someone who knows *that person* as well, what they think this person's colour is and why. See how close your answers are or not.

YOUR CHARACTERS COLOUR
Read the given character description just as you would an audition, **assign a colour to that character.** Now take that colour you chose and **allow it to infuse into your entire body**, affecting your every move, your speaking, the way you see the world etc. **Take any book** you have, flip to a random page and **read the text as this Colour/Character**. **Tip**: Be specific, choose a colour that excites you and don't be afraid to get creative.

CHARACTER DESCRIPTION: [JORDAN] Jordan is a dedicated and idealistic urban gardener, transforming neglected city spaces into lush green havens. Dressed in comfortable, earthy-toned clothing, often with soil on their hands and a sunhat, Jordan is a familiar and welcoming presence in the neighbourhood. They run community gardening workshops, sharing their knowledge and passion for sustainable living. Their character is a harmonious blend of environmental activism, community spirit, and a deep connection to nature, striving to make the urban world greener, one plant at a time.

CHOOSE THEIR COLOUR - 4 Minutes [Set Timer]
THEIR COLOUR:

CHOOSE THEIR SONG - 4 Minutes [Set Timer]
THEIR SONG:

READ PASSAGE FROM BOOK - 2 Minutes [Set Timer]

FREEFORM DANCE - 2 minutes - [Set Timer]
Put on the selected music and **engage in freeform dancing**, anchored in your colour/character, Allow your body to move spontaneously and without inhibition. This can help you tap into your creative instincts and develop physical expressiveness *while staying in character.* **Tip**: Journal about the differences as opposed to how you normally dance.

JOURNAL YOUR EXPERIENCE - 1 Minute [Set Timer]

WORKOUT COMPLETED [ ]

Whatever you decide is your motivation in the scene, the opposite of that is also true and should be in it.
Michael Shurtleff

HISTORICAL RESEARCH

We are in the information era and have access to the world and its rich history at our fingertips. This exploration is not about 'learning facts'; it's a journey to the heart of human experience. The empathy and the understanding, especially on the things you disagree with, are incredibly valuable. If you look closely, you'll find the way people think, at different times in history, their attitudes, choices, and the way they move their bodies can teach you so much about us, right now. Fill your toolbox so it's overflowing with information and ideas to pull from so your imagination has so much to play with.

PHYSICAL WARMUP - 2 minutes - [Set Timer]
Freeform Dance: Put on some music and engage in freeform dancing. Allow your body to move spontaneously and without inhibition. This can help you tap into your creative instincts and develop physical expressiveness. **Tip**: Try music you've never listened to.

RESEARCH - 13 Minutes [Set Timer]
YouTube, streaming platforms, the internet or books, **research the given era/person/moment in time,** journal or make notes on your device, so when you want to find this information, it's organized and readily accessible. As you go, **write anything and everything _you_ find fascinating. Tip:** If the topic doesn't interest you, choose your own, or take a chance and still research it, but from a different perspective. Physicalities, voice, ideals, etc. Trust your body that when you see something interesting, you'll know. **Extra**: Speak it out and copy their movements. Our memory recall is massively affected by our bodies. Be specific and when you re-read your notes, you'll be amazed by how much your mind and body remember.

TOPIC:
The French New Wave Cinema (Late 1950s - 1960s) - The Perspective of Jean-Paul Belmondo: Jean-Paul Belmondo, a prominent French actor, offers an insightful look into the French New Wave cinema movement. Known for his roles in films like "Breathless" (1960) and "Pierrot le Fou" (1965), Belmondo's casual, charismatic screen presence and non-traditional approach to acting made him a symbol of the movement. There is considerable footage of his films and interviews so you can study his naturalistic acting style, ability to blend charm and depth in his performances, and his contribution to a cinematic revolution that broke away from traditional filmmaking norms.

WORKOUT COMPLETED [ ]

Humour [in a scene] is not jokes. It is that attitude toward being alive without which you would long ago have jumped off the 59th Street Bridge.
Michael Shurtleff

BELIEF

Beliefs are the convictions that something exists or is true, especially without proof. That is also the definition of what we do as actors. We play make-believe. Our beliefs shape our world, especially our beliefs about ourselves and it works for the characters you play. Understand your beliefs and how they influence your mind, body and spirit, then you will be able to better understand others, so you can embody them. Allow the beliefs of your character to colour your perception of your world and your interaction with everything in it. "Acting is the best magic trick in the world. We applaud performances not because it's real, but because you made us believe."

VOCAL WORK - 2 Minutes - [Set timer]

Lip Trills: Close your lips together lightly, like you're going to blow a raspberry. Then, blow air through your closed lips while making sounds. You should feel a tickling sensation. Pick a song and Lip Trill along with it. **Tip**: Stretch your range as much as you can and pick a song you've never listened to.

BELIEF WORKOUT

Get your journal or write in here. **Define your personal belief/view** on the given subject. **Grab any book you own,** flip to a random page and **read it out loud,** colouring the words and intention with your belief system. **Tip:** Write trigger words you can hook into in the future: **Optimism-** Always smiling, grateful, opportunity, sunshine yellow.

YOUR PERSONAL BELIEF

Public Affection - 7 Minutes [Set Timer]

_____
_____
_____
_____

READ WITH BELIEF - 2 Minutes [Set Timer]

CHARACTERS BELIEF

Public Affection

Disgusting. Nobody wants to see that. Sure, at home in private but drives me crazy how many people think touching and kissing around others is okay. It's selfish and nobody wants to see that.

READ WITH CHARACTERS BELIEF - 2 Minutes [Set Timer]
Forget your personal view and **fully embrace the character's belief. Read out loud again.**

JOURNAL YOUR EXPERIENCE - 2 Minutes [Set Timer]

_____
_____
_____
_____

WORKOUT COMPLETED [ ]

PERFORMANCE STRATEGY
14 DAY REVIEW

TAKE A MOMENT OF REFLECTION AND BREAKDOWN WHERE YOU ARE RIGHT NOW IN YOUR CAREER AND AS AN ACTOR. THE MORE SPECIFIC YOU ARE THE MORE CLEAR YOU CAN SEE WHERE YOU ARE NOW SO YOU CAN GET TO WHERE YOU WANT TO GO FASTER

★ ★ ★ ★ ★

Stephen King: His first novel, "Carrie," was rejected multiple times before finally being published, launching his career as a best-selling author.

DATE:

MY WHY
WHY ARE YOU DOING WHAT YOU ARE DOING
BE SPECIFIC

MY MAIN GOALS
IN-ORDER OF IMPORTANCE

1.

   Action Step(s):

2.

   Action Step(s):

3.

   Action Step(s):

FROM THE LAST 14 DAYS
5 STAR RATING

YOUR KEY POINTS AND TAKEAWAYS - WHY THAT AMOUNT OF STAR RATING, LIKES, DISLIKES, THE BIGGEST LESSON YOU LEARNED, GOOD OR BAD:

STRENGTHS:

WEAKNESSES:

IMPROVEMENT STRATEGY
HOW CAN YOU IMPROVE ON THESE AREAS FOR THE NEXT 14 DAYS:

GOAL FROM LAST :
DID YOU ACHIEVE IT?

WHY OR WHY NOT?

GOAL FOR THE NEXT 14 EXERCISES
THE MORE SPECIFIC YOU ARE THE GREATER THE RESULT

   Action Step(s):

The point is to find an action that YOU want to do. What gets YOU going? What gets you HOT? Only YOU know.
A practical handbook for the actor

MY WHY:

GOAL(s):

PHYSICAL WARMUP - COSMIC ORBIT - 1 minute [Set Timer]
Celestial Movement: Imagine you're moving through space, orbiting around planets and stars. Your movements are both weightless and full of gravity's tug. **Tip**: Let your body float and then fall, as if you're both the moon in orbit and the comet pulled by a planet's influence.

VOCAL WORK - DIALOGUE WITH ECHO - 3 minutes [Set Timer]
Call and Response: Choose a phrase and project it as if calling out to a vast canyon. After each call, listen for the echo in your imagination and respond with a softer, nuanced tone. **Tip**: Use this exercise to play with volume control and emotional inflection.

EMOTIONAL RECALL - ANTICIPATORY NERVES - 5 minutes [Set Timer]
Edge of Action: Recall a time when you were on the edge of doing something significant—stepping on stage, proposing, a moment before a competition. Capture that mix of nerves, excitement, and anticipation. **Tip**: Let your body's movements oscillate between hesitation and the urge to spring forward.

ANIMAL WORK - OCTOPUS FLUIDITY

Research - 2 minutes [Set Timer]
Observe the octopus, its fluid motion, and its ability to squeeze through tight spaces with ease.

Animal Exercise 3 minutes [Set Timer]
Emulate the octopus's movements by making your body as fluid and malleable as possible. Flow across the space with smooth, rippling motions. **Tip**: Imagine your limbs are the tentacles, reaching and pulling through water, and allow your body to articulate with similar flexibility and grace.

Discovery Journal - 1 Minute [Set Timer]
3 Main Characteristics: (Whatever stands out to YOU to embody the essence)

_____
_____
_____
_____
_____

WORKOUT COMPLETED [ ]

I think the most liberating thing I did early on was to free myself from any concern with my looks as they pertained to my work.
Meryl Streep

SCRIPT ANALYSIS for RELATIONSHIPS & SPECIFICITY - 15 minutes [Set Timer]
Choose your character, circle everything in this script you have a relationship with. Including people, places, things, smells, time of day etc. **Write what your relationship with those items are** and **be specific.** The more specific and fun you have with your relationships, the more interesting your characters will be and the more fun the audience has. **Tip:** Everything isn't in the scene. Use your imagination to create details, <u>only if</u> it's contextually appropriate. **Extra:** Write your > ***Objective, win or lose? Consequence of failing?*** *The Who What Where When Why.*

Title: **Unspoken Words**
INT. COZY YET MESSY APARTMENT - EVENING
A small apartment filled with memories. Tense. KATE and ETHAN, a couple going through a challenging phase, sit across from each other. The table cluttered with old photos and paperwork.

KATE
(thumb through a photo album)
Remember this? Our trip to the coast?

ETHAN
Yeah. You hated that beach.

KATE
I hated the sand. But I loved the seafood.

ETHAN
Yes. You. Did. And this one. Your art show... You were so nervous.

KATE
So nervous. You were my rock that night...

There's a pause as they both look at the photos, lost in memories.

ETHAN
Kate, where did we go wrong?

KATE
I don't know. Maybe we grew apart. Maybe we stopped listening.

ETHAN
I still love you.

KATE
(tears in her eyes)
I love you too. But love isn't always enough.

ETHAN
Is there any way... any chance we could try again?

KATE
(pulls her hand away gently)
We've tried, Ethan. Sometimes, the bravest thing we can do is let go.

ETHAN
So, this is it? The end of our story?

KATE
Not the end. Just a different chapter. For both of us.

Ethan nods, tears brimming. Kate wipes away a tear, trying to stay composed.

KATE
I'll always cherish what we had. Always.

ETHAN
I just wish...

KATE
Some wishes don't come true. But we'll be okay.

They sit in silence, the weight of their unspoken words filling the room.

WORKOUT COMPLETED [ ]

All an actor has is their blind faith that
they are who they say they are today,
in any scene.
Meryl Streep

IMAGINATION

We have a lot of tools in our arsenal as actors but **I believe imagination is the most powerful.** "If you hook into the character's belief system and you believe it 100%, there is no way the audience won't." - Meryl Streep "Imagination is more important than knowledge for knowledge is limited. - Einstein. Everyone has an Imagination but it must be worked out to get stronger. Think of your imagination as a limitless playground. In this space, you can be anyone, go anywhere, and do anything. **Have the courage to allow yourself to play!**

Solo Imaginary World Exploration - 6 Minutes [Set Timer]

Find a quiet space to relax and focus. **Close your eyes** and **let your imagination run wild. Tip:** Engage all your senses to explore this environment. Touch, taste, smell etc. Allow your emotions to guide you. **Extra:** After you establish this world in your imagination, you could introduce characters and have a dialogue with them. Are they friends or foes?

IMAGINARY WORLD: Floating Monasteries in the Sky: Traverse ancient monasteries on solitary sky islands, interacting with wise monks.

JOURNAL YOUR EXPERIENCE - 2 Minutes [Set Timer]

_____
_____
_____
_____
_____
_____

Your Characters Filter - 5 Minutes [Set Timer]

Everyone including the characters you play see the world through their own specific perspective/filter. I like to use the word filter because you can take out a filter, clean it, change its style, colour, an optimist or a pessimist, comedian or a nihilist, etc. **Find a quiet space** to focus. **Close your eyes and let go of your personal thoughts and emotions** to make space for your characters. **Open your eyes, and allow the filter provided to effect everything around you. Tip:** Explore wherever you are and interact with the objects. **Extra:** How does *this* character walk and move in their world?

FILTER: Rebellious Outlaw: Views rules and norms with contempt and seeks to challenge them.

JOURNAL YOUR EXPERIENCE - 2 Minutes [Set Timer]

_____
_____
_____
_____
_____
_____

WORKOUT COMPLETED [ ]

Acting is all about honesty. If you can fake that, you've got it made.
George Burns

CHARACTER STUDY "PEOPLE WATCHING"

Actors are required to portray characters that are believable and relatable. You don't have to agree with them but you have to understand them. Walk like them, talk like them, see the world like them. So, in order to fill our toolbox, we have to **go out into the world and study**. Then practice them over and over so we can "walk in their shoes', comfortably and confidently. Study their movements, mannerisms, the "vibe" they give off, the clothes they wear etc. **Fill your toolbox with the rhythms and idiosyncrasies of human behaviour.**

OBSERVATION CHARACTER STUDY - 15 Minutes [Set Timer]

Find a busy place where you can **sit and observe.** Choose anyone you find interesting. **Write down what stands out about them.** *The way they sit, drink their coffee, walk, talk, interact with others etc.* **Tip**: **Mirror them immediately**. This will help memorize the feeling of that character so whenever you come back to these characters you're discovering, your body will remember. **Extra**: Before you go to sleep, read over the characters from today and reenact their movements.

_____
_____
_____
_____
_____
_____
_____
_____
_____
_____
_____
_____
_____
_____
_____
_____
_____
_____
_____
_____

COLOURS: We as humans respond to colours like frequencies. If you pay attention closely, you can see everyone has their own 'colour' that defines their core. An essence that informs how they operate and move through the world.

WHAT COLOUR ARE THEY:

WORKOUT COMPLETED [ ]

Life beats down and crushes the soul and art
reminds you that you have one.
Stella Adler

VOICE & DICTION

I wish I had learned this at the beginning of my career. The confidence to communicate clearly and powerfully is a game-changer for you as an actor. **Think of your voice as a musical instrument that needs regular tuning. This workout is your daily tuning session,** ensuring that your instrument is always ready. "The word 'theatre' comes from the Greeks. It means the seeing place. It is the place people come to see the truth about life and the social situation." - Stella Adler. Embrace this workout as a key to unlocking and portraying *that* truth by letting your voice be the vehicle that transports your audience into the heart of your story.

READ PASSAGE - 30 Seconds [Set Timer]
Speak the passage and take note of its quality. **Tip**: Record Audio to compare afterward.

"The desert sings a song of solitude. Sands shift, the sun beats down, and the vast emptiness speaks volumes in its silent grandeur. At night, the cool air brings whispers of ancient travellers under the starry sky.

RELAXATION - 1 Minute [Set Timer]
Deep Breathing: Sit and Inhale deeply through your nose, filling your lungs, then exhale slowly through your mouth. Imagine stress leaving your body with each breath.

Nay Nay Nay - 1 Minute [Set Timer]
Pick a song and sing the word "Nay" repeatedly. Start with a comfortable pitch and gradually move the sound from your nose to your chest, ensuring each "Nay" is clear and resonant. Stretch your range as best you can to strengthen.

Sustained 'S' - 2 Minutes [Set Timer]
Inhale deeply and then exhale slowly, making a continuous 's' sound. Keep the sound as even and steady as you can. Always push a little longer than you think you can.

Vowel Pronunciation Drill - 2 Minutes [Set Timer]
Slowly go through each vowel sound **(A, E, I, O, U)**, **holding and exaggerating each sound. Combine them with consonants** (e.g., ba, be, bi, bo, bu). Pay attention to the clarity and sharpness of each sound. Repeat a few times before moving to the next.

Lip Trills - 3 minutes - [Set timer]
Close your lips together lightly, like you're going to blow a raspberry. Then, blow air through your closed lips while making sounds. You should feel a tickling sensation. Pick a song and Lip Trill the whole along with it. **Tip**: Stretch your range as much as you can and pick a song you've never listened to.

The Cork Exercise - 4 Minutes [Set Timer]
Place a cork between your teeth and try to read a passage aloud. This forces your articulation muscles to work harder. If you don't have a cork, bite down gently on your thumb. You can use the following text for this exercise:

READ PASSAGE AGAIN - 30 Seconds [Set Timer]
Speak the passage and take note of its quality. **Tip**: Record Audio to compare.

Discovery Journal - 1 Minute [Set Timer]

WORKOUT COMPLETED [ ]

I love acting. It is so much more real than life.
Oscar Wilde

SUBTEXT

Subtext is what lies beneath the surface of our words. It's the hidden layer of meaning, driven by the character's internal thoughts, emotions, desires, and motivations. Subtext is one of my favourite things as an actor because so much can be said with one simple line of dialogue. The power of "Hello" can be exciting if you told that person years ago "If I ever see you again, I'll kill you. Maybe it's the most beautiful person you've ever seen. Now, say "hello". *Subtext* shows the audience what your relationship with the characters/places/situations are, without having to explain it. We experience it every day and it is our job to create characters that interact as we do.

VOCAL WORK - 3 minutes - [Set Timer]
Lip Trills: Close your lips together lightly, like you're going to blow a raspberry. Then, blow air through your closed lips while making sounds. You should feel a tickling sensation. Pick a song and Lip Trill along with it. **Tip**: Stretch your range as much as you can and pick a song you've never listened to.

SUBTEXT PRACTICE
Use the line of dialogue provided and practice each of these subtexts **out loud.** Move on to the next, only when you believe yourself. Trust that you will know when *that* is. Before you begin, **pick a spot to look at and imagine** in detail, **who you are speaking with**. **Tip**: *Sometimes* we mean exactly what we are saying. Look for that too. **Extra**: Substitute someone you have a strong relationship with in real life, good or bad, and see it's affect.

Initial Line: "I just found out that the old library in town is being turned into a luxury hotel."
Your Response Line: "Really? I wonder who bought it. The library was such a landmark. It's odd thinking of it as a hotel now. It had its own charm, didn't it? What are your thoughts about this transformation?"

SUBTEXTS - 6 Minutes [Set Timer]
[ ] Sentimental: You have fond memories of the library and feel a sense of loss.
[ ] Cynical: You think it's just another example of commercialism taking over.
[ ] Indifferent: You rarely visited the library and aren't affected by the change.
[ ] Optimistic: You see it as a positive development and good use of space.
[ ] Suspicious: You suspect there's more to the story behind this conversion.
[ ] Your Own Subtext

RELATIONSHIP SUBTEXTS - 6 Minutes [Set Timer]
[ ] The Friend that never leaves you alone.
[ ] Your disabled little brother.
[ ] Best friend you've known since you were 6 years old.
[ ] Co-worker with terrible Body Oder.
[ ] Your siblings best friend who is also your secret crush.
[ ] Your Own Subtext

Discovery Journal

_____
_____
_____
_____

WORKOUT COMPLETED [ ]

Simply defined, an action is the physical pursuance of a specific goal. Physical action is the main building block of an actor's technique because it is the one thing that you, the actor, can consistently do on-stage. Choosing a good action is an invaluable skill that can only be developed by long, hard practice.
A practical handbook for the actor

EMOTIONS

The 'moment before', **the emotional preparation, is the most important key to a great scene.** If you start any scene *without* an emotional preparation it feels like trying to drive a car in neutral. The preparation is the uphill climb of every rollercoaster; Once you grind all the way to the top, the chains let go and the rest of the ride takes care of itself. "No one wants to see a play or a movie and look at technical proficiency. You want to be moved, you want a human experience, you want to feel less alone" - Viola Davis. **Practice your emotions over and over** so when it's time, you aren't worried "Will I get there?" **You're imagination and emotions should be a tinderbox, so easy to light up. All it take is half a spark.**

EULOGY - 12 Minutes [Set Timer]

Find a quiet comfortable space. Choose someone in your life who is alive and important to you. Create an imaginary reason for why they have died. Now start from the point of the phone call— Imagine who calls, what they say and what you say. Eventually find yourself at the funeral, about to begin the eulogy. See the casket, is it open or closed?? What is that person wearing and any other details for yourself. Before you begin to speak, look into the audience and see who is there- Family, friends etc **Then begin the eulogy. Tip**: Be as specific as you can with everything. **Inside of specificity is where you will find the triggers to your heart.** Let your imagination take you wherever you want in this exercise. **Example**: Placing her favourite sheep stuffed animal in the casket, tucked under her arm like she always held it, then kissing her goodbye one last time.

DISCOVERY JOURNAL - 3 Minutes [Set Timer]

Make sure to **include the specific triggers** you experience because you can use these **TRIGGER MOMENTS** in the future instead of repeating the *entire* exercise.

___

WORKOUT COMPLETED [ ]

If you get an impulse in a scene, no matter how wrong it seems, follow the impulse. It might be something and if it ain't... take two.
Jack Nicholson

THE CORK EXERCISE - 4 Minutes [Set Timer]

Place a cork between your teeth and read a passage aloud. This forces your articulation muscles to work harder. If you don't have a cork, bite down gently on your thumb. You can use the following text for this exercise:

"At the heart of the bustling city, the park offers a respite from the concrete jungle. Trees sway gently in the breeze, birds chirp merrily, and people stroll along the paths, lost in thought or laughter, a green oasis amidst the urban sprawl."

WRITE A LETTER - 10 Minutes [Set Timer]

Get a piece of paper or write this in your device. **Take a moment** to let this situation and relationship sink in. Then let your imagination run wild and **write them a letter.**

Your Character: Morgan, a dedicated and experienced nurse in a hospice care facility.

Other Character: Riley, the family member of a patient who passed away under Morgan's care, who has publicly accused Morgan of negligence, despite no evidence.

Relationship: Morgan's relationship with Riley was initially cordial and professional, built on providing care and support during a difficult time. However, the accusation has not only hurt Morgan professionally but also personally, as it goes against everything Morgan stands for in their career.

Context of the Letter: Feeling a mixture of hurt, frustration, and a need to set the record straight, Morgan decides to write a letter to Riley. This letter is an expression of Morgan's dedication to their patients, a defence against the unfounded accusations, and an attempt to provide comfort and understanding to Riley, who is clearly in pain from their loss.

Discovery Journal - 1 minute [Set Timer]

_____
_____
_____
_____

WORKOUT COMPLETED [ ]

Its what I learn from the great actors that I work with. Stillness. That's all and that's the hardest thing.
Morgan Freeman

VOCAL WORK - 3 minutes [Set timer]
Lip Trills: Close your lips together lightly, like you're going to blow a raspberry. Then, blow air through your closed lips while making sounds. You should feel a tickling sensation. Pick a song and Lip Trill along with it. **Tip**: Stretch your range as much as you can and pick a song you've never listened to.

VERBAL IMPROV - 10 Minutes [Set Timer]

Find a space where you are comfortable and free to express yourself. Take a moment to **let this situation, character and prompt, sink in**. Then let your imagination run wild: **Picture who you are talking to** then **begin with the prompt** and **continue to verbalize everything** this character would say. **Tip**: This is exploration! There is no "getting it right". BE BRAVE to explore and discover.

Character: Jordan, a professional musician known for their passion and commitment to authenticity, discovers that their bandmate, Casey, known for being the pragmatic one, has been plagiarizing music for their latest album. As someone who values originality, Jordan is deeply troubled by this.

Prompt: "Casey, I've realized some of our music isn't original. We need to address this now."

Who are you talking to:

Describe them in two specific words:

Discovery Journal - 2 minutes [Set Timer]
_____
_____
_____
_____
_____
_____
_____
_____

WORKOUT COMPLETED [ ]

The best way to guarantee a loss is to quit.
Morgan Freeman

SELF AWARENESS

The more you understand yourself, the more you are able to understand and develop your characters. Like you, your characters have thoughts, beliefs, traumas, passions etc. When you become aware of your own and start to see how those experiences and beliefs have shaped your life, how you operate and view the world, then you can develop your characters that are much more rich and vivid.

PHYSICAL WARMUP - 2 minutes [Set Timer]
Freeform Dance: Put on some music and engage in freeform dancing. Allow your body to move spontaneously and without inhibition. This can help you tap into your creative instincts and develop physical expressiveness. **Tip**: Try music you've never listened to.

CURRENT EMOTIONAL INVENTORY - 3 Minutes [Set Timer]
Write down and **record your current emotions**. Identify what you're feeling at this moment and why. **Tip**: Be as specific as you can, **don't disregard anything.** You can also **scan your body** to see how and where your current emotion is affecting you. Your posture, the way you walk, bouncing foot, sore neck etc

CURRENT EMOTIONAL STATE:

SELF DISCOVERY QUESTIONS - 10 Minutes [Set Timer]
I suggest a journal or writing it in your phone's notes so you don't run out of space here.

What do I believe is the meaning or purpose of life?

Why? Where does that come from? How does that make you view the world?

WORKOUT COMPLETED [ ]

I think you should take your job seriously, but not yourself. That is the best combination.
Dame Judi Dench

IMAGINATION

We have a lot of tools in our arsenal as actors but I believe imagination is the most powerful. "If you hook into the character's belief system and you believe it 100%, there is no way the audience won't." - Meryl Streep. Everyone has an Imagination but it must be worked out to get stronger. Think of your imagination as a limitless playground. In this space, you can be anyone, go anywhere, and do anything. **Have the courage to allow yourself to play!**

VOCAL WORK - 2 Minutes - [Set timer]
Lip Trills: Close your lips together lightly, like you're going to blow a raspberry. Then, blow air through your closed lips while making sounds. You should feel a tickling sensation. Pick a song and Lip Trill along with it. **Tip**: Stretch your range as much as you can and pick a song you've never listened to.

IMPROVISED STORYTELLING - 5 Minutes [Set Timer]
Speak out the scenario provided and continue the story! Focus on vivid details, character development and how the main character overcomes the main obstacle. **Tip**: Try not to stop speaking so you don't have time to "think". Allow your imagination to keep moving forward without interruption. **Tip:** Record these stories on your device, in case it's great but more importantly to see your progress as you go on.

STARTING POINT: You are Harper, a novice hiker who, during a solo trek, stumbles upon a hidden cave with walls covered in intricate, unknown symbols. Curiosity leads you to touch one of the symbols and it begins to glow brighter and brighter until—

IMAGINARY WORLD EXPLORATION - 6 Minutes [Set Timer]

Find a quiet space to relax and focus. **Close your eyes** and let your imagination run wild. **Tip:** Engage all your senses to explore this environment. Touch, taste, smell etc and allow your emotions to guide you. **Extra:** After you explore this world with your senses, you could introduce characters and have a dialogue with them. Are they friends or foes?

IMAGINARY WORLD: SHOCKING HAPPINESS: The busiest city you've ever experienced where everyone is smiling ear to ear. You realize that every time you aren't smiling you get a sharp and painful shock down your spine. Except... you see one person in the crowd of smiles who isn't affected.

JOURNAL YOUR EXPERIENCE - 2 Minutes [Set Timer]

_____
_____
_____
_____
_____
_____
_____
_____

WORKOUT COMPLETED [ ]

When I was young, people said, You need a backup career. I've come across many actors like me who didn't have a backup. That drive and will made it work.
Clive Owen

ANCHORING INTO YOUR CHARACTER COLOUR & MUSIC

Anchoring yourself into your character is vital. It's one of the most freeing feelings when you understand their *essence* because everything they do, how they do it and what their purpose is, becomes so clear to you and the audience. Every choice you make after you find your *anchor*, feels easy, because you're acting from who and what your character is at the core. You can call it an essence, an aura, vibe, energy etc. We all have it and feel it from everyone around us. There are many ways into your character but music and colour are my favourite. Music can inform the script, your character, even each scene. Colours, I think you will find, can work incredibly because we as humans respond to colours like frequencies. Colours evoke many feelings and if you pay attention closely, you can see everyone has their own 'colour' that defines their core. An essence that informs how they operate and move through the world.

THEIR COLOUR - 2 Minutes [Set Timer]
Think of **someone you know**, and **define them with a colour**. **Tip**: Trust yourself. Your initial colour is usually close. **Tip**: Start with basic colours then eventually become much more specific. **Example**: Corinna is an earthy green with rays of sunlight flowing through the green. **Extra**: Ask someone who knows *that person* as well, what they think this person's colour is and why. See how close your answers are or not.

YOUR CHARACTERS COLOUR
Read the given character description just as you would an audition, **assign a colour to that character.** Now take that colour you chose and **allow it to infuse into your entire body**, affecting your every move, your speaking, the way you see the world etc. **Take any book** you have, flip to a random page and **read the text as this Colour/Character**. **Tip**: Be specific, choose a colour that excites you and don't be afraid to get creative.

CHARACTER DESCRIPTION: [SKYLER] Skyler is a fearless parkour enthusiast, known for their breathtaking urban free-running videos. They navigate the city's rooftops and alleyways with astonishing agility and grace, always wearing comfortable yet durable clothing suitable for their daring feats. Skyler's social media is filled with clips of their high-energy escapades, inspiring a generation of followers with their philosophy of overcoming physical and mental barriers. Despite their online fame, Skyler remains humble and approachable, often seen mentoring younger enthusiasts in the art of parkour. Their character is a dynamic mix of athleticism, fearlessness, and a motivational spirit.

CHOOSE THEIR COLOUR - 4 Minutes [Set Timer]
THEIR COLOUR:

CHOOSE THEIR SONG - 4 Minutes [Set Timer]
THEIR SONG:

READ PASSAGE FROM BOOK - 2 Minutes [Set Timer]

FREEFORM DANCE - 2 minutes - [Set Timer]
Put on the selected music and **engage in freeform dancing, anchored in your colour/character,** Allow your body to move spontaneously and without inhibition. This can help you tap into your creative instincts and develop physical expressiveness *while staying in character.* **Tip**: Journal about the differences as opposed to how you normally dance.

JOURNAL YOUR EXPERIENCE - 1 Minute [Set Timer]

WORKOUT COMPLETED [ ]

If I get rejected for a part, I pick myself up and say OK, not today, maybe tomorrow.
Liam Neeson

HISTORICAL RESEARCH

We are in the information era and have access to the world and its rich history at our fingertips. This exploration is not about 'learning facts'; it's a journey to the heart of human experience. The empathy and the understanding, especially on the things you disagree with, are incredibly valuable. If you look closely, you'll find the way people think, at different times in history, their attitudes, choices, and the way they move their bodies can teach you so much about us, right now. Fill your toolbox so it's overflowing with information and ideas to pull from so your imagination has so much to play with.

PHYSICAL WARMUP - 2 minutes - [Set Timer]
Freeform Dance: Put on some music and engage in freeform dancing. Allow your body to move spontaneously and without inhibition. This can help you tap into your creative instincts and develop physical expressiveness. **Tip**: Try music you've never listened to.

RESEARCH - 13 Minutes [Set Timer]
YouTube, streaming platforms, the internet or books, **research the given era/person/moment in time,** journal or make notes on your device, so when you want to find this information, it's organized and readily accessible. As you go, **write anything and everything _you_ find fascinating. Tip**: If the topic doesn't interest you, choose your own, or take a chance and still research it, but from a different perspective. Physicalities, voice, ideals, etc. Trust your body that when you see something interesting, you'll know. **Extra**: Speak it out and copy their movements. Our memory recall is massively affected by our bodies. Be specific and when you re-read your notes, you'll be amazed by how much your mind and body remember.

TOPIC:
The Space Race (1957-1975) - The Perspective of Yuri Gagarin: Yuri Gagarin, a Soviet pilot and cosmonaut, offers a unique viewpoint on the Space Race. As the first human to journey into outer space and orbit the Earth in 1961, Gagarin became an international hero and a symbol of Soviet space achievement. Footage of Gagarin, including his training, the preparations for his historic flight, post-flight interviews, and public appearances, provides actors with material to study his demeanour, the way he carried himself under immense pressure, and his interactions with the public and officials. Gagarin's story is one of courage, national pride, and the human quest for exploration, making him a compelling figure for actors studying characters who deal with groundbreaking achievements and their aftermath.

WORKOUT COMPLETED [ ]

The function of the actor is to make the
audience imagine for the moment, that real
things are happening to real people.
George Bernard Shaw

BELIEF

Beliefs are the convictions that something exists or is true, especially without proof. That is also the definition of what we do as actors. We play make-believe. Our beliefs shape our world, especially our beliefs about ourselves and it works for the characters you play. Understand your beliefs and how they influence your mind, body and spirit, then you will be able to better understand others, so you can embody them. Allow the beliefs of your character to colour your perception of your world and your interaction with everything in it. "Acting is the best magic trick in the world. We applaud performances not because it's real, but because you made us believe."

VOCAL WORK - 2 Minutes - [Set timer]

Lip Trills: Close your lips together lightly, like you're going to blow a raspberry. Then, blow air through your closed lips while making sounds. You should feel a tickling sensation. Pick a song and Lip Trill along with it. **Tip**: Stretch your range as much as you can and pick a song you've never listened to.

BELIEF WORKOUT

Get your journal or write in here. **Define your personal belief/view** on the given subject. **Grab any book you own,** flip to a random page and **read it out loud,** colouring the words and intention with your belief system. **Tip:** Write trigger words you can hook into in the future: **Optimism-** Always smiling, grateful, opportunity, sunshine yellow.

YOUR PERSONAL BELIEF

Empathy - 7 Minutes [Set Timer]

_____
_____
_____
_____

READ WITH BELIEF - 2 Minutes [Set Timer]

CHARACTERS BELIEF

Empathy

I consider myself an empath. I love that everyone comes to me and feels supported by how much I can listen and understand. I feel other's emotions very deeply and think that word needs more of us. More love and understanding with everything and everyone.

READ WITH CHARACTERS BELIEF - 2 Minutes [Set Timer]

Forget your personal view and **fully embrace the character's belief. Read out loud again.**

JOURNAL YOUR EXPERIENCE - 2 Minutes [Set Timer]

_____
_____
_____
_____
_____

WORKOUT COMPLETED [ ]

PERFORMANCE STRATEGY
14 DAY REVIEW

TAKE A MOMENT OF REFLECTION AND BREAKDOWN WHERE YOU ARE RIGHT NOW IN YOUR CAREER AND AS AN ACTOR. THE MORE SPECIFIC YOU ARE THE MORE CLEAR YOU CAN SEE WHERE YOU ARE NOW SO YOU CAN GET TO WHERE YOU WANT TO GO FASTER

★ ★ ★ ★ ★

Vincent van Gogh: Only sold one painting during his lifetime but is now regarded as one of the most influential figures in the history of Western art.

DATE:

MY WHY
WHY ARE YOU DOING WHAT YOU ARE DOING
BE SPECIFIC

MY MAIN GOALS
IN-ORDER OF IMPORTANCE

1.

   Action Step(s):

2.

   Action Step(s):

3.

   Action Step(s):

FROM THE LAST 14 DAYS
5 STAR RATING

YOUR KEY POINTS AND TAKEAWAYS - WHY THAT AMOUNT OF STAR RATING, LIKES, DISLIKES, THE BIGGEST LESSON YOU LEARNED, GOOD OR BAD:

STRENGTHS:

WEAKNESSES:

IMPROVEMENT STRATEGY
HOW CAN YOU IMPROVE ON THESE AREAS FOR THE NEXT 14 DAYS:

GOAL FROM LAST :
DID YOU ACHIEVE IT?

WHY OR WHY NOT?

GOAL FOR THE NEXT 14 EXERCISES
THE MORE SPECIFIC YOU ARE THE GREATER THE RESULT

   Action Step(s):

The formula to happiness and success is just being actually yourself, in the most vivid possible way you can.
Meryl Streep

MY WHY:

GOAL(s):

PHYSICAL WARMUP - RHYTHMIC PULSE - 1 minute [Set Timer]
Percussive Movements: Engage in a series of movements that have a natural rhythm or beat, like a pulsating dance. Transition between smooth, lyrical motions and sharp, staccato beats. **Tip:** Feel the heartbeat of the movement through your body, let it guide you and try to vary the intensity of your movements.

VOCAL WORK - SIREN SONGS - 3 minutes [Set Timer]
Pitch Exploration: Glide your voice up and down through your entire range in a single breath, like a siren moving through the air. Start soft and slow, then increase volume and speed. **Tip:** Visualize your voice as a physical entity moving through space, soaring high and swooping low, filling the room.

EMOTIONAL RECALL - WISTFUL LONGING - 5 minutes [Set Timer]
Yearning Emotion: Think back to a time when you longed for something or someone. Sink into that feeling of desire and let it be expressed through your posture, facial expressions, and gestures. **Tip**: Build the emotion from a place of internal yearning and let it gradually manifest in your outward expressions.

ANIMAL WORK - CHAMELEON'S POISE

Research - 2 minutes [Set Timer]
Investigate the chameleon, its slow, deliberate movements, and its ability to change colours in response to the environment.

Animal Exercise - 3 minutes [Set Timer]
Emulate the chameleon's deliberate and precise movements. Slow your pace down significantly, and with each movement, imagine changing colours and blending into your surroundings. **Tip:** Integrate the chameleon's observational stillness with sudden, purposeful motions, embodying its unique blend of patience and precision.

Discovery Journal - 1 Minute [Set Timer]
3 Main Characteristics: (Whatever stands out to YOU to embody the essence)

_____
_____
_____
_____
_____
_____

WORKOUT COMPLETED [ ]

To act means to do so you must have something specific to do onstage or you will immediately stop acting. This is why physical action is so very important for The actor.
A practical handbook for the actor

SCRIPT ANALYSIS for **RELATIONSHIPS & SPECIFICITY** - 15 minutes [Set Timer]
Choose your character, circle everything in this script you have a relationship with. Including people, places, things, smells, time of day etc. **Write what your relationship with those items are** and **be specific**. The more specific and fun you have with your relationships, the more interesting your characters will be and the more fun the audience has. **Tip:** Everything isn't in the scene. Use your imagination to create details, only if it's contextually appropriate. **Extra:** Write your > **Objective, win or lose? Consequence of failing?** The **Who What Where When Why.**

Title: **Midnight Serenade**
INT. DOWNTOWN SIDEWALK CAFÉ - LATE NIGHT
A small, intimate sidewalk café in the heart of the city, lit by string lights. LILA (mid-20s, a dreamy poet) sits alone at a table, writing in a notebook. Across the street, SAM (early 30s, an amateur musician with a gentle demeanour), is packing up his guitar after a street performance. He notices Lila...

SAM
Excuse me, I couldn't help but notice you are... a poet?

LILA
Just some thoughts on paper.

SAM
I'm Sam. I was playing across the street. Just saying some *thoughts on paper* out loud.

LILA
That was you? Your music... I like it.

SAM
Thank you. What do you write about?

LILA
All the normal stuff. The beauty in the mundane.

SAM
My mom used to say... "The extraordinary in the ordinary."

LILA
I like that. The world needs more of the extraordinary.

SAM
Do you think I could hear one of your poems?

LILA
If I can hear one of your songs.

Sam smiles and takes out his guitar, beginning to play a soft, melodious tune. Lila listens, then begins to recite a poem in rhythm with the music.

LILA
(reciting)
In the quiet of the night, under the watchful moon's light...

Their impromptu performance creates a magical atmosphere, drawing the attention of a few late-night café goers. The small crowd claps as they finish.

SAM
I liked that. A lot.
LILA
So, did they.
SAM
One more?

She smiles as she turns the page in her journal. They play another as the café fades into the background, the city's night rhythm enveloping them.

WORKOUT COMPLETED [ ]

With the courage to begin and the discipline to endure. Victory becomes a matter of time.
It all starts with the shoes.
Stella Adler

IMAGINATION

We have a lot of tools in our arsenal as actors but **I believe imagination is the most powerful.** "If you hook into the character's belief system and you believe it 100%, there is no way the audience won't." - Meryl Streep "Imagination is more important than knowledge for knowledge is limited. - Einstein. Everyone has an Imagination but it must be worked out to get stronger. Think of your imagination as a limitless playground. In this space, you can be anyone, go anywhere, and do anything. **Have the courage to allow yourself to play!**

Solo Imaginary World Exploration - 6 Minutes [Set Timer]

Find a quiet space to relax and focus. **Close your eyes** and **let your imagination run wild. Tip:** Engage all your senses to explore this environment. Touch, taste, smell etc. Allow your emotions to guide you. **Extra:** After you establish this world in your imagination, you could introduce characters and have a dialogue with them. Are they friends or foes?

IMAGINARY WORLD: Bioluminescent Jungle on a Moonlit Night: Explore a jungle aglow with bioluminescent plants and creatures under the moon.

JOURNAL YOUR EXPERIENCE - 2 Minutes [Set Timer]

_____
_____
_____
_____
_____
_____
_____

Your Characters Filter - 5 Minutes [Set Timer]

Everyone including the characters you play see the world through their own specific perspective/filter. I like to use the word filter because you can take out a filter, clean it, change its style, colour, an optimist or a pessimist, comedian or a nihilist, etc. **Find a quiet space** to focus. **Close your eyes and let go of your personal thoughts and emotions** to make space for your characters. **Open your eyes, and allow the filter provided to effect everything around you. Tip**: Explore wherever you are and interact with the objects. **Extra:** How does *this* character walk and move in their world?

FILTER: Compassionate Healer: Perceives the pain in others and seeks to alleviate it.

JOURNAL YOUR EXPERIENCE - 2 Minutes [Set Timer]

_____
_____
_____
_____
_____
_____
_____

WORKOUT COMPLETED [ ]

What is acting but lying and what is good lying but convincing lying?
Lawrence Olivier

CHARACTER STUDY "PEOPLE WATCHING"

Actors are required to portray characters that are believable and relatable. You don't have to agree with them but you have to understand them. Walk like them, talk like them, see the world like them. So, in order to fill our toolbox, we have to **go out into the world and study**. Then practice them over and over so we can "walk in their shoes', comfortably and confidently. Study their movements, mannerisms, the "vibe" they give off, the clothes they wear etc. **Fill your toolbox with the rhythms and idiosyncrasies of human behaviour.**

OBSERVATION CHARACTER STUDY - 15 Minutes [Set Timer]

Find a busy place where you can **sit and observe.** Choose anyone you find interesting. **Write down what stands out about them.** *The way they sit, drink their coffee, walk, talk, interact with others etc.* **Tip: Mirror them immediately.** This will help memorize the feeling of that character so whenever you come back to these characters you're discovering, your body will remember. **Extra**: Before you go to sleep, read over the characters from today and reenact their movements.

_____
_____
_____
_____
_____
_____
_____
_____
_____
_____
_____
_____
_____
_____
_____
_____
_____
_____
_____
_____
_____
_____
_____
_____

COLOURS: We as humans respond to colours like frequencies. If you pay attention closely, you can see everyone has their own 'colour' that defines their core. An essence that informs how they operate and move through the world.

WHAT COLOUR ARE THEY:

WORKOUT COMPLETED [ ]

All an actor has is their blind faith that they are who they say they are today, in any scene.
Meryl Streep

VOICE & DICTION

I wish I had learned this at the beginning of my career. The confidence to communicate clearly and powerfully is a game-changer for you as an actor. **Think of your voice as a musical instrument that needs regular tuning. This workout is your daily tuning session,** ensuring that your instrument is always ready. "The word 'theatre' comes from the Greeks. It means the seeing place. It is the place people come to see the truth about life and the social situation." - Stella Adler. Embrace this workout as a key to unlocking and portraying *that* truth by letting your voice be the vehicle that transports your audience into the heart of your story.

READ PASSAGE - 30 Seconds [Set Timer]
Speak the passage and take note of its quality. **Tip**: Record Audio to compare afterward.

"Deep within the rainforest, a mysterious melody plays. Leaves flutter, raindrops patter, and the dense canopy hides wonders untold. Creatures move unseen, adding their voices to this vibrant symphony of life."

RELAXATION - 1 Minute [Set Timer]
Deep Breathing: Sit and Inhale deeply through your nose, filling your lungs, then exhale slowly through your mouth. Imagine stress leaving your body with each breath.

Nay Nay Nay - 1 Minute [Set Timer]
Pick a song and sing the word "Nay" repeatedly. Start with a comfortable pitch and gradually move the sound from your nose to your chest, ensuring each "Nay" is clear and resonant. Stretch your range as best you can to strengthen.

Sustained 'S' - 2 Minutes [Set Timer]
Inhale deeply and then exhale slowly, making a continuous 's' sound. Keep the sound as even and steady as you can. Always push a little longer than you think you can.

Vowel Pronunciation Drill - 2 Minutes [Set Timer]
Slowly go through each vowel sound **(A, E, I, O, U)**, **holding and exaggerating each sound. Combine them with consonants** (e.g., ba, be, bi, bo, bu). Pay attention to the clarity and sharpness of each sound. Repeat a few times before moving to the next.

Lip Trills - 3 minutes - [Set timer]
Close your lips together lightly, like you're going to blow a raspberry. Then, blow air through your closed lips while making sounds. You should feel a tickling sensation. Pick a song and Lip Trill the whole along with it. **Tip**: Stretch your range as much as you can and pick a song you've never listened to.

The Cork Exercise - 4 Minutes [Set Timer]
Place a cork between your teeth and try to read a passage aloud. This forces your articulation muscles to work harder. If you don't have a cork, bite down gently on your thumb. You can use the following text for this exercise:

READ PASSAGE AGAIN - 30 Seconds [Set Timer]
Speak the passage and take note of its quality. **Tip**: Record Audio to compare.

Discovery Journal - 1 Minute [Set Timer]

WORKOUT COMPLETED [ ]

I mean honestly, I look at acting like it's my job to disappear. The best acting is invisible.
Michael Shannon

SUBTEXT

Subtext is what lies beneath the surface of our words. It's the hidden layer of meaning, driven by the character's internal thoughts, emotions, desires, and motivations. Subtext is one of my favourite things as an actor because so much can be said with one simple line of dialogue. The power of "Hello" can be exciting if you told that person years ago "If I ever see you again, I'll kill you. Maybe it's the most beautiful person you've ever seen. Now, say "hello". *Subtext* shows the audience what your relationship with the characters/places/situations are, without having to explain it. We experience it every day and it is our job to create characters that interact as we do.

VOCAL WORK - 3 minutes - [Set Timer]
Lip Trills: Close your lips together lightly, like you're going to blow a raspberry. Then, blow air through your closed lips while making sounds. You should feel a tickling sensation. Pick a song and Lip Trill along with it. **Tip**: Stretch your range as much as you can and pick a song you've never listened to.

SUBTEXT PRACTICE
Use the line of dialogue provided and practice each of these subtexts **out loud.** Move on to the next, only when you believe yourself. Trust that you will know when *that* is. Before you begin, **pick a spot to look at and imagine** in detail, **who you are speaking with**. **Tip**: *Sometimes* we mean exactly what we are saying. Look for that too. **Extra**: Substitute someone you have a strong relationship with in real life, good or bad, and see it's affect.

Initial Line: "I just found out they're bringing back the old summer carnival after ten years."
Your Response Line: "Really? That's great. The carnival always had an air of mystery and thrill about it. Brings back memories. Are you going to go?"

SUBTEXTS - 6 Minutes [Set Timer]
[ ] Thrill-Seeker: You crave the adrenaline rush the carnival always provided.
[ ] Romanticized: You associate the carnival with a passionate summer fling.
[ ] Deeply Nostalgic: You yearn for the carefree days of youth it represents.
[ ] Intensely Skeptical: You've always felt there was something unsettling about the carnival.
[ ] Overwhelmed: The sensory overload of the carnival both excites and intimidates you.
[ ] Your Own Subtext

RELATIONSHIP SUBTEXTS - 6 Minutes [Set Timer]
[ ] The Ex who kissed you on the Ferris wheel.
[ ] The Long-Lost Friend you used to roam the carnival with.
[ ] The Rival from your teenage years you'd always encounter there.
[ ] The Protective Older Sibling who used to watch over you.
[ ] The Charismatic Stranger you had an unforgettable encounter with.
[ ] Your Own Subtext

Discovery Journal

_____
_____
_____
_____
_____

WORKOUT COMPLETED [ ]

I don't want to 'play' a character. If Im going to do something dramatic, I want it to be inspired. I want it to be passionate.
Miles Teller

EMOTIONS

The 'moment before', **the emotional preparation, is the most important key to a great scene.** If you start any scene *without* an emotional preparation it feels like trying to drive a car in neutral. The preparation is the uphill climb of every rollercoaster; Once you grind all the way to the top, the chains let go and the rest of the ride takes care of itself. "No one wants to see a play or a movie and look at technical proficiency. You want to be moved, you want a human experience, you want to feel less alone" - Viola Davis. **Practice your emotions over and over** so when it's time, you aren't worried "Will I get there?" **You're imagination and emotions should be a tinderbox, so easy to light up. All it take is half a spark.**

EULOGY - 12 Minutes [Set Timer]

Find a quiet comfortable space. Choose someone in your life who is alive and important to you. Create an imaginary reason for why they have died. Now start from the point of the phone call— Imagine who calls, what they say and what you say. Eventually find yourself at the funeral, about to begin the eulogy. See the casket, is it open or closed?? What is that person wearing and any other details for yourself. Before you begin to speak, look into the audience and see who is there- Family, friends etc **Then begin the eulogy.** **Tip**: Be as specific as you can with everything. **Inside of specificity is where you will find the triggers to your heart.** Let your imagination take you wherever you want in this exercise. **Example**: Placing her favourite sheep stuffed animal in the casket, tucked under her arm like she always held it, then kissing her goodbye one last time.

DISCOVERY JOURNAL - 3 Minutes [Set Timer]

Make sure to **include the specific triggers** you experience because you can use these **TRIGGER MOMENTS** in the future instead of repeating the *entire* exercise.

WORKOUT COMPLETED [ ]

I don't know what acting is, but I enjoy it.
Anthony Hopkins

THE CORK EXERCISE - 4 Minutes [Set Timer]
Place a cork between your teeth and read a passage aloud. This forces your articulation muscles to work harder. If you don't have a cork, bite down gently on your thumb. You can use the following text for this exercise:

> "In the hush of the library, rows of books stand sentinel, guardians of knowledge and history. The gentle rustle of pages turning and the soft tapping of keyboards create a symphony of quiet study, a sanctuary for seekers of wisdom."

WRITE A LETTER - 10 Minutes [Set Timer]
Get a piece of paper or write this in your device. **Take a moment** to let this situation and relationship sink in. Then let your imagination run wild and **write them a letter.**

Your Character: Jordan, a successful entrepreneur who recently discovered a significant betrayal.
Other Character: Alex, a trusted business partner and long-time friend, has been secretly undermining Jordan's business for personal gain.

Relationship: Jordan and Alex's relationship was built on years of mutual respect and shared successes in their business ventures. The revelation of Alex's duplicity not only threatens the business but also shatters the trust and friendship that Jordan values deeply.

Context of the Letter: Reeling from the shock and hurt of this betrayal, Jordan writes a letter to Alex. This letter is an outlet for Jordan's feelings of betrayal, disappointment, and anger. It's a confrontation of the broken trust, an attempt to understand Alex's motives, and perhaps a final goodbye to a friendship that meant the world to Jordan.

Discovery Journal - 1 minute [Set Timer]
_____
_____
_____

WORKOUT COMPLETED [ ]

No matter what people tell you, words and
ideas can change the world.
Robin Williams

VOCAL WORK - 3 minutes - [Set Timer]

Lip Trills: Close your lips together lightly, like you're going to blow a raspberry. Then, blow air through your closed lips while making sounds. You should feel a tickling sensation. Pick a song and Lip Trill along with it. **Tip**: Stretch your range as much as you can and pick a song you've never listened to.

VERBAL IMPROV - 10 Minutes [Set Timer]

Find a space where you are comfortable and free to express yourself. Take a moment to **let this situation, character and prompt, sink in**. Then let your imagination run wild: **Picture who you are talking to** then **begin with *the prompt*** and **continue to verbalize everything** this character would say. **Tip**: This is exploration! There is no "getting it right". BE BRAVE to explore and discover.

Character: Taylor, a community organizer known for their dedication to social justice, uncovers that their colleague, Harper, generally respected for their calm demeanour, has been manipulating community funds. Taylor's upbringing in a financially struggling community makes this breach of trust particularly painful.

Prompt: "Harper, I've found discrepancies in our fund allocations. We should talk about this immediately."

Who are you talking to:

Describe them in two specific words:

Discovery Journal - 2 minutes [Set Timer]

_____
_____
_____
_____
_____
_____
_____

WORKOUT COMPLETED [ ]

The actor is an athlete of the heart.
I always tell the truth. Even when I lie.
Al Pacino

SELF AWARENESS

The more you understand yourself, the more you are able to understand and develop your characters. Like you, your characters have thoughts, beliefs, traumas, passions etc. When you become aware of your own and start to see how those experiences and beliefs have shaped your life, how you operate and view the world, then you can develop your characters that are much more rich and vivid.

PHYSICAL WARMUP - 2 minutes [Set Timer]

Freeform Dance: Put on some music and engage in freeform dancing. Allow your body to move spontaneously and without inhibition. This can help you tap into your creative instincts and develop physical expressiveness. **Tip**: Try music you've never listened to.

CURRENT EMOTIONAL INVENTORY - 3 Minutes [Set Timer]

Write down and **record your current emotions**. Identify what you're feeling at this moment and why. **Tip**: Be as specific as you can, **don't disregard anything.** You can also **scan your body** to see how and where your current emotion is affecting you. Your posture, the way you walk, bouncing foot, sore neck etc

CURRENT EMOTIONAL STATE:

SELF DISCOVERY QUESTIONS - 10 Minutes [Set Timer]

I suggest a journal or writing it in your phone's notes so you don't run out of space here.

What traits do I admire in others? (Extra: Name the person and why you admire it so much)

How do I show empathy or compassion?

WORKOUT COMPLETED [ ]

Don't you find it odd that when you're a kid, everyone, all the world, encourages you to follow your dreams. But when you're older, somehow they act offended if you even try.
Ethan Hawke

IMAGINATION

We have a lot of tools in our arsenal as actors but I believe imagination is the most powerful. "If you hook into the character's belief system and you believe it 100%, there is no way the audience won't." - Meryl Streep. Everyone has an Imagination but it must be worked out to get stronger. Think of your imagination as a limitless playground. In this space, you can be anyone, go anywhere, and do anything. **Have the courage to allow yourself to play!**

VOCAL WORK - 2 minutes - [Set Timer]
Lip Trills: Close your lips together lightly, like you're going to blow a raspberry. Then, blow air through your closed lips while making sounds. You should feel a tickling sensation. Pick a song and Lip Trill along with it. **Tip**: Stretch your range as much as you can and pick a song you've never listened to.

IMPROVISED STORYTELLING - 5 Minutes [Set Timer]
Speak out the scenario provided and continue the story! Focus on vivid details, character development and how the main character overcomes the main obstacle. **Tip**: Try not to stop speaking so you don't have time to "think". Allow your imagination to keep moving forward without interruption. **Tip:** Record these stories on your device, in case it's great but more importantly to see your progress as you go on.

STARTING POINT: You are Sam, a professional linguist who receives a mysterious package containing an ancient scroll with a language that no one has been able to decipher. As you begin to analyze and translate the script, you realize it says "Run Sam. Now." You hear commotion outside your door and get a horrible feeling... As women in suits with guns, burst through the door, you stuff the scroll into your pocket and—

IMAGINARY WORLD EXPLORATION - 6 Minutes [Set Timer]

Find a quiet space to relax and focus. **Close your eyes** and let your imagination run wild. **Tip:** Engage all your senses to explore this environment. Touch, taste, smell etc and allow your emotions to guide you. **Extra:** After you explore this world with your senses, you could introduce characters and have a dialogue with them. Are they friends or foes?

IMAGINARY WORLD: GELATINOUS REALM - Christmas is everywhere. As you venture through the town you realize every home you enter is a memory from each of your Christmases.

JOURNAL YOUR EXPERIENCE - 2 Minutes [Set Timer]

___

WORKOUT COMPLETED [ ]

Do what you have to do, to do what
you want to do.
Unknown

ANCHORING INTO YOUR CHARACTER COLOUR & MUSIC

Anchoring yourself into your character is vital. It's one of the most freeing feelings when you understand their *essence* because everything they do, how they do it and what their purpose is, becomes so clear to you and the audience. Every choice you make after you find your *anchor*, feels easy, because you're acting from who and what your character is at the core. You can call it an essence, an aura, vibe, energy etc. We all have it and feel it from everyone around us. There are many ways into your character but music and colour are my favourite. Music can inform the script, your character, even each scene. Colours, I think you will find, can work incredibly because we as humans respond to colours like frequencies. Colours evoke many feelings and if you pay attention closely, you can see everyone has their own 'colour' that defines their core. An essence that informs how they operate and move through the world.

THEIR COLOUR - 2 Minutes [Set Timer]
Think of **someone you know**, and **define them with a colour**. **Tip**: Trust yourself. Your initial colour is usually close. **Tip**: Start with basic colours then eventually become much more specific. **Example**: Corinna is an earthy green with rays of sunlight flowing through the green. **Extra**: Ask someone who knows *that person* as well, what they think this person's colour is and why. See how close your answers are or not.

YOUR CHARACTERS COLOUR
Read the given character description just as you would an audition, **assign a colour to that character.** Now take that colour you chose and **allow it to infuse into your entire body,** affecting your every move, your speaking, the way you see the world etc. **Take any book** you have, flip to a random page and **read the text as this Colour/Character**. **Tip**: Be specific, choose a colour that excites you and don't be afraid to get creative.

CHARACTER DESCRIPTION: [AVERY] Avery is a mysterious antique dealer with a knack for finding rare and unusual items. Their shop is an eclectic mix of history and mystery, with Avery often seen examining a new peculiar artifact. Dressed in vintage attire that matches the shop's aura, Avery has a mysterious and captivating presence. They possess an extensive knowledge of antiques and their histories, often sharing intriguing tales about their acquisitions. Despite their warm and engaging demeanour, there's a secretive side hinting at a darker past.

CHOOSE THEIR COLOUR - 4 Minutes [Set Timer]
THEIR COLOUR:

CHOOSE THEIR SONG - 4 Minutes [Set Timer]
THEIR SONG:

READ PASSAGE FROM BOOK - 2 Minutes [Set Timer]

FREEFORM DANCE - 2 minutes - [Set Timer]
Put on the selected music and **engage in freeform dancing, anchored in your colour/character,** Allow your body to move spontaneously and without inhibition. This can help you tap into your creative instincts and develop physical expressiveness *while staying in character.* **Tip**: Journal about the differences as opposed to how you normally dance.

JOURNAL YOUR EXPERIENCE - 1 Minute [Set Timer]
____
____
____
____

WORKOUT COMPLETED [ ]

Dreams are great. In fact, dreams are necessary in life or no one would ever go anywhere! But a dream without a goal, and without action, has no opportunity to come true.
Denzel Washington

HISTORICAL RESEARCH

We are in the information era and have access to the world and its rich history at our fingertips. This exploration is not about 'learning facts'; it's a journey to the heart of human experience. The empathy and the understanding, especially on the things you disagree with, are incredibly valuable. If you look closely, you'll find the way people think, at different times in history, their attitudes, choices, and the way they move their bodies can teach you so much about us, right now. Fill your toolbox so it's overflowing with information and ideas to pull from so your imagination has so much to play with.

PHYSICAL WARMUP - 2 minutes - [Set Timer]
Freeform Dance: Put on some music and engage in freeform dancing. Allow your body to move spontaneously and without inhibition. This can help you tap into your creative instincts and develop physical expressiveness. **Tip**: Try music you've never listened to.

RESEARCH - 13 Minutes [Set Timer]
YouTube, streaming platforms, the internet or books, **research the given era/person/moment in time,** journal or make notes on your device, so when you want to find this information, it's organized and readily accessible. As you go, **write anything and everything _you_ find fascinating. Tip:** If the topic doesn't interest you, choose your own, or take a chance and still research it, but from a different perspective. Physicalities, voice, ideals, etc. Trust your body that when you see something interesting, you'll know. **Extra**: Speak it out and copy their movements. Our memory recall is massively affected by our bodies. Be specific and when you re-read your notes, you'll be amazed by how much your mind and body remember.

TOPIC:
The Vietnam War Era (1955-1975) - The Perspective of Walter Cronkite: Walter Cronkite, a renowned American broadcast journalist, offers an insightful perspective on the Vietnam War era. Known as "the most trusted man in America," Cronkite's broadcasts, especially his critical commentary following the Tet Offensive in 1968, significantly influenced public opinion on the war. There is extensive footage of his newscasts and reports, which actors can study to capture his authoritative yet empathetic journalistic style, his ability to convey complex issues clearly, and his role in shaping media coverage during a tumultuous period in American history. Cronkite's demeanour and delivery make him a compelling figure for actors exploring the intersection of media, politics, and public sentiment.

_____
_____
_____
_____
_____
_____
_____
_____
_____
_____
_____
_____

WORKOUT COMPLETED [ ]

Never compromise on who you are. You are born with the capacity to achieve greatness if you so desire. Learning to say no is a critical element to accessing that greatness. Your choices will define you; so make them the right ones.
Denzel Washington

BELIEF

Beliefs are the convictions that something exists or is true, especially without proof. That is also the definition of what we do as actors. We play make-believe. Our beliefs shape our world, especially our beliefs about ourselves and it works for the characters you play. Understand your beliefs and how they influence your mind, body and spirit, then you will be able to better understand others, so you can embody them. Allow the beliefs of your character to colour your perception of your world and your interaction with everything in it. "Acting is the best magic trick in the world. We applaud performances not because it's real, but because you made us believe."

VOCAL WORK - 2 minutes - [Set Timer]

Lip Trills: Close your lips together lightly, like you're going to blow a raspberry. Then, blow air through your closed lips while making sounds. You should feel a tickling sensation. Pick a song and Lip Trill along with it. **Tip**: Stretch your range as much as you can and pick a song you've never listened to.

BELIEF WORKOUT

Get your journal or write in here. **Define your personal belief/view** on the given subject. **Grab any book you own,** flip to a random page and **read it out loud,** colouring the words and intention with your belief system. **Tip:** Write trigger words you can hook into in the future: **Optimism-** Always smiling, grateful, opportunity, sunshine yellow.

YOUR PERSONAL BELIEF

Right & Wrong - 7 Minutes [Set Timer]

_____
_____
_____
_____

READ WITH BELIEF - 2 Minutes [Set Timer]

CHARACTERS BELIEF

Right & Wrong

The ends always justify the means. Traditional morals are constraints for the weak. I believe in the supremacy of power and intellect. For me, morality is a chessboard, and I am the grandmaster, moving pieces at my will.

READ WITH CHARACTERS BELIEF - 2 Minutes [Set Timer]
Forget your personal view and **fully embrace the character's belief. Read out loud again.**

JOURNAL YOUR EXPERIENCE - 2 Minutes [Set Timer]

_____
_____
_____
_____

WORKOUT COMPLETED [ ]

PERFORMANCE STRATEGY
14 DAY REVIEW

TAKE A MOMENT OF REFLECTION AND BREAKDOWN WHERE YOU ARE RIGHT NOW IN YOUR CAREER AND AS AN ACTOR.
THE MORE SPECIFIC YOU ARE THE MORE CLEAR YOU CAN SEE WHERE YOU ARE NOW SO YOU CAN GET TO WHERE YOU WANT TO GO FASTER

★   ★   ★   ★   ★

Walt Disney: His first animation company went bankrupt. He later found monumental success with Disney, creating a lasting legacy in the entertainment industry.

DATE:

MY WHY
WHY ARE YOU DOING WHAT YOU ARE DOING
BE SPECIFIC

MY MAIN GOALS
IN-ORDER OF IMPORTANCE

1.

   Action Step(s):

2.

   Action Step(s):

3.

   Action Step(s):

FROM THE LAST 14 DAYS
5 STAR RATING

YOUR KEY POINTS AND TAKEAWAYS - WHY THAT AMOUNT OF STAR RATING, LIKES, DISLIKES, THE BIGGEST LESSON YOU LEARNED, GOOD OR BAD:

STRENGTHS:

WEAKNESSES:

IMPROVEMENT STRATEGY
HOW CAN YOU IMPROVE ON THESE AREAS FOR THE NEXT 14 DAYS:

GOAL FROM LAST :
DID YOU ACHIEVE IT?

WHY OR WHY NOT?

GOAL FOR THE NEXT 14 EXERCISES
THE MORE SPECIFIC YOU ARE THE GREATER THE RESULT

   Action Step(s):

One of the things about acting is it
allows you to live other peoples lives
without having to pay the price.
Robert De Niro

MY WHY:

GOAL(s):

PHYSICAL WARMUP - ELEMENTAL DANCE - 1 minute [Set Timer]
Nature's Rhythm: Dance as if you are the wind, then transition to the solidity of earth, the fluidity of water, and the ferocity of fire. **Tip**: Allow each element to inform the quality of your movement; be as changeable as the breeze, as grounded as the earth, as fluid as water, and as unpredictable as fire.

VOCAL WORK - WHISPERED SECRETS - 3 minutes [Set Timer]
Whispered Tones: Whisper a monologue or a series of phrases. Focus on articulation and the breath behind the whisper. Gradually, let your whispers grow into full voice. **Tip**: Notice how whispering affects your vocal cords and how it feels when the voice is released into a full sound.

EMOTIONAL RECALL - PENSIVE MOMENTS - 5 minutes [Set Timer]
Reflective Solitude: Recall a moment of deep contemplation or decision-making. Re-live the thoughts, the inner turmoil, and the moments of silence that surrounded it. **Tip**: Let your body reflect the mental journey, from the stillness of thought to the action that followed.

ANIMAL WORK - MAJESTIC EAGLE

Research - 2 minutes [Set Timer]
Study the eagle's characteristics, focusing on its powerful gaze, the spread of its wings, and the decisiveness of its dive.

Animal Exercise 3 minutes [Set Timer]
Embody the eagle's commanding presence. Spread your arms like wings, move with assuredness, and strike with precision. **Tip**: Imagine the feeling of soaring and the sudden focus as you dive for your prey, embodying the eagle's keen eyes and fierce determination.

Discovery Journal - 1 Minute [Set Timer]
3 Main Characteristics: (Whatever stands out to YOU to embody the essence)

_____
_____
_____
_____
_____
_____

WORKOUT COMPLETED [ ]

Acting is like a high wire act. Your margin for error is very slim.
Christine Baranski

SCRIPT ANALYSIS for **RELATIONSHIPS & SPECIFICITY** - 15 minutes [Set Timer]

Choose your character, circle everything in this script you have a relationship with. Including people, places, things, smells, time of day etc. **Write what your relationship with those items are** and **be specific.** The more specific and fun you have with your relationships, the more interesting your characters will be and the more fun the audience has. **Tip:** Everything isn't in the scene. Use your imagination to create details, only if it's contextually appropriate. **Extra:** Write your > **Objective, win or lose? Consequence of failing?** The **Who What Where When Why.**

Title: **Chance Encounters**
INT. QUIRKY BOOKSTORE - AFTERNOON
*A cozy bookstore, stacks of books and vintage posters. **JAMIE**: introspective, is browsing through the literature section. **ALEX**, spontaneous, accidentally bumps into **JAMIE**, the books fall—*

ALEX
Oh no, I'm so sorry! I'm a walking disaster today.

JAMIE
It's okay. Happens to the best of us.

ALEX
Ah, 'To Kill a Mockingbird'. A classic. You a fan of Harper Lee?

JAMIE
More like a fan of anything that can transport me to another world.

ALEX
I get that.
(Reading the title of another one of the books she dropped)
"How to introduce yourself to a really pretty stranger?"

JAMIE
What? That's not the book I— *(Checking the book)* Clever. Jamie.

ALEX
I'm Alex. Nice to meet you, Jamie.
They begin re-shelving the books together.

ALEX(cont'd)
So, what's your favourite 'world' to escape to?

JAMIE
Hmm, that's tough. I'd say anywhere that challenges the way I think.

ALEX
I'm more of a 'fantasy world' kind of person. Dragons, wizards—

JAMIE
Fantasy is great. It's like stepping into a dream.

ALEX
You ever thought of writing your own book?

JAMIE
Sometimes. But I think I'm better at reading them than writing them.

ALEX
I bet you'd write something amazing. You have that 'writerly' look. I think it's the shoes.

JAMIE
Writerly look, huh? That's a new one.
They finish stacking the books.

ALEX
There's a coffee shop next door. After you find you're next 'challenge', would you, maybe like to grab a coffee? Tea? Hot chocolate?

JAMIE
I'd like that. All three.
They laugh as he bumps into the bookshelf as he turns to walk away... They laugh again.

WORKOUT COMPLETED [ ]

Acting makes you look at life and try to understand it in a beautiful way.
Clemence Poesy

IMAGINATION

We have a lot of tools in our arsenal as actors but **I believe imagination is the most powerful.** "If you hook into the character's belief system and you believe it 100%, there is no way the audience won't." - Meryl Streep "Imagination is more important than knowledge for knowledge is limited. - Einstein. Everyone has an Imagination but it must be worked out to get stronger. Think of your imagination as a limitless playground. In this space, you can be anyone, go anywhere, and do anything. **Have the courage to allow yourself to play!**

Solo Imaginary World Exploration - 6 Minutes [Set Timer]

Find a quiet space to relax and focus. **Close your eyes** and **let your imagination run wild. Tip:** Engage all your senses to explore this environment. Touch, taste, smell etc. Allow your emotions to guide you. **Extra:** After you establish this world in your imagination, you could introduce characters and have a dialogue with them. Are they friends or foes?

IMAGINARY WORLD: Giant's Abandoned Playroom: Navigate an environment from a miniature perspective in a giant's playroom.

JOURNAL YOUR EXPERIENCE - 2 Minutes [Set Timer]

_____
_____
_____
_____
_____
_____
_____

Your Characters Filter - 5 Minutes [Set Timer]

Everyone including the characters you play see the world through their own specific perspective/filter. I like to use the word filter because you can take out a filter, clean it, change its style, colour, an optimist or a pessimist, comedian or a nihilist, etc. **Find a quiet space** to focus. **Close your eyes and let go of your personal thoughts and emotions** to make space for your characters. **Open your eyes, and allow the filter provided to effect everything around you. Tip:** Explore wherever you are and interact with the objects. **Extra:** How does *this* character walk and move in their world?

FILTER: Mischievous Imp: Loves to create chaos and stir up trouble playfully.

JOURNAL YOUR EXPERIENCE - 2 Minutes [Set Timer]

_____
_____
_____
_____
_____
_____
_____

WORKOUT COMPLETED [ ]

The training process is nothing more than
the process of making the use of these
tools habitual. Once they are habitual,
the actor need not think about them.
Only then is he free to play.
A practical handbook for the actor

CHARACTER STUDY "PEOPLE WATCHING"

Actors are required to portray characters that are believable and relatable. You don't have to agree with them but you have to understand them. Walk like them, talk like them, see the world like them. So, in order to fill our toolbox, we have to **go out into the world and study**. Then practice them over and over so we can "walk in their shoes', comfortably and confidently. Study their movements, mannerisms, the "vibe" they give off, the clothes they wear etc. **Fill your toolbox with the rhythms and idiosyncrasies of human behaviour.**

OBSERVATION CHARACTER STUDY - 15 Minutes [Set Timer]

Find a busy place where you can **sit and observe.** Choose anyone you find interesting. **Write down what stands out about them.** *The way they sit, drink their coffee, walk, talk, interact with others etc.* **Tip**: **Mirror them immediately**. This will help memorize the feeling of that character so whenever you come back to these characters you're discovering, your body will remember. **Extra**: Before you go to sleep, read over the characters from today and reenact their movements.

_____
_____
_____
_____
_____
_____
_____
_____
_____
_____
_____
_____
_____
_____
_____
_____
_____
_____
_____
_____
_____

COLOURS: We as humans respond to colours like frequencies. If you pay attention closely, you can see everyone has their own 'colour' that defines their core. An essence that informs how they operate and move through the world.

WHAT COLOUR ARE THEY:

WORKOUT COMPLETED [ ]

There is no overacting, only untrue acting.
Stellan Skarsgard

VOICE & DICTION

I wish I had learned this at the beginning of my career. The confidence to communicate clearly and powerfully is a game-changer for you as an actor. **Think of your voice as a musical instrument that needs regular tuning. This workout is your daily tuning session,** ensuring that your instrument is always ready. "The word 'theatre' comes from the Greeks. It means the seeing place. It is the place people come to see the truth about life and the social situation." - Stella Adler. Embrace this workout as a key to unlocking and portraying *that* truth by letting your voice be the vehicle that transports your audience into the heart of your story.

READ PASSAGE - 30 Seconds [Set Timer]
Speak the passage and take note of its quality. **Tip**: Record Audio to compare afterward.

"Under the starlit sky, the night whispers softly. Stars twinkle, the moon glows, and the quiet darkness hums with the beauty of the cosmos. The vast universe unfolds above, a tapestry of light and mystery."

RELAXATION - 1 Minute [Set Timer]
Deep Breathing: Sit and Inhale deeply through your nose, filling your lungs, then exhale slowly through your mouth. Imagine stress leaving your body with each breath.

Nay Nay Nay - 1 Minute [Set Timer]
Pick a song and sing the word "Nay" repeatedly. Start with a comfortable pitch and gradually move the sound from your nose to your chest, ensuring each "Nay" is clear and resonant. Stretch your range as best you can to strengthen.

Sustained 'S' - 2 Minutes [Set Timer]
Inhale deeply and then exhale slowly, making a continuous 's' sound. Keep the sound as even and steady as you can. Always push a little longer than you think you can.

Vowel Pronunciation Drill - 2 Minutes [Set Timer]
Slowly go through each vowel sound **(A, E, I, O, U)**, **holding and exaggerating each sound. Combine them with consonants** (e.g., ba, be, bi, bo, bu). Pay attention to the clarity and sharpness of each sound. Repeat a few times before moving to the next.

Lip Trills - 3 minutes - [Set timer]
Close your lips together lightly, like you're going to blow a raspberry. Then, blow air through your closed lips while making sounds. You should feel a tickling sensation. Pick a song and Lip Trill the whole along with it. **Tip**: Stretch your range as much as you can and pick a song you've never listened to.

The Cork Exercise - 4 Minutes [Set Timer]
Place a cork between your teeth and try to read a passage aloud. This forces your articulation muscles to work harder. If you don't have a cork, bite down gently on your thumb. You can use the following text for this exercise:

READ PASSAGE AGAIN - 30 Seconds [Set Timer]
Speak the passage and take note of its quality. **Tip**: Record Audio to compare.

Discovery Journal - 1 Minute [Set Timer]

WORKOUT COMPLETED [ ]

I think everything in life is art. What you do. How you dress. The way you love someone and how you talk. Your smile and your personality. What you believe in and all your dreams. The way you drink your tea and how you decorate your home. Or party. Your grocery list. The food you make. How your writing looks. And the way you feel. Life is art.
Helena Bonham Carter

SUBTEXT

Subtext is what lies beneath the surface of our words. It's the hidden layer of meaning, driven by the character's internal thoughts, emotions, desires, and motivations. Subtext is one of my favourite things as an actor because so much can be said with one simple line of dialogue. The power of "Hello" can be exciting if you told that person years ago "If I ever see you again, I'll kill you. Maybe it's the most beautiful person you've ever seen. Now, say "hello". *Subtext* shows the audience what your relationship with the characters/places/situations are, without having to explain it. We experience it every day and it is our job to create characters that interact as we do.

VOCAL WORK - 3 minutes - [Set Timer]
Lip Trills: Close your lips together lightly, like you're going to blow a raspberry. Then, blow air through your closed lips while making sounds. You should feel a tickling sensation. Pick a song and Lip Trill along with it. **Tip**: Stretch your range as much as you can and pick a song you've never listened to.

SUBTEXT PRACTICE
Use the line of dialogue provided and practice each of these subtexts **out loud.** Move on to the next, only when you believe yourself. Trust that you will know when *that* is. Before you begin, **pick a spot to look at and imagine** in detail, **who you are speaking with**. **Tip**: *Sometimes* we mean exactly what we are saying. Look for that too. **Extra**: Substitute someone you have a strong relationship with in real life, good or bad, and see it's affect.

Initial Line: "I heard that the old treehouse we used to play in is being torn down next week."
Your Response Line: "No way, really? That treehouse was our secret fortress. I remember that summer we built it. I can't believe it's actually going. Who is tearing it down?"

SUBTEXTS - 6 Minutes [Set Timer]
[ ] Deeply Sentimental: You're mourning the loss of a cherished symbol of your youth.
[ ] Bitter: You resent the changing landscape that's erasing your past.
[ ] Philosophical: You reflect on the impermanence of things and life's transitions.
[ ] Indifferent: You've moved on and the treehouse no longer holds meaning for you.
[ ] Resigned: You accept it as an inevitable part of growing up and moving on.
[ ] Your Own Subtext

RELATIONSHIP SUBTEXTS - 6 Minutes [Set Timer]
[ ] The Childhood Best Friend who shared countless adventures there.
[ ] The First Crush who carved your initials in the treehouse.
[ ] The Sibling who always felt left out of the treehouse gang.
[ ] The Neighbor who always complained about the noise you made.
[ ] The Parent who's now nostalgic about your younger days.
[ ] Your Own Subtext

Discovery Journal
_____
_____
_____

WORKOUT COMPLETED [ ]

THE FIVE - Relationship, Immediate Objective, Super objective, Consequence of failing & Underlying fear.
Konstantin Stanislavski

EMOTIONS

The 'moment before', **the emotional preparation, is the most important key to a great scene.** If you start any scene *without* an emotional preparation it feels like trying to drive a car in neutral. The preparation is the uphill climb of every rollercoaster; Once you grind all the way to the top, the chains let go and the rest of the ride takes care of itself. "No one wants to see a play or a movie and look at technical proficiency. You want to be moved, you want a human experience, you want to feel less alone" - Viola Davis. **Practice your emotions over and over** so when it's time, you aren't worried "Will I get there?" **You're imagination and emotions should be a tinderbox, so easy to light up. All it take is half a spark.**

EULOGY - 12 Minutes [Set Timer]

Find a quiet comfortable space. Choose someone in your life who is alive and important to you. Create an imaginary reason for why they have died. Now start from the point of the phone call— Imagine who calls, what they say and what you say. Eventually find yourself at the funeral, about to begin the eulogy. See the casket, is it open or closed?? What is that person wearing and any other details for yourself. Before you begin to speak, look into the audience and see who is there- Family, friends etc **Then begin the eulogy. Tip**: Be as specific as you can with everything. **Inside of specificity is where you will find the triggers to your heart.** Let your imagination take you wherever you want in this exercise. **Example**: Placing her favourite sheep stuffed animal in the casket, tucked under her arm like she always held it, then kissing her goodbye one last time.

DISCOVERY JOURNAL - 3 Minutes [Set Timer]

Make sure to **include the specific triggers** you experience because you can use these **TRIGGER MOMENTS** in the future instead of repeating the *entire* exercise.

_____
_____
_____
_____
_____
_____
_____
_____
_____
_____
_____
_____
_____
_____
_____
_____
_____
_____
_____
_____

WORKOUT COMPLETED [ ]

Acting is the best magic trick in the world.
Victor Zinck Jr

THE CORK EXERCISE - 4 Minutes [Set Timer]
Place a cork between your teeth and read a passage aloud. This forces your articulation muscles to work harder. If you don't have a cork, bite down gently on your thumb. You can use the following text for this exercise:

"In the early hours of the morning, the city park is a haven of tranquillity. Joggers tread softly on the paths, squirrels scamper in the grass, and the distant hum of the city seems worlds away."

WRITE A LETTER - 10 Minutes [Set Timer]
Get a piece of paper or write this in your device. **Take a moment** to let this situation and relationship sink in. Then let your imagination run wild and **write them a letter.**

Your Character: Alex, a child protective services worker who has dedicated their career to helping vulnerable children.
Other Character: Casey, the parent of a child Alex was involved in removing from their home due to safety concerns, who has since made significant life changes.

Relationship: Alex's professional duty required making difficult decisions, including the heart-wrenching choice to remove Casey's child from their care. This decision was made with the child's best interests in mind but left both Alex and Casey grappling with complex emotions.

Context of the Letter: After learning that Casey has turned their life around and is seeking to regain custody, Alex is compelled to write a letter. This letter is a reflection on the painful decision made, an acknowledgment of Casey's efforts to change, and a personal expression of hope for the child's future. It's an emotionally charged communication, balancing professional boundaries with the deep human impact of such cases.

Discovery Journal - 1 minute [Set Timer]
_____
_____
_____
_____

WORKOUT COMPLETED [ ]

If I believe it 100% there's no way the
audience can believe otherwise.
Meryl Streep

VOCAL WORK - 3 minutes - [Set Timer]
Lip Trills: Close your lips together lightly, like you're going to blow a raspberry. Then, blow air through your closed lips while making sounds. You should feel a tickling sensation. Pick a song and Lip Trill along with it. **Tip**: Stretch your range as much as you can and pick a song you've never listened to.

VERBAL IMPROV - 10 Minutes [Set Timer]

Find a space where you are comfortable and free to express yourself. Take a moment to **let this situation, character and prompt, sink in**. Then let your imagination run wild: **Picture who you are talking to** then **begin with *the prompt*** and **continue to verbalize everything** this character would say. **Tip**: This is exploration! There is no "getting it right". BE BRAVE to explore and discover.

Character: Alex, a software developer known for their integrity and innovation, learns that their project teammate, Riley, typically seen as laid-back and easygoing, has been stealing code from competitors. Alex's past experience with intellectual property theft makes them sensitive to this issue.

Prompt: "Riley, I know about the code theft. We need to discuss the implications of your actions."

Who are you talking to:

Describe them in two specific words:

Discovery Journal - 2 minutes [Set Timer]

_____
_____
_____
_____
_____
_____
_____

WORKOUT COMPLETED [ ]

The greater the obstacles the more passion
you will bring to overcoming and winning.
Unknown

SELF AWARENESS

The more you understand yourself, the more you are able to understand and develop your characters. Like you, your characters have thoughts, beliefs, traumas, passions etc. When you become aware of your own and start to see how those experiences and beliefs have shaped your life, how you operate and view the world, then you can develop your characters that are much more rich and vivid.

PHYSICAL WARMUP - 2 minutes [Set Timer]
Freeform Dance: Put on some music and engage in freeform dancing. Allow your body to move spontaneously and without inhibition. This can help you tap into your creative instincts and develop physical expressiveness. **Tip**: Try music you've never listened to.

CURRENT EMOTIONAL INVENTORY - 3 Minutes [Set Timer]
Write down and **record your current emotions**. Identify what you're feeling at this moment and why. **Tip**: Be as specific as you can, **don't disregard anything.** You can also **scan your body** to see how and where your current emotion is affecting you. Your posture, the way you walk, bouncing foot, sore neck etc

CURRENT EMOTIONAL STATE:

SELF DISCOVERY QUESTIONS - 10 Minutes [Set Timer]
I suggest a journal or writing it in your phone's notes so you don't run out of space here.

What makes me feel most alive and Why? (Describe the feeling it gives you)

How do I handle loneliness or solitude? (Describe the feeling as specific as you can)

WORKOUT COMPLETED [ ]

I know very little about acting, Im just
a gifted faker.
Robert Downey Jr

IMAGINATION

We have a lot of tools in our arsenal as actors but I believe imagination is the most powerful. "If you hook into the character's belief system and you believe it 100%, there is no way the audience won't." - Meryl Streep. Everyone has an Imagination but it must be worked out to get stronger. Think of your imagination as a limitless playground. In this space, you can be anyone, go anywhere, and do anything. **Have the courage to allow yourself to play!**

VOCAL WORK - 2 minutes - [Set Timer]
Lip Trills: Close your lips together lightly, like you're going to blow a raspberry. Then, blow air through your closed lips while making sounds. You should feel a tickling sensation. Pick a song and Lip Trill along with it. **Tip**: Stretch your range as much as you can and pick a song you've never listened to.

IMPROVISED STORYTELLING - 5 Minutes [Set Timer]
Speak out the scenario provided and continue the story! Focus on vivid details, character development and how the main character overcomes the main obstacle. **Tip**: Try not to stop speaking so you don't have time to "think". Allow your imagination to keep moving forward without interruption. **Tip**: Record these stories on your device, in case it's great but more importantly to see your progress as you go on.

STARTING POINT: You are Taylor, a skilled cartographer who comes across an ancient, uncharted island while updating marine maps. Intrigued by this discovery, you set out on an expedition to explore the island. Upon arrival, you find that the island is home to a lost civilization with advanced knowledge and technology.

IMAGINARY WORLD EXPLORATION - 6 Minutes [Set Timer]

Find a quiet space to relax and focus. **Close your eyes** and let your imagination run wild. **Tip:** Engage all your senses to explore this environment. Touch, taste, smell etc and allow your emotions to guide you. **Extra:** After you explore this world with your senses, you could introduce characters and have a dialogue with them. Are they friends or foes?

IMAGINARY WORLD: LULLABY MEADOW - A gentle meadow where the soft strains of a lullaby fill the air, lulling you into a state of peaceful serenity. Wildflowers sway in harmony with the soothing melody, creating a restful oasis. A powerful roar you've never heard can be heard in the distance.

JOURNAL YOUR EXPERIENCE - 2 Minutes [Set Timer]

_____
_____
_____
_____
_____
_____

WORKOUT COMPLETED [ ]

Nod say yes and then do whatever the fuck you were going to do in the first place.
Robert Downey Jr

ANCHORING INTO YOUR CHARACTER COLOUR & MUSIC

Anchoring yourself into your character is vital. It's one of the most freeing feelings when you understand their *essence* because everything they do, how they do it and what their purpose is, becomes so clear to you and the audience. Every choice you make after you find your *anchor*, feels easy, because you're acting from who and what your character is at the core. You can call it an essence, an aura, vibe, energy etc. We all have it and feel it from everyone around us. There are many ways into your character but music and colour are my favourite. Music can inform the script, your character, even each scene. Colours, I think you will find, can work incredibly because we as humans respond to colours like frequencies. Colours evoke many feelings and if you pay attention closely, you can see everyone has their own 'colour' that defines their core. An essence that informs how they operate and move through the world.

THEIR COLOUR - 2 Minutes [Set Timer]
Think of **someone you know**, and **define them with a colour**. **Tip**: Trust yourself. Your initial colour is usually close. **Tip**: Start with basic colours then eventually become much more specific. **Example**: Corinna is an earthy green with rays of sunlight flowing through the green. **Extra**: Ask someone who knows *that person* as well, what they think this person's colour is and why. See how close your answers are or not.

YOUR CHARACTERS COLOUR
Read the given character description just as you would an audition, **assign a colour to that character.** Now take that colour you chose and **allow it to infuse into your entire body**, affecting your every move, your speaking, the way you see the world etc. **Take any book** you have, flip to a random page and **read the text as this Colour/Character**. **Tip**: Be specific, choose a colour that excites you and don't be afraid to get creative.

CHARACTER DESCRIPTION: [LUCAS] Lucas is a talented but struggling playwright, pouring his soul into scripts that blend reality with fantastical elements. His small, chaotic apartment doubles as his writing space, filled with stacks of scripts and books. Lucas often appears dishevelled, lost in his thoughts, with a perpetually furrowed brow as he wrestles with writer's block and the pursuit of the perfect story. Despite facing rejection and financial difficulties, he remains committed to his craft, driven by a deep passion for storytelling and theatre. Lucas' character is a complex mix of creative brilliance, vulnerability, and resilience, embodying the struggles and triumphs of an artist.

CHOOSE THEIR COLOUR - 4 Minutes [Set Timer]
THEIR COLOUR:

CHOOSE THEIR SONG - 4 Minutes [Set Timer]
THEIR SONG:

READ PASSAGE FROM BOOK - 2 Minutes [Set Timer]

FREEFORM DANCE - 2 minutes - [Set Timer]
Put on the selected music and **engage in freeform dancing, anchored in your colour/character,** Allow your body to move spontaneously and without inhibition. This can help you tap into your creative instincts and develop physical expressiveness *while staying in character.* **Tip**: Journal about the differences as opposed to how you normally dance.

JOURNAL YOUR EXPERIENCE - 1 Minute [Set Timer]

WORKOUT COMPLETED [ ]

Emotional Power is maybe the most valuable
thing an actor can have.
Christopher Walken

HISTORICAL RESEARCH

We are in the information era and have access to the world and its rich history at our fingertips. This exploration is not about 'learning facts'; it's a journey to the heart of human experience. The empathy and the understanding, especially on the things you disagree with, are incredibly valuable. If you look closely, you'll find the way people think, at different times in history, their attitudes, choices, and the way they move their bodies can teach you so much about us, right now. Fill your toolbox so it's overflowing with information and ideas to pull from so your imagination has so much to play with.

PHYSICAL WARMUP - 2 minutes - [Set Timer]
Freeform Dance: Put on some music and engage in freeform dancing. Allow your body to move spontaneously and without inhibition. This can help you tap into your creative instincts and develop physical expressiveness. **Tip**: Try music you've never listened to.

RESEARCH - 13 Minutes [Set Timer]
YouTube, streaming platforms, the internet or books, **research the given era/person/moment in time,** journal or make notes on your device, so when you want to find this information, it's organized and readily accessible. As you go, **write anything and everything _you_ find fascinating. Tip**: If the topic doesn't interest you, choose your own, or take a chance and still research it, but from a different perspective. Physicalities, voice, ideals, etc. Trust your body that when you see something interesting, you'll know. **Extra**: Speak it out and copy their movements. Our memory recall is massively affected by our bodies. Be specific and when you re-read your notes, you'll be amazed by how much your mind and body remember.

TOPIC:
The Challenger Space Shuttle Disaster (1986) - The Perspective of Christa McAuliffe: Christa McAuliffe, a high school teacher selected to be the first civilian astronaut, offers a unique perspective on the Challenger Space Shuttle disaster. As a participant in the Teacher in Space Project, McAuliffe underwent extensive training and was set to conduct experiments and teach lessons from space. There is available footage of McAuliffe during her training and interviews, providing actors with material to study her demeanour, speech, and enthusiasm for the mission. Her involvement and subsequent tragic fate in the Challenger disaster present a deeply human story set against a backdrop of space exploration and national tragedy.

_____
_____
_____
_____
_____
_____
_____
_____
_____
_____
_____
_____
_____
_____
_____
_____
_____

WORKOUT COMPLETED [ ]

Its funny, in a way the actor is a writer. Its not like the two things are so separate as to be like apples and oranges. The writer and the actor are one.
Sam Shepard

BELIEF

Beliefs are the convictions that something exists or is true, especially without proof. That is also the definition of what we do as actors. We play make-believe. Our beliefs shape our world, especially our beliefs about ourselves and it works for the characters you play. Understand your beliefs and how they influence your mind, body and spirit, then you will be able to better understand others, so you can embody them. Allow the beliefs of your character to colour your perception of your world and your interaction with everything in it. "Acting is the best magic trick in the world. We applaud performances not because it's real, but because you made us believe."

VOCAL WORK - 2 minutes - [Set Timer]
Lip Trills: Close your lips together lightly, like you're going to blow a raspberry. Then, blow air through your closed lips while making sounds. You should feel a tickling sensation. Pick a song and Lip Trill along with it. **Tip**: Stretch your range as much as you can and pick a song you've never listened to.

BELIEF WORKOUT

Get your journal or write in here. **Define your personal belief/view** on the given subject. **Grab any book you own,** flip to a random page and **read it out loud,** colouring the words and intention with your belief system. **Tip:** Write trigger words you can hook into in the future: **Optimism-** Always smiling, grateful, opportunity, sunshine yellow.

YOUR PERSONAL BELIEF

Right & Wrong - 7 Minutes [Set Timer]

_____
_____
_____
_____

READ WITH BELIEF - 2 Minutes [Set Timer]

CHARACTERS BELIEF

Right & Wrong

"Do to others as you wish to be done upon you" I truly stand by that quote. I'm not perfect but I pride myself in how good of a person I am. Right and wrong is an easy choice for me and I feel strong because I love that about myself.

READ WITH CHARACTERS BELIEF - 2 Minutes [Set Timer]
Forget your personal view and **fully embrace the character's belief.** Read out loud again.

JOURNAL YOUR EXPERIENCE - 2 Minutes [Set Timer]

_____
_____
_____
_____

WORKOUT COMPLETED [ ]

PERFORMANCE STRATEGY
14 DAY REVIEW

TAKE A MOMENT OF REFLECTION AND BREAKDOWN WHERE YOU ARE RIGHT NOW IN YOUR CAREER AND AS AN ACTOR.
THE MORE SPECIFIC YOU ARE THE MORE CLEAR YOU CAN SEE WHERE YOU ARE NOW SO YOU CAN GET TO WHERE YOU WANT TO GO FASTER

★ ★ ★ ★ ★

Elvis Presley: The iconic "King of Rock and Roll" was initially told he couldn't sing. He went on to become one of the most significant cultural icons of the 20th century.

DATE:

MY WHY
WHY ARE YOU DOING WHAT YOU ARE DOING
BE SPECIFIC

MY MAIN GOALS
IN-ORDER OF IMPORTANCE

1.

   Action Step(s):

2.

   Action Step(s):

3.

   Action Step(s):

FROM THE LAST 14 DAYS
5 STAR RATING

YOUR KEY POINTS AND TAKEAWAYS - WHY THAT AMOUNT OF STAR RATING, LIKES, DISLIKES, THE BIGGEST LESSON YOU LEARNED, GOOD OR BAD:

STRENGTHS:

WEAKNESSES:

IMPROVEMENT STRATEGY
HOW CAN YOU IMPROVE ON THESE AREAS FOR THE NEXT 14 DAYS:

GOAL FROM LAST :
DID YOU ACHIEVE IT?

WHY OR WHY NOT?

GOAL FOR THE NEXT 14 EXERCISES
THE MORE SPECIFIC YOU ARE THE GREATER THE RESULT

   Action Step(s):

If you tell the truth about how you're
feeling it becomes funny.
Larry David

MY WHY:

GOAL(s):

PHYSICAL WARMUP - 1 minute [Set Timer]
Freeform Dance: Put on some music and engage in freeform dancing. Allow your body to move spontaneously and without inhibition. This can help you tap into your creative instincts and develop physical expressiveness. **Tip**: Try music you've never listened to.

VOCAL WORK - ECHO PATTERNING - 3 minutes [Set Timer]
Resonance Play: Make a sound, any sound, and then play with its echo, repeating it at different volumes and pitches. Imagine the sound bouncing off of distant walls, even if you're in an open space. **Tip**: Use this exercise to explore the full range of your voice, finding new colours and textures.

EMOTIONAL RECALL - BITTERSWEET MEMORY - 5 minutes - [Set Timer]
Complex Emotion: Think of a memory that is both sweet and sorrowful, a goodbye or a bittersweet victory. Allow this dual feeling to inhabit your body, expressing it through movement that sways between joy and sadness. **Tip**: Focus on the transition between emotions, and how one can seamlessly blend into the other.

ANIMAL WORK - SERPENTINE GRACE

Research - 2 minutes [Set Timer]
Investigate the fluid, sinuous motion of snakes. Pay attention to the undulating rhythm and the way a snake can move with swift strikes and languid motion.

Animal Exercise 3 minutes [Set Timer]

Channel the snake's movement, letting your body ripple and glide across the floor or through the air. **Tip**: Allow your spine to articulate the undulating motion and use your breath to initiate the smooth, continuous flow of movement.

Discovery Journal - 1 Minute [Set Timer]
3 Main Characteristics: (Whatever stands out to YOU to embody the essence)

_____
_____
_____
_____
_____

WORKOUT COMPLETED [ ]

I always thought the idea of education was
to learn to think for yourself.
Robin Williams

SCRIPT ANALYSIS for **RELATIONSHIPS & SPECIFICITY** - 15 minutes [Set Timer]
Choose your character, circle everything in this script you have a relationship with. Including people, places, things, smells, time of day etc. **Write what your relationship with those items are** and **be specific.** The more specific and fun you have with your relationships, the more interesting your characters will be and the more fun the audience has. **Tip:** Everything isn't in the scene. Use your imagination to create details, only if it's contextually appropriate. **Extra:** Write your > **Objective, win or lose? Consequence of failing?** The **Who What Where When Why.**

Title: **Shattered Vows**
EXT. DESERTED CITY STREET - LATE NIGHT
A quiet, empty street under the glow of a streetlight. **DETECTIVE BRETT**, mid-30s, off-duty and simmering, confronts **ERIC**, late 30s, the 'other guy', who's clearly uncomfortable and remorseful.

DETECTIVE BRETT
I saw your texts on his phone. Emails. *Pictures.*
ERIC
(looking down, guiltily)
Michael, I...
Michael's calmness scares Eric...
DETECTIVE BRETT
How long has this been going on?
ERIC
It wasn't planned. I swear to you.
DETECTIVE BRETT
How long?
ERIC
8 Months. 9... 9 Months.
DETECTIVE BRETT
9. When?
ERIC
At the Halloween party you two threw. I didn't—
DETECTIVE BRETT
Shut up, right now. I mean it. You say another word and I'll beat you to death with my bare hands.
ERIC
You're a cop...
BRETT
Exactly. (Eric stays quiet, after a long moment...) I'm sorry.
ERIC
(barely audible)
I'm sorry, Michael.
DETECTIVE BRETT
I loved him... You need to leave.

Michael turns and walks away, leaving Eric standing alone under the streetlight, the silence speaking volumes of regret and heartbreak.

WORKOUT COMPLETED [ ]

Acting is about fact. You just have to believe that you are the person you're playing and that what is happening is happening to you.
Ivana Chubbuck

IMAGINATION

We have a lot of tools in our arsenal as actors but **I believe imagination is the most powerful.** "If you hook into the character's belief system and you believe it 100%, there is no way the audience won't." - Meryl Streep "Imagination is more important than knowledge for knowledge is limited. - Einstein. Everyone has an Imagination but it must be worked out to get stronger. Think of your imagination as a limitless playground. In this space, you can be anyone, go anywhere, and do anything. **Have the courage to allow yourself to play!**

Solo Imaginary World Exploration - 6 Minutes [Set Timer]

Find a quiet space to relax and focus. **Close your eyes** and **let your imagination run wild. Tip:** Engage all your senses to explore this environment. Touch, taste, smell etc. Allow your emotions to guide you. **Extra:** After you establish this world in your imagination, you could introduce characters and have a dialogue with them. Are they friends or foes?

IMAGINARY WORLD: Volcanic Isle of Mythical Creatures: Brave the beauty and danger of an island with an active volcano and mythical creatures.

JOURNAL YOUR EXPERIENCE - 2 Minutes [Set Timer]

_____
_____
_____
_____
_____

Your Characters Filter - 5 Minutes [Set Timer]

Everyone including the characters you play see the world through their own specific perspective/filter. I like to use the word filter because you can take out a filter, clean it, change its style, colour, an optimist or a pessimist, comedian or a nihilist, etc. **Find a quiet space** to focus. **Close your eyes and let go of your personal thoughts and emotions** to make space for your characters. **Open your eyes, and allow the filter provided to effect everything around you. Tip**: Explore wherever you are and interact with the objects. **Extra:** How does *this* character walk and move in their world?

FILTER: Vigilant Guardian: Always alert and looking out for potential threats.

JOURNAL YOUR EXPERIENCE - 2 Minutes [Set Timer]

_____
_____
_____
_____
_____
_____
_____

WORKOUT COMPLETED [ ]

It is your flaws, your insecurities and your fears that make you special… for both the character you play and you.
Unknown

CHARACTER STUDY "PEOPLE WATCHING"

Actors are required to portray characters that are believable and relatable. You don't have to agree with them but you have to understand them. Walk like them, talk like them, see the world like them. So, in order to fill our toolbox, we have to **go out into the world and study**. Then practice them over and over so we can "walk in their shoes', comfortably and confidently. Study their movements, mannerisms, the "vibe" they give off, the clothes they wear etc. **Fill your toolbox with the rhythms and idiosyncrasies of human behaviour.**

OBSERVATION CHARACTER STUDY - 15 Minutes [Set Timer]

Find a busy place where you can **sit and observe.** Choose anyone you find interesting. **Write down what stands out about them.** *The way they sit, drink their coffee, walk, talk, interact with others etc.* **Tip: Mirror them immediately.** This will help memorize the feeling of that character so whenever you come back to these characters you're discovering, your body will remember. **Extra**: Before you go to sleep, read over the characters from today and reenact their movements.

___

COLOURS: We as humans respond to colours like frequencies. If you pay attention closely, you can see everyone has their own 'colour' that defines their core. An essence that informs how they operate and move through the world.

WHAT COLOUR ARE THEY:

WORKOUT COMPLETED [ ]

Learn the rules like a pro so you can break them like an artist.
Pablo Picasso

VOICE & DICTION

I wish I had learned this at the beginning of my career. The confidence to communicate clearly and powerfully is a game-changer for you as an actor. **Think of your voice as a musical instrument that needs regular tuning. This workout is your daily tuning session,** ensuring that your instrument is always ready. "The word 'theatre' comes from the Greeks. It means the seeing place. It is the place people come to see the truth about life and the social situation." - Stella Adler. Embrace this workout as a key to unlocking and portraying *that* truth by letting your voice be the vehicle that transports your audience into the heart of your story.

READ PASSAGE - 30 Seconds [Set Timer]
Speak the passage and take note of its quality. **Tip**: Record Audio to compare afterward.

> "Autumn arrives in a dance of colour. Leaves turn gold and red, the air crisps, and every step through the fallen leaves tells a story of change. The scent of harvest fills the air, signalling the end of summer's reign."

RELAXATION - 1 Minute [Set Timer]
Deep Breathing: Sit and Inhale deeply through your nose, filling your lungs, then exhale slowly through your mouth. Imagine stress leaving your body with each breath.

Nay Nay Nay - 1 Minute [Set Timer]
Pick a song and sing the word "Nay" repeatedly. Start with a comfortable pitch and gradually move the sound from your nose to your chest, ensuring each "Nay" is clear and resonant. Stretch your range as best you can to strengthen.

Sustained 'S' - 2 Minutes [Set Timer]
Inhale deeply and then exhale slowly, making a continuous 's' sound. Keep the sound as even and steady as you can. Always push a little longer than you think you can.

Vowel Pronunciation Drill - 2 Minutes [Set Timer]
Slowly go through each vowel sound **(A, E, I, O, U), holding and exaggerating each sound. Combine them with consonants** (e.g., ba, be, bi, bo, bu). Pay attention to the clarity and sharpness of each sound. Repeat a few times before moving to the next.

Lip Trills - 3 minutes - [Set timer]
Close your lips together lightly, like you're going to blow a raspberry. Then, blow air through your closed lips while making sounds. You should feel a tickling sensation. Pick a song and Lip Trill the whole along with it. **Tip**: Stretch your range as much as you can and pick a song you've never listened to.

The Cork Exercise - 4 Minutes [Set Timer]
Place a cork between your teeth and try to read a passage aloud. This forces your articulation muscles to work harder. If you don't have a cork, bite down gently on your thumb. You can use the following text for this exercise:

READ PASSAGE AGAIN - 30 Seconds [Set Timer]
Speak the passage and take note of its quality. **Tip**: Record Audio to compare.

Discovery Journal - 1 Minute [Set Timer]

WORKOUT COMPLETED [ ]

If you're not having fun, you've made
the wrong choices.
Ivana Chubbuck

SUBTEXT

Subtext is what lies beneath the surface of our words. It's the hidden layer of meaning, driven by the character's internal thoughts, emotions, desires, and motivations. Subtext is one of my favourite things as an actor because so much can be said with one simple line of dialogue. The power of "Hello" can be exciting if you told that person years ago "If I ever see you again, I'll kill you. Maybe it's the most beautiful person you've ever seen. Now, say "hello". *Subtext* shows the audience what your relationship with the characters/places/situations are, without having to explain it. We experience it every day and it is our job to create characters that interact as we do.

VOCAL WORK - 3 minutes - [Set Timer]
Lip Trills: Close your lips together lightly, like you're going to blow a raspberry. Then, blow air through your closed lips while making sounds. You should feel a tickling sensation. Pick a song and Lip Trill along with it. **Tip**: Stretch your range as much as you can and pick a song you've never listened to.

SUBTEXT PRACTICE
Use the line of dialogue provided and practice each of these subtexts **out loud.** Move on to the next, only when you believe yourself. Trust that you will know when *that* is. Before you begin, **pick a spot to look at and imagine** in detail, **who you are speaking with**. **Tip**: *Sometimes* we mean exactly what we are saying. Look for that too. **Extra**: Substitute someone you have a strong relationship with in real life, good or bad, and see it's affect.

Initial Line: "The diner where we had our first job is closing down after 40 years."
Your Response Line: "Hamburger Mary's? 10 Years working there. So many memories in that place. Had my first kiss there. It's strange to think it won't be there anymore. Do you remember the night we...?"

SUBTEXTS - 6 Minutes [Set Timer]
[ ] Reflective: You're pondering how much life has changed since those days.
[ ] Melancholic: You feel a deep sense of loss for a place tied to so many memories.
[ ] Unaffected: You've outgrown your past and the diner's closing doesn't impact you.
[ ] Grateful: You're thankful for the experiences and lessons learned there.
[ ] Regretful: You lament missed opportunities and connections from that time.
[ ] Your Own Subtext

RELATIONSHIP SUBTEXTS - 6 Minutes [Set Timer]
[ ] The Co-Worker who became a lifelong friend.
[ ] The First Love that started with shy smiles across the counter.
[ ] The Mentor who taught you invaluable life skills.
[ ] The Rival who always tried to outdo you in every task.
[ ] The Regular Customer who became part of your life story.
[ ] Your Own Subtext

Discovery Journal

_____
_____
_____
_____

WORKOUT COMPLETED [ ]

Great art is always life or death circumstances.
Unknown

EMOTIONS

The 'moment before', **the emotional preparation, is the most important key to a great scene.** If you start any scene without an emotional preparation it feels like trying to drive a car in neutral. The preparation is the uphill climb of every rollercoaster; Once you grind all the way to the top, the chains let go and the rest of the ride takes care of itself. "No one wants to see a play or a movie and look at technical proficiency. You want to be moved, you want a human experience, you want to feel less alone" - Viola Davis. **Practice your emotions over and over** so when it's time, you aren't worried "Will I get there?" **You're imagination and emotions should be a tinderbox, so easy to light up. All it take is half a spark.**

EULOGY - 12 Minutes [Set Timer]

Find a quiet comfortable space. Choose someone in your life who is alive and important to you. Create an imaginary reason for why they have died. Now start from the point of the phone call— Imagine who calls, what they say and what you say. Eventually find yourself at the funeral, about to begin the eulogy. See the casket, is it open or closed?? What is that person wearing and any other details for yourself. Before you begin to speak, look into the audience and see who is there- Family, friends etc **Then begin the eulogy.** **Tip**: Be as specific as you can with everything. **Inside of specificity is where you will find the triggers to your heart.** Let your imagination take you wherever you want in this exercise. **Example**: Placing her favourite sheep stuffed animal in the casket, tucked under her arm like she always held it, then kissing her goodbye one last time.

DISCOVERY JOURNAL - 3 Minutes [Set Timer]

Make sure to **include the specific triggers** you experience because you can use these **TRIGGER MOMENTS** in the future instead of repeating the *entire* exercise.

WORKOUT COMPLETED [ ]

Safe choices create safe results.
Take risks!
Unknown

THE CORK EXERCISE - 4 Minutes [Set Timer]

Place a cork between your teeth and read a passage aloud. This forces your articulation muscles to work harder. If you don't have a cork, bite down gently on your thumb. You can use the following text for this exercise:

> "At the riverside, water flows tirelessly, carving its path through the landscape. Birds swoop over the surface, their reflections fleeting in the rippling water. Trees line the banks, their leaves whispering secrets to the stream."

WRITE A LETTER - 10 Minutes [Set Timer]

Get a piece of paper or write this in your device. **Take a moment** to let this situation and relationship sink in. Then let your imagination run wild and **write them a letter.**

Your Character: Taylor, a renowned investigative journalist.

Other Character: Jordan, a whistleblower who provided Taylor with crucial information for a high-profile case, but later retracted their statements, leading to a public controversy and putting Taylor's credibility at risk.

Relationship: Taylor and Jordan shared a brief but intense professional relationship built on trust and the pursuit of truth. Taylor's career and reputation hinged on the information Jordan provided. Jordan's sudden retraction not only jeopardized the case but also raised questions about Taylor's journalistic integrity.

Context of the Letter: Feeling betrayed and professionally endangered, Taylor writes a letter to Jordan. This letter is a mix of professional outrage, a quest for the truth behind Jordan's retraction, and an attempt to understand the motivations and pressures that might have led to such a drastic change of heart. It's an expression of the personal and professional turmoil caused by this turn of events.

Discovery Journal - 1 minute [Set Timer]

_____
_____
_____
_____
_____

WORKOUT COMPLETED [ ]

You're only given one little spark of madness.
You mustn't lose it.
Robin Williams

VOCAL WORK - 3 minutes - [Set Timer]

Lip Trills: Close your lips together lightly, like you're going to blow a raspberry. Then, blow air through your closed lips while making sounds. You should feel a tickling sensation. Pick a song and Lip Trill along with it. **Tip**: Stretch your range as much as you can and pick a song you've never listened to.

VERBAL IMPROV - 10 Minutes [Set Timer]

Find a space where you are comfortable and free to express yourself. Take a moment to **let this situation, character and prompt, sink in**. Then let your imagination run wild: **Picture who you are talking to** then **begin with *the prompt*** and **continue to verbalize everything** this character would say. **Tip**: This is exploration! There is no "getting it right". BE BRAVE to explore and discover.

Character: Sam, kind, sincere and funny, recently proposed to the love of their life and has never been happier. Sam comes home early to surprise them with their favourite flowers and finds them in bed with another person. Your best friend, Jo. After you break off the engagement, you go over to Jo's house — **'Knock Knock Knock'**

Prompt: "We, need to talk."

Who are you talking to:

Describe them in two specific words:

Discovery Journal - 2 minutes [Set Timer]

_____
_____
_____
_____
_____
_____
_____
_____
_____

WORKOUT COMPLETED [ ]

Establish boundaries... then cross them.
Unknown

SELF AWARENESS

The more you understand yourself, the more you are able to understand and develop your characters. Like you, your characters have thoughts, beliefs, traumas, passions etc. When you become aware of your own and start to see how those experiences and beliefs have shaped your life, how you operate and view the world, then you can develop your characters that are much more rich and vivid.

PHYSICAL WARMUP - 2 minutes [Set Timer]

Freeform Dance: Put on some music and engage in freeform dancing. Allow your body to move spontaneously and without inhibition. This can help you tap into your creative instincts and develop physical expressiveness. **Tip**: Try music you've never listened to.

CURRENT EMOTIONAL INVENTORY - 3 Minutes [Set Timer]

Write down and **record your current emotions**. Identify what you're feeling at this moment and why. **Tip**: Be as specific as you can, **don't disregard anything.** You can also **scan your body** to see how and where your current emotion is affecting you. Your posture, the way you walk, bouncing foot, sore neck etc

CURRENT EMOTIONAL STATE:

SELF DISCOVERY QUESTIONS - 10 Minutes [Set Timer]

I suggest a journal or writing it in your phone's notes so you don't run out of space here.

What am I afraid to admit about myself?

How have I changed in the last five years?

WORKOUT COMPLETED [ ]

No matter how dark it is,
always find the humour.
Unknown

IMAGINATION

We have a lot of tools in our arsenal as actors but I believe imagination is the most powerful. "If you hook into the character's belief system and you believe it 100%, there is no way the audience won't." - Meryl Streep. Everyone has an Imagination but it must be worked out to get stronger. Think of your imagination as a limitless playground. In this space, you can be anyone, go anywhere, and do anything. **Have the courage to allow yourself to play!**

VOCAL WORK - 2 minutes - [Set Timer]
Lip Trills: Close your lips together lightly, like you're going to blow a raspberry. Then, blow air through your closed lips while making sounds. You should feel a tickling sensation. Pick a song and Lip Trill along with it. **Tip**: Stretch your range as much as you can and pick a song you've never listened to.

- 5 Minutes [Set Timer]
Speak out the scenario provided and continue the story! Focus on vivid details, character development and how the main character overcomes the main obstacle. **Tip**: Try not to stop speaking so you don't have time to "think". Allow your imagination to keep moving forward without interruption. **Tip:** Record these stories on your device, in case it's great but more importantly to see your progress as you go on.

STARTING POINT: You are Morgan, a young musician who inherits an ancient violin from a distant relative. Upon playing it, you discover that the violin's melodies can manipulate everyone around you. But it only lasts 60 seconds. You leave the house and decide your first visit will be—

IMAGINARY WORLD EXPLORATION - 6 Minutes [Set Timer]

Find a quiet space to relax and focus. **Close your eyes** and let your imagination run wild. **Tip:** Engage all your senses to explore this environment. Touch, taste, smell etc and allow your emotions to guide you. **Extra:** After you explore this world with your senses, you could introduce characters and have a dialogue with them. Are they friends or foes?

IMAGINARY WORLD: THE SHADOWED MAZE - Picture a sprawling labyrinthine maze where towering hedges cast elongated, ominous shadows. The ground beneath your feet is cold and damp, and eerie whispers echo through the air.

JOURNAL YOUR EXPERIENCE - 2 Minutes [Set Timer]

_____
_____
_____
_____
_____
_____
_____

WORKOUT COMPLETED [ ]

You are in relationship with absolutely
everything in the scene.
Relationship creates character.
Victor Zinck Jr

ANCHORING INTO YOUR CHARACTER COLOUR & MUSIC

Anchoring yourself into your character is vital. It's one of the most freeing feelings when you understand their *essence* because everything they do, how they do it and what their purpose is, becomes so clear to you and the audience. Every choice you make after you find your *anchor*, feels easy, because you're acting from who and what your character is at the core. You can call it an essence, an aura, vibe, energy etc. We all have it and feel it from everyone around us. There are many ways into your character but music and colour are my favourite. Music can inform the script, your character, even each scene. Colours, I think you will find, can work incredibly because we as humans respond to colours like frequencies. Colours evoke many feelings and if you pay attention closely, you can see everyone has their own 'colour' that defines their core. An essence that informs how they operate and move through the world.

THEIR COLOUR - 2 Minutes [Set Timer]
Think of **someone you know**, and **define them with a colour**. **Tip**: Trust yourself. Your initial colour is usually close. **Tip**: Start with basic colours then eventually become much more specific. **Example**: Corinna is an earthy green with rays of sunlight flowing through the green. **Extra**: Ask someone who knows *that person* as well, what they think this person's colour is and why. See how close your answers are or not.

YOUR CHARACTERS COLOUR
Read the given character description just as you would an audition, **assign a colour to that character.** Now take that colour you chose and **allow it to infuse into your entire body**, affecting your every move, your speaking, the way you see the world etc. **Take any book** you have, flip to a random page and **read the text as this Colour/Character**. **Tip**: Be specific, choose a colour that excites you and don't be afraid to get creative.

CHARACTER DESCRIPTION: [BLAKE] Blake is a skilled urban climber and photographer, capturing breathtaking views from the tops of skyscrapers and other urban structures. Dressed in gear suitable for scaling buildings, including a camera slung over their shoulder, Blake is always ready for the next climb. Their social media is filled with stunning aerial shots of the city, gaining them a considerable following. Despite their adventurous and daring public persona, Blake is introspective and thoughtful, often contemplating the beauty and isolation of urban landscapes from their unique vantage points. Their character embodies a blend of fearlessness, artistic vision, and a reflective appreciation of the urban environment from perspectives few dare to explore.

CHOOSE THEIR COLOUR - 4 Minutes [Set Timer]
THEIR COLOUR:

CHOOSE THEIR SONG - 4 Minutes [Set Timer]
THEIR SONG:

READ PASSAGE FROM BOOK - 2 Minutes [Set Timer]

FREEFORM DANCE - 2 minutes - [Set Timer]
Put on the selected music and **engage in freeform dancing, anchored in your colour/character,** Allow your body to move spontaneously and without inhibition. This can help you tap into your creative instincts and develop physical expressiveness *while staying in character.* **Tip**: Journal about the differences as opposed to how you normally dance.

JOURNAL YOUR EXPERIENCE - 1 Minute [Set Timer]

WORKOUT COMPLETED [ ]

Just say the lines and COMMIT.
Unknown

HISTORICAL RESEARCH

We are in the information era and have access to the world and its rich history at our fingertips. This exploration is not about 'learning facts'; it's a journey to the heart of human experience. The empathy and the understanding, especially on the things you disagree with, are incredibly valuable. If you look closely, you'll find the way people think, at different times in history, their attitudes, choices, and the way they move their bodies can teach you so much about us, right now. Fill your toolbox so it's overflowing with information and ideas to pull from so your imagination has so much to play with.

PHYSICAL WARMUP - 2 minutes - [Set Timer]
Freeform Dance: Put on some music and engage in freeform dancing. Allow your body to move spontaneously and without inhibition. This can help you tap into your creative instincts and develop physical expressiveness. **Tip**: Try music you've never listened to.

RESEARCH - 13 Minutes [Set Timer]
YouTube, streaming platforms, the internet or books, **research the given era/person/moment in time,** journal or make notes on your device, so when you want to find this information, it's organized and readily accessible. As you go, **write anything and everything _you_ find fascinating. Tip:** If the topic doesn't interest you, choose your own, or take a chance and still research it, but from a different perspective. Physicalities, voice, ideals, etc. Trust your body that when you see something interesting, you'll know. **Extra**: Speak it out and copy their movements. Our memory recall is massively affected by our bodies. Be specific and when you re-read your notes, you'll be amazed by how much your mind and body remember.

TOPIC:
The Battle of Gettysburg (1863) - The Perspective of Elizabeth Thorn: Elizabeth Thorn played a significant but less recognized role during the Battle of Gettysburg in the American Civil War. As the caretaker of the Evergreen Cemetery at Gettysburg, she took on the grim task of burying the dead in the aftermath of the battle, despite being six months pregnant at the time. Her diary entries and later accounts provide a poignant and personal perspective on the impact of the battle on the local community and the often-overlooked contributions of women during wartime.

WORKOUT COMPLETED [ ]

The most important thing is that you believe
that you're meant to be an actor.
Then you will be.
Kate Winslet

BELIEF

Beliefs are the convictions that something exists or is true, especially without proof. That is also the definition of what we do as actors. We play make-believe. Our beliefs shape our world, especially our beliefs about ourselves and it works for the characters you play. Understand your beliefs and how they influence your mind, body and spirit, then you will be able to better understand others, so you can embody them. Allow the beliefs of your character to colour your perception of your world and your interaction with everything in it. "Acting is the best magic trick in the world. We applaud performances not because it's real, but because you made us believe."

VOCAL WORK - 2 minutes - [Set Timer]
Lip Trills: Close your lips together lightly, like you're going to blow a raspberry. Then, blow air through your closed lips while making sounds. You should feel a tickling sensation. Pick a song and Lip Trill along with it. **Tip**: Stretch your range as much as you can and pick a song you've never listened to.

BELIEF WORKOUT

Get your journal or write in here. **Define your personal belief/view** on the given subject. **Grab any book you own,** flip to a random page and **read it out loud,** colouring the words and intention with your belief system. **Tip:** Write trigger words you can hook into in the future: **Optimism-** Always smiling, grateful, opportunity, sunshine yellow.

YOUR PERSONAL BELIEF

Responsibility - 7 Minutes [Set Timer]

_____
_____
_____
_____

READ WITH BELIEF - 2 Minutes [Set Timer]

CHARACTERS BELIEF

Responsibility
Gives me anxiety. So many things to worry about as I get older. I hate being a grown-up, it's exhausting. I do what I need to do but just enough so I can relax. I try not to worry about the future but it's impossible not to!

READ WITH CHARACTERS BELIEF - 2 Minutes [Set Timer]
Forget your personal view and **fully embrace the character's belief. Read out loud again.**

JOURNAL YOUR EXPERIENCE - 2 Minutes [Set Timer]

_____
_____
_____

WORKOUT COMPLETED [ ]

PERFORMANCE STRATEGY
14 DAY REVIEW

TAKE A MOMENT OF REFLECTION AND BREAKDOWN WHERE YOU ARE RIGHT NOW IN YOUR CAREER AND AS AN ACTOR.
THE MORE SPECIFIC YOU ARE THE MORE CLEAR YOU CAN SEE WHERE YOU ARE NOW SO YOU CAN GET TO WHERE YOU WANT TO GO FASTER

★ ★ ★ ★ ★

Joanne J.K. Rowling: Before becoming one of the world's best-selling authors with the "Harry Potter" series, Rowling was a single mother living on welfare.

DATE:

MY WHY
WHY ARE YOU DOING WHAT YOU ARE DOING
BE SPECIFIC

MY MAIN GOALS
IN-ORDER OF IMPORTANCE

1.

    Action Step(s):

2.

    Action Step(s):

3.

    Action Step(s):

FROM THE LAST 14 DAYS
5 STAR RATING

YOUR KEY POINTS AND TAKEAWAYS - WHY THAT AMOUNT OF STAR RATING, LIKES, DISLIKES, THE BIGGEST LESSON YOU LEARNED, GOOD OR BAD:

STRENGTHS:

WEAKNESSES:

IMPROVEMENT STRATEGY
HOW CAN YOU IMPROVE ON THESE AREAS FOR THE NEXT 14 DAYS:

GOAL FROM LAST :
DID YOU ACHIEVE IT?

WHY OR WHY NOT?

GOAL FOR THE NEXT 14 EXERCISES
THE MORE SPECIFIC YOU ARE THE GREATER THE RESULT

    Action Step(s):

I shut my eyes in order to see.
Paul Gauguin

MY WHY:

GOAL(s):

PHYSICAL WARMUP - AIR SCULPTING - 1 minute [Set Timer]
Spatial Exploration: Use your hands and body to sculpt the air around you, as if you are shaping invisible clay. Allow your body to flow freely, creating and interacting with the shapes you imagine in the space. **Tip**: Let your movements be fluid and continuous, imagine the air has a tangible quality to it that you can mould.

VOCAL WORK - TONAL CASCADES - 3 minutes [Set Timer]
Tonal Shifts: Begin with a middle-range tone and slide your voice up and down through scales, like a cascade of water flowing over rocks. Notice how each note resonates in different parts of your body and face. **Tip**: Concentrate on the smooth transition between notes, feeling the natural wave of your voice as it travels through the scale.

EMOTIONAL RECALL - 5 minutes [Set Timer]
Joyful Climax: Recall the most euphoric moment of your life. Visualize the setting, the smells, and the sounds, and let this joy flood through you. Express this euphoria through expansive, open movements. **Tip**: Let your breath be your guide, inhaling with the buildup of joy and exhaling with expressive movements, amplifying the emotional experience.

ANIMAL WORK - SLY FOX

Research - 2 minutes [Set Timer]
Delve into the cunning nature of the fox, its stealth, and its acute senses. **Tip**: Pay attention to the fox's adaptability and how it responds to its environment.

Animal Exercise - 3 minutes [Set Timer]
Imitate the fox's stealthy gait and sudden pounces. **Tip**: Use your senses to heighten your awareness, move with purpose and agility, and react quickly as if you are navigating through the forest.

Discovery Journal - 1 Minute [Set Timer]
3 Main Characteristics: (Whatever stands out to YOU to embody the essence)

_____
_____
_____
_____

WORKOUT COMPLETED [ ]

You have a voice an artist. It's just getting your own confidence. And you find just by doing it and that confidence will come.
Tom Cruise

SCRIPT ANALYSIS for RELATIONSHIPS & SPECIFICITY - 15 minutes [Set Timer]
Choose your character, circle everything in this script you have a relationship with. Including people, places, things, smells, time of day etc. **Write what your relationship with those items are** and **be specific**. The more specific and fun you have with your relationships, the more interesting your characters will be and the more fun the audience has. **Tip:** Everything isn't in the scene. Use your imagination to create details, only if it's contextually appropriate. **Extra:** Write your > **Objective, win or lose? Consequence of failing?** The **Who What Where When Why.**

Title: A New Chapter
EXT. FAMILY HOME DRIVEWAY - EARLY MORNING
The first light of dawn casts a gentle glow on a modest family home. **DAVID**, 18, stands next to a packed car, a mix of excitement and apprehension in his eyes. **FATHER**, late 40s, loving and visibly emotional, faces him, trying to muster a brave smile.

FATHER
Well, this is it, huh?
DAVID
Yeah, Dad. Don't do it... Don't cry.
FATHER
I still see that little boy who wouldn't let go of my hand on his first day at school.
DAVID
I think I've grown a bit since then.
FATHER
(smiling through tears)
Just a bit. Your mom... she would've been so proud.
DAVID
(wistfully)
I wish she could see this.
FATHER
She sees you, son. She's been with us every step of the way. (then) You're ready for this. You're going to do great things.
DAVID
I'm going to miss you, Dad. Are you going to be, okay?
FATHER
(laughter and tears)
No... But this is your time now. Remember, we're always with you and call me. Every day.
DAVID
I will. (Off his look) I will. I promise.
They embrace tightly, a lifetime of love and shared struggles in their hold.
FATHER
Go on now. Go write your story. Write it in the stars.
DAVID
I Love you, Dad.
FATHER
Love you more, son.

David gets into the car, giving one last look to his father. The father waves, watching as the car pulls away. He stands there, a proud but emotional figure, as a new chapter begins for both of them.

WORKOUT COMPLETED [ ]

Your emotional preparation is the
engine to the scene.
Victor Zinck Jr

IMAGINATION

We have a lot of tools in our arsenal as actors but **I believe imagination is the most powerful.** "If you hook into the character's belief system and you believe it 100%, there is no way the audience won't." - Meryl Streep "Imagination is more important than knowledge for knowledge is limited. - Einstein. Everyone has an Imagination but it must be worked out to get stronger. Think of your imagination as a limitless playground. In this space, you can be anyone, go anywhere, and do anything. **Have the courage to allow yourself to play!**

Solo Imaginary World Exploration - 6 Minutes [Set Timer]

Find a quiet space to relax and focus. **Close your eyes** and **let your imagination run wild. Tip:** Engage all your senses to explore this environment. Touch, taste, smell etc. Allow your emotions to guide you. **Extra:** After you establish this world in your imagination, you could introduce characters and have a dialogue with them. Are they friends or foes?

IMAGINARY WORLD: Futuristic Dystopia: Navigate a high-tech world dominated by AI, with towering skyscrapers and neon-lit streets.

JOURNAL YOUR EXPERIENCE - 2 Minutes [Set Timer]

_____
_____
_____
_____
_____

Your Characters Filter - 5 Minutes [Set Timer]

Everyone including the characters you play see the world through their own specific perspective/filter. I like to use the word filter because you can take out a filter, clean it, change its style, colour, an optimist or a pessimist, comedian or a nihilist, etc. **Find a quiet space** to focus. **Close your eyes and let go of your personal thoughts and emotions** to make space for your characters. **Open your eyes, and allow the filter provided to effect everything around you. Tip**: Explore wherever you are and interact with the objects. **Extra:** How does *this* character walk and move in their world?

FILTER: Cynical Realist: Always looking for the hidden catch or downside in situations.

JOURNAL YOUR EXPERIENCE - 2 Minutes [Set Timer]

_____
_____
_____
_____
_____
_____

WORKOUT COMPLETED [ ]

If there was a gym for actors where they were allowed to fail every day, we would see some superb performances.
Gary Oldman

CHARACTER STUDY "PEOPLE WATCHING"

Actors are required to portray characters that are believable and relatable. You don't have to agree with them but you have to understand them. Walk like them, talk like them, see the world like them. So, in order to fill our toolbox, we have to **go out into the world and study**. Then practice them over and over so we can "walk in their shoes', comfortably and confidently. Study their movements, mannerisms, the "vibe" they give off, the clothes they wear etc. **Fill your toolbox with the rhythms and idiosyncrasies of human behaviour.**

OBSERVATION CHARACTER STUDY - 15 Minutes [Set Timer]

Find a busy place where you can **sit and observe.** Choose anyone you find interesting. **Write down what stands out about them**. *The way they sit, drink their coffee, walk, talk, interact with others etc.* **Tip:** **Mirror them immediately**. This will help memorize the feeling of that character so whenever you come back to these characters you're discovering, your body will remember. **Extra:** Before you go to sleep, read over the characters from today and reenact their movements.

COLOURS: We as humans respond to colours like frequencies. If you pay attention closely, you can see everyone has their own 'colour' that defines their core. An essence that informs how they operate and move through the world.

WHAT COLOUR ARE THEY:

WORKOUT COMPLETED [ ]

Your preparation is completely different than your acting. Preparation is design. Acting is improvising inside that design.
Victor Zinck Jr

VOICE and DICTION

I wish I had learned this at the beginning of my career. The confidence to communicate clearly and powerfully is a game-changer for you as an actor. **Think of your voice as a musical instrument that needs regular tuning. This workout is your daily tuning session,** ensuring that your instrument is always ready. "The word 'theatre' comes from the Greeks. It means the seeing place. It is the place people come to see the truth about life and the social situation." - Stella Adler. Embrace this workout as a key to unlocking and portraying *that* truth by letting your voice be the vehicle that transports your audience into the heart of your story.

READ PASSAGE - 30 Seconds [Set Timer]
Speak the passage and take note of its quality. **Tip**: Record Audio to compare afterward.

> "Winter blankets the world in hush. Snowflakes fall gently, ice glistens, and the serene silence holds the promise of renewal. The chill in the air whispers of cozy nights by the fire, sharing stories and warmth."

RELAXATION - 2 Minutes [Set Timer]
Deep Breathing (1 minute) Sit or stand comfortably. Inhale deeply through your nose, filling your lungs, then exhale slowly through your mouth. Imagine stress leaving your body with each breath.
Neck Rolls (30 seconds) Gently roll your head in a circular motion, first clockwise, then counterclockwise, to release neck tension.
Conclude with one more minute of deep, rhythmic breathing, feeling the relaxation spread throughout your entire body. **(30 seconds)**

Sustained 'S' - 2 Minutes [Set Timer]
Inhale deeply and then exhale slowly, making a continuous 's' sound. Keep the sound as even and steady as you can. Do this for 1 minute, rest, then another minute.

Vowel Pronunciation Drill - 2 Minutes [Set Timer]
Slowly go through each vowel sound **(A, E, I, O, U)**, **holding and exaggerating each sound. Combine them with consonants** (e.g., ba, be, bi, bo, bu). Pay attention to the clarity and sharpness of each sound. Repeat a few times before moving to the next.

Resonance Exercises - 3 Minutes [Set Timer]
Practice the "Ng" exercise: say the word "sing" and hold the "ng" at the end. Feel the vibration in your nasal cavity. Experiment with moving the resonance to different parts of your face and head, like your chest or the front of your face, to feel different vibrations.

The Cork Exercise - 4 Minutes [Set Timer]
Place a cork between your teeth and try to read a passage aloud. This forces your articulation muscles to work harder. If you don't have a cork, bite down gently on your thumb. You can use the following text for this exercise:

READ PASSAGE AGAIN - 30 Seconds [Set Timer]
Speak the passage and take note of its quality. **Tip**: Record Audio to compare.

Discovery Journal - 1 Minute [Set Timer]

_____
_____
_____

WORKOUT COMPLETED [ ]

Our deepest fear is not that we are inadequate. Our deepest fear is that we are powerful beyond measure.
Coach Carter, Coach Carter

SUBTEXT

Subtext is what lies beneath the surface of our words. It's the hidden layer of meaning, driven by the character's internal thoughts, emotions, desires, and motivations. Subtext is one of my favourite things as an actor because so much can be said with one simple line of dialogue. The power of "Hello" can be exciting if you told that person years ago "If I ever see you again, I'll kill you. Maybe it's the most beautiful person you've ever seen. Now, say "hello". *Subtext* shows the audience what your relationship with the characters/places/situations are, without having to explain it. We experience it every day and it is our job to create characters that interact as we do.

VOCAL WORK - 3 minutes - [Set Timer]
Lip Trills: Close your lips together lightly, like you're going to blow a raspberry. Then, blow air through your closed lips while making sounds. You should feel a tickling sensation. Pick a song and Lip Trill along with it. **Tip**: Stretch your range as much as you can and pick a song you've never listened to.

SUBTEXT PRACTICE
Use the line of dialogue provided and practice each of these subtexts **out loud.** Move on to the next, only when you believe yourself. Trust that you will know when *that* is. Before you begin, **pick a spot to look at and imagine** in detail, **who you are speaking with.** **Tip**: *Sometimes* we mean exactly what we are saying. Look for that too. **Extra**: Substitute someone you have a strong relationship with in real life, good or bad, and see it's affect.

Initial Line: "I bumped into Coach Thompson at the grocery store. He hasn't changed a bit."
Your Response Line: "Coach Thompson, really? Blast from the past. Remember those gruelling practice sessions? He was tough. I wonder if he still remembers us. Did he say anything?"

SUBTEXTS - 6 Minutes [Set Timer]
[ ] Respectful: You still hold a deep respect for the coach's influence in your life.
[ ] Secret Hate: The coach did something to you, that you've never told anyone.
[ ] Curious: You're intrigued about how he views those times now.
[ ] Indifferent: Your sports days are long behind you, and you feel little connection.
[ ] Proud: You look back at those times as foundational to who you are today.
[ ] Your Own Subtext

RELATIONSHIP SUBTEXTS - 6 Minutes [Set Timer]
[ ] The Teammate who shared triumphs and defeats with you.
[ ] The Rival who always tried to outshine you in front of the coach.
[ ] The Younger Sibling who idolized the coach and followed in your footsteps.
[ ] The Parent who never missed a game and was your biggest fan.
[ ] The Old Friend who drifted away after the team disbanded.
[ ] Your Own Subtext

Discovery Journal
_____
_____
_____
_____

WORKOUT COMPLETED [ ]

If you're not willing to risk, you cannot grow. If you cannot grow, you cannot become your best. If you cannot become your best, you cannot be happy. If you cannot be happy, what else is there?
Les Brown

EMOTIONS

The 'moment before', **the emotional preparation, is the most important key to a great scene.** If you start any scene *without* an emotional preparation it feels like trying to drive a car in neutral. The preparation is the uphill climb of every rollercoaster; Once you grind all the way to the top, the chains let go and the rest of the ride takes care of itself. "No one wants to see a play or a movie and look at technical proficiency. You want to be moved, you want a human experience, you want to feel less alone" - Viola Davis. **Practice your emotions over and over** so when it's time, you aren't worried "Will I get there?" **You're imagination and emotions should be a tinderbox, so easy to light up. All it take is half a spark.**

EULOGY - 12 Minutes [Set Timer]

Find a quiet comfortable space. Choose someone in your life who is alive and important to you. Create an imaginary reason for why they have died. Now start from the point of the phone call— Imagine who calls, what they say and what you say. Eventually find yourself at the funeral, about to begin the eulogy. See the casket, is it open or closed?? What is that person wearing and any other details for yourself. Before you begin to speak, look into the audience and see who is there- Family, friends etc **Then begin the eulogy.** **Tip**: Be as specific as you can with everything. **Inside of specificity is where you will find the triggers to your heart.** Let your imagination take you wherever you want in this exercise. **Example**: Placing her favourite sheep stuffed animal in the casket, tucked under her arm like she always held it, then kissing her goodbye one last time.

DISCOVERY JOURNAL - 3 Minutes [Set Timer]

Make sure to **include the specific triggers** you experience because you can use these **TRIGGER MOMENTS** in the future instead of repeating the *entire* exercise.

___
___
___
___
___
___
___
___
___
___
___
___
___
___
___
___
___
___
___

WORKOUT COMPLETED [ ]

I don't get acting jobs because of my looks.
Alec Baldwin

THE CORK EXERCISE - 4 Minutes [Set Timer]
Place a cork between your teeth and read a passage aloud. This forces your articulation muscles to work harder. If you don't have a cork, bite down gently on your thumb. You can use the following text for this exercise:

> "High above, on the mountain peak, the view is breathtaking. Clouds drift below, casting moving shadows over the landscape. The air is thin and crisp, a reward for the arduous climb."

WRITE A LETTER - 10 Minutes [Set Timer]
Get a piece of paper or write this in your device. **Take a moment** to let this situation AND relationship sink in. Then let your imagination run wild and **write them a letter.**

Your Character: Liam, a veteran returning from service, struggling to readjust to civilian life.
Other Character: The family of a fellow soldier and close friend who died in combat, saving Liam's life.

Relationship: Liam's bond with his fallen comrade was forged in the intensity of shared experiences on the battlefield. The family, while proud of their loved one's heroism, is grieving deeply. Liam's survival, intertwined with their loss, creates a complex emotional connection between him and the family.

Context of the Letter: Battling with survivor's guilt and a profound sense of loss, Liam decides to write a letter to the family of his fallen friend. The letter is an expression of his sorrow, gratitude, and the weight of living a life that was saved at such a great cost. It's a tribute to his friend's memory, an attempt to convey the unspoken bond between soldiers, and a heartfelt acknowledgment of the family's grief.

Discovery Journal - 1 minute [Set Timer]

_____
_____
_____
_____
_____
_____

WORKOUT COMPLETED [ ]

No good movie is too long and no bad
movie is short enough.
Roger Ebert

VOCAL WORK - 3 minutes - [Set Timer]
Lip Trills: Close your lips together lightly, like you're going to blow a raspberry. Then, blow air through your closed lips while making sounds. You should feel a tickling sensation. Pick a song and Lip Trill along with it. **Tip**: Stretch your range as much as you can and pick a song you've never listened to.

VERBAL IMPROV - 10 Minutes [Set Timer]

Find a space where you are comfortable and free to express yourself. Take a moment to **let this situation, character and prompt, sink in**. Then let your imagination run wild: **Picture who you are talking to** then **begin with *the prompt*** and **continue to verbalize everything** this character would say. **Tip**: This is exploration! There is no "getting it right". BE BRAVE to explore and discover.

Character: Casey, a fitness coach known for their motivational skills and health advocacy, discovers that their business partner, Taylor, often considered the 'life of the party', has been promoting unhealthy weight loss supplements to clients. Casey's own struggle with body image issues heightens the impact of this discovery.

Prompt: "Taylor, we need to discuss the supplements you've been recommending to our clients."

Discovery Journal - 2 minutes [Set Timer]

Who are you talking to:

Describe them in two specific words:

Discovery Journal - 2 minutes [Set Timer]

_____
_____
_____
_____
_____
_____
_____
_____
_____
_____

WORKOUT COMPLETED [ ]

You have to really believe not only in yourself;
you have to believe that the world is actually
worth your sacrifices.
Zaha Hadid

SELF AWARENESS

The more you understand yourself, the more you are able to understand and develop your characters. Like you, your characters have thoughts, beliefs, traumas, passions etc. When you become aware of your own and start to see how those experiences and beliefs have shaped your life, how you operate and view the world, then you can develop your characters that are much more rich and vivid.

PHYSICAL WARMUP - 2 minutes [Set Timer]

Freeform Dance: Put on some music and engage in freeform dancing. Allow your body to move spontaneously and without inhibition. This can help you tap into your creative instincts and develop physical expressiveness. **Tip**: Try music you've never listened to.

CURRENT EMOTIONAL INVENTORY - 3 Minutes [Set Timer]

Write down and **record your current emotions**. Identify what you're feeling at this moment and why. **Tip**: Be as specific as you can, **don't disregard anything.** You can also **scan your body** to see how and where your current emotion is affecting you. Your posture, the way you walk, bouncing foot, sore neck etc

CURRENT EMOTIONAL STATE:

SELF DISCOVERY QUESTIONS - 10 Minutes [Set Timer]

I suggest a journal or writing it in your phone's notes so you don't run out of space here.

How do I define beauty or attractiveness?

What legacy do I want to leave behind?

WORKOUT COMPLETED [ ]

The best performances are those which are charged with emotional power.
Unknown

IMAGINATION

We have a lot of tools in our arsenal as actors but I believe imagination is the most powerful. "If you hook into the character's belief system and you believe it 100%, there is no way the audience won't." - Meryl Streep. Everyone has an Imagination but it must be worked out to get stronger. Think of your imagination as a limitless playground. In this space, you can be anyone, go anywhere, and do anything. **Have the courage to allow yourself to play!**

VOCAL WORK - 2 minutes - [Set Timer]

Lip Trills: Close your lips together lightly, like you're going to blow a raspberry. Then, blow air through your closed lips while making sounds. You should feel a tickling sensation. Pick a song and Lip Trill along with it. **Tip**: Stretch your range as much as you can and pick a song you've never listened to.

IMPROVISED STORYTELLING - 5 Minutes [Set Timer]

Speak out the scenario provided and continue the story! Focus on vivid details, character development AND how the main character overcomes the main obstacle. **Tip**: Try not to stop speaking so you don't have time to "think". Allow your imagination to keep moving forward without interruption. **Tip**: Record these stories on your device, in case it's great but more importantly to see your progress as you go on.

STARTING POINT: You are Alex, a landscape architect who stumbles upon an old, forgotten garden hidden behind an overgrown hedge in the city park. As you begin to restore the garden, you find that each plant and flower has unique properties – some can induce vivid dreams, others can recall forgotten memories, and a few can even show glimpses of possible futures. You bring the flowers home and make tea... Unsure of which to try first you close your eyes and grab—

IMAGINARY WORLD EXPLORATION - 6 Minutes [Set Timer]

Find a quiet space to relax AND focus. **Close your eyes** and let your imagination run wild. **Tip:** Engage all your senses to explore this environment. Touch, taste, smell etc and allow your emotions to guide you. **Extra:** After you explore this world with your senses, you could introduce characters and have a dialogue with them. Are they friends or foes?

IMAGINARY WORLD: THE ECHOING MIRROR - In this flourishing landscape, everything is a little bigger than it usually is and even more interestingly, whatever emotions you have within you, are mimicked by the weather.

JOURNAL YOUR EXPERIENCE - 2 Minutes [Set Timer]

_____
_____
_____
_____
_____
_____
_____

WORKOUT COMPLETED [ ]

Learn to live with self-awareness, not self-involvement.
Ivana Chubbuck

ANCHORING INTO YOUR CHARACTER COLOUR & MUSIC

Anchoring yourself into your character is vital. It's one of the most freeing feelings when you understand their *essence* because everything they do, how they do it and what their purpose is, becomes so clear to you and the audience. Every choice you make after you find your *anchor*, feels easy, because you're acting from who and what your character is at the core. You can call it an essence, an aura, vibe, energy etc. We all have it and feel it from everyone around us. There are many ways into your character but music and colour are my favourite. Music can inform the script, your character, even each scene. Colours, I think you will find, can work incredibly because we as humans respond to colours like frequencies. Colours evoke many feelings and if you pay attention closely, you can see everyone has their own 'colour' that defines their core. An essence that informs how they operate and move through the world.

THEIR COLOUR - 2 Minutes [Set Timer]
Think of **someone you know**, and **define them with a colour**. **Tip**: Trust yourself. Your initial colour is usually close. **Tip**: Start with basic colours then eventually become much more specific. **Example**: Corinna is an earthy green with rays of sunlight flowing through the green. **Extra**: Ask someone who knows *that person* as well, what they think this person's colour is and why. See how close your answers are or not.

YOUR CHARACTERS COLOUR
Read the given character description just as you would an audition, **assign a colour to that character.** Now take that colour you chose and **allow it to infuse into your entire body**, affecting your every move, your speaking, the way you see the world etc. **Take any book** you have, flip to a random page and **read the text as this Colour/Character**. **Tip**: Be specific, choose a colour that excites you and don't be afraid to get creative.

CHARACTER DESCRIPTION: [QUINCY] Quincy is a daring investigative journalist known for uncovering hidden truths and exposing corruption. Their attire is practical yet sharp, reflecting a readiness to pursue wherever it leads. Quincy's small, cluttered office is filled with notes, recordings, and clippings from their various investigations. Despite the risks, Quincy is driven by a relentless pursuit of justice and truth. They have a natural ability to connect with sources and a knack for getting information others can't. Quincy's character combines a tenacious spirit with a strong moral compass.

CHOOSE THEIR COLOUR - 4 Minutes [Set Timer]
THEIR COLOUR:

CHOOSE THEIR SONG - 4 Minutes [Set Timer]
THEIR SONG:

READ PASSAGE FROM BOOK - 2 Minutes [Set Timer]

FREEFORM DANCE - 2 minutes - [Set Timer]
Put on the selected music and **engage in freeform dancing, anchored in your colour/character,** Allow your body to move spontaneously and without inhibition. This can help you tap into your creative instincts and develop physical expressiveness *while staying in character.* **Tip**: Journal about the differences as opposed to how you normally dance.

JOURNAL YOUR EXPERIENCE - 1 Minute [Set Timer]

WORKOUT COMPLETED [ ]

Acting isn't something you do. Instead of doing it, it occurs. If you're going to start with logic, you might as well give up. You can have conscious preparation, but you have unconscious results.
Lee Strasberg

HISTORICAL RESEARCH

We are in the information era and have access to the world and its rich history at our fingertips. This exploration is not about 'learning facts'; it's a journey to the heart of human experience. The empathy and the understanding, especially on the things you disagree with, are incredibly valuable. If you look closely, you'll find the way people think, at different times in history, their attitudes, choices, and the way they move their bodies can teach you so much about us, right now. Fill your toolbox so it's overflowing with information and ideas to pull from so your imagination has so much to play with.

PHYSICAL WARMUP - 2 minutes - [Set Timer]
Freeform Dance: Put on some music and engage in freeform dancing. Allow your body to move spontaneously and without inhibition. This can help you tap into your creative instincts and develop physical expressiveness. **Tip**: Try music you've never listened to.

RESEARCH - 13 Minutes [Set Timer]
YouTube, streaming platforms, the internet or books, **research the given era/person/moment in time,** journal or make notes on your device, so when you want to find this information, it's organized and readily accessible. As you go, **write anything and everything _you_ find fascinating. Tip:** If the topic doesn't interest you, choose your own, or take a chance and still research it, but from a different perspective. Physicalities, voice, ideals, etc. Trust your body that when you see something interesting, you'll know. **Extra**: Speak it out and copy their movements. Our memory recall is massively affected by our bodies. Be specific and when you re-read your notes, you'll be amazed by how much your mind and body remember.

TOPIC:
The Titanic Sinking (1912) - The Perspective of Violet Jessop:
Violet Jessop, a stewardess and nurse, offers a unique perspective on the Titanic disaster. She not only survived the sinking of the Titanic in 1912 but also the earlier collision of its sister ship, the RMS Olympic, and later the sinking of the HMHS Britannic during World War I. Her memoirs provide a firsthand account of these maritime disasters, offering insights into the experiences of a crew member during some of the most famous shipwrecks in history.

_____
_____
_____
_____
_____
_____
_____
_____
_____
_____
_____
_____
_____
_____

WORKOUT COMPLETED [ ]

There's nothing more boring than
uncomplicated happiness.
Cate Blanchett

BELIEF

Beliefs are the convictions that something exists or is true, especially without proof. That is also the definition of what we do as actors. We play make-believe. Our beliefs shape our world, especially our beliefs about ourselves and it works for the characters you play. Understand your beliefs and how they influence your mind, body and spirit, then you will be able to better understand others, so you can embody them. Allow the beliefs of your character to colour your perception of your world and your interaction with everything in it. "Acting is the best magic trick in the world. We applaud performances not because it's real, but because you made us believe."

VOCAL WORK - 2 Minutes - [Set timer]

Lip Trills: Close your lips together lightly, like you're going to blow a raspberry. Then, blow air through your closed lips while making sounds. You should feel a tickling sensation. Pick a song and Lip Trill along with it. **Tip**: Stretch your range as much as you can and pick a song you've never listened to.

BELIEF WORKOUT

Get your journal or write in here. **Define your personal belief/view** on the given subject. **Grab any book you own,** flip to a random page and **read it out loud,** colouring the words and intention with your belief system. **Tip:** Write trigger words you can hook into in the future: **Optimism-** Always smiling, grateful, opportunity, sunshine yellow.

YOUR PERSONAL BELIEF

Mistakes- 7 Minutes [Set Timer]

_____
_____
_____
_____

READ WITH BELIEF - 2 Minutes [Set Timer]

CHARACTERS BELIEF

Mistakes

Mistakes are just failures, plain and simple. Something I should have avoided and won't make the same mistake twice. My mother always said, "In this house, perfection is the expectation, not the exception."

READ WITH CHARACTERS BELIEF - 2 Minutes [Set Timer]

Forget your personal view and **fully embrace the character's belief. Read out loud again.**

JOURNAL YOUR EXPERIENCE - 2 Minutes [Set Timer]

_____
_____
_____
_____

WORKOUT COMPLETED [ ]

PERFORMANCE STRATEGY
14 DAY REVIEW

TAKE A MOMENT OF REFLECTION AND BREAKDOWN WHERE YOU ARE RIGHT NOW IN YOUR CAREER AND AS AN ACTOR.
THE MORE SPECIFIC YOU ARE THE MORE CLEAR YOU CAN SEE WHERE YOU ARE NOW SO YOU CAN GET TO WHERE YOU WANT TO GO FASTER

★ ★ ★ ★ ★

J.R.R. Tolkien: Initially rejected by several publishers, Tolkien's "The Lord of the Rings" series went on to become a cornerstone of fantasy literature.

DATE:

MY WHY
WHY ARE YOU DOING WHAT YOU ARE DOING
BE SPECIFIC

MY MAIN GOALS
IN-ORDER OF IMPORTANCE

1.

    Action Step(s):

2.

    Action Step(s):

3.

    Action Step(s):

FROM THE LAST 14 DAYS
5 STAR RATING

YOUR KEY POINTS AND TAKEAWAYS - WHY THAT AMOUNT OF STAR RATING, LIKES, DISLIKES, THE BIGGEST LESSON YOU LEARNED, GOOD OR BAD:

STRENGTHS:

WEAKNESSES:

IMPROVEMENT STRATEGY
HOW CAN YOU IMPROVE ON THESE AREAS FOR THE NEXT 14 DAYS:

GOAL FROM LAST :
DID YOU ACHIEVE IT?

WHY OR WHY NOT?

GOAL FOR THE NEXT 14 EXERCISES
THE MORE SPECIFIC YOU ARE THE GREATER THE RESULT

    Action Step(s):

We tell ourselves stories in order to live.
Julianne Moore

MY WHY:

GOAL(s):

PHYSICAL WARMUP - SHADOW MIMICRY - 1 minute [Set Timer]
Mime Shadows: Play with the shadows in the room using your body, creating shapes and stories with your movements. **Tip**: Imagine your shadow is a character of its own, and interact with it as if it has a mind of its own.

VOCAL WORK - 3 minutes [Set Timer]
Humming Waves: Start with a low hum and gradually increase in volume and pitch, like a wave rising, then let it fall away again. **Tip**: Feel the vibration of your voice in your chest and let it ripple out through your body.

EMOTIONAL RECALL - 5 minutes [Set Timer]
Frustration Release: Remember a time when you were utterly frustrated. Envision the scenario in detail, then release that frustration through controlled, deliberate movements. **Tip**: Channel the energy of the frustration into each movement as if physically pushing the emotion out of your body.

ANIMAL WORK - MANTIS SHRIMP

Research - 2 minutes [Set Timer]
Explore the vibrant world of the mantis shrimp, noted for its extraordinary vision and lightning-fast predatory skills.

Animal Exercise - 3 minutes [Set Timer]
Emulate the mantis shrimp's striking motion with quick, sharp arm movements. **Tip**: Imagine the spectrum of colours it sees and reflect that in the dynamic energy of your movements.

Discovery Journal - 1 Minute [Set Timer]
3 Main Characteristics: (Whatever stands out to YOU to embody the essence)
_____
_____
_____
_____
_____
_____

WORKOUT COMPLETED [ ]

The only thing an actor owes his public is not to bore them.
Marlon Brando

SCRIPT ANALYSIS for RELATIONSHIPS & SPECIFICITY - 15 minutes [Set Timer]
Choose your character, circle everything in this script you have a relationship with. Including people, places, things, smells, time of day etc. **Write what your relationship with those items are and be specific.** The more specific and fun you have with your relationships, the more interesting your characters will be and the more fun the audience has. **Tip:** Everything isn't in the scene. Use your imagination to create details, only if it's contextually appropriate. **Extra:** Write your > **Objective, win or lose? Consequence of failing?** The **Who What Where When Why.**

Title: **Recipe for Disaster**
INT. SMALL FAMILY RESTAURANT KITCHEN - EVENING
The kitchen is cramped and bustling with activity. Chefs and waiters rush about, but the focus is on GIOVANNI (50s, a charismatic but hot-headed chef) and ANNA (30s, his level-headed but under-appreciated sister and business partner). They argue amidst the chaos.

ANNA
It's called fusion, Gio. It's innovative. The customers love it.
GIOVANNI
Innovative? Aye, aye, aye! Pasta does not belong with curry!
ANNA
It's getting us the best reviews we've had in years!
GIOVANNI
Look at this! This isn't cooking; it's a circus act!
ANNA
The kitchen needs organization, not just passion, Gio.
GIOVANNI
Passion is the soul of cooking! Without it, food is just... fuel!
ANNA
And without a solid plan, a restaurant is just... chaos.
GIOVANNI
You're turning my kitchen into a joke.
ANNA
A joke? Last time I checked, we co-own this place.
GIOVANNI
I should have never agreed to this partnership.
ANNA
I'm starting to regret it myself.
Giovanni throws his hands up in exasperation. Just then, a waiter rushes in.
WAITER
Chef, the customers are asking for more of the Spicy Thai Spaghetti!
GIOVANNI
More? What is wrong with people?
ANNA
Maybe it's time for the old dog to learn some new tricks.
GIOVANNI
Aye, aye, aye! *(to chefs)* What are you waiting for?! Pasta, pasta pasta!
ANNA
Pasta, pasta, pasta.
Giovanni grabs some ingredients... Anna tries to hide her amusement.

WORKOUT COMPLETED [ ]

I'm curious about other people. That's the essence of my acting. I'm interested in what it would be like to be you.
Meryl Streep

IMAGINATION

We have a lot of tools in our arsenal as actors but **I believe imagination is the most powerful.** "If you hook into the character's belief system and you believe it 100%, there is no way the audience won't." - Meryl Streep "Imagination is more important than knowledge for knowledge is limited. - Einstein. Everyone has an Imagination but it must be worked out to get stronger. Think of your imagination as a limitless playground. In this space, you can be anyone, go anywhere, and do anything. **Have the courage to allow yourself to play!**

Solo Imaginary World Exploration - 6 Minutes [Set Timer]

Find a quiet space to relax and focus. **Close your eyes** and **let your imagination run wild. Tip:** Engage all your senses to explore this environment. Touch, taste, smell etc. Allow your emotions to guide you. **Extra:** After you establish this world in your imagination, you could introduce characters and have a dialogue with them. Are they friends or foes?

IMAGINARY WORLD: Abandoned Amusement Park at Night: Unravel the mysteries of a once-joyous, now eerie amusement park.

JOURNAL YOUR EXPERIENCE - 2 Minutes [Set Timer]

_____
_____
_____
_____
_____
_____

Your Characters Filter - 5 Minutes [Set Timer]

Everyone including the characters you play see the world through their own specific perspective/filter. I like to use the word filter because you can take out a filter, clean it, change its style, colour, an optimist or a pessimist, comedian or a nihilist, etc. **Find a quiet space** to focus. **Close your eyes and let go of your personal thoughts and emotions** to make space for your characters. **Open your eyes, and allow the filter provided to effect everything around you. Tip:** Explore wherever you are and interact with the objects. **Extra:** How does _this_ character walk and move in their world?

FILTER: Melancholic Poet: Finds beauty and sadness intertwined in all experiences.

JOURNAL YOUR EXPERIENCE - 2 Minutes [Set Timer]

_____
_____
_____
_____
_____
_____

WORKOUT COMPLETED [ ]

The right sort of practice carried out over a sufficient period of time leads to improvement. Nothing else.
Anders Ericsson

CHARACTER STUDY "PEOPLE WATCHING"

Actors are required to portray characters that are believable and relatable. You don't have to agree with them but you have to understand them. Walk like them, talk like them, see the world like them. So, in order to fill our toolbox, we have to **go out into the world and study**. Then practice them over and over so we can "walk in their shoes', comfortably and confidently. Study their movements, mannerisms, the "vibe" they give off, the clothes they wear etc. **Fill your toolbox with the rhythms and idiosyncrasies of human behaviour.**

OBSERVATION CHARACTER STUDY - 15 Minutes [Set Timer]

Find a busy place where you can **sit and observe.** Choose anyone you find interesting. **Write down what stands out about them**. *The way they sit, drink their coffee, walk, talk, interact with others etc.* **Tip: Mirror them immediately**. This will help memorize the feeling of that character so whenever you come back to these characters you're discovering, your body will remember. **Extra**: Before you go to sleep, read over the characters from today and reenact their movements.

_____
_____
_____
_____
_____
_____
_____
_____
_____
_____
_____
_____
_____
_____
_____
_____
_____
_____
_____
_____
_____
_____

COLOURS: We as humans respond to colours like frequencies. If you pay attention closely, you can see everyone has their own 'colour' that defines their core. An essence that informs how they operate and move through the world.

WHAT COLOUR ARE THEY:

WORKOUT COMPLETED [ ]

To grasp the full significance of life is the actor's duty; to interpret it is his problem; and to express it his dedication.
James Dean

VOICE & DICTION

I wish I had learned this at the beginning of my career. The confidence to communicate clearly and powerfully is a game-changer for you as an actor. **Think of your voice as a musical instrument that needs regular tuning. This workout is your daily tuning session,** ensuring that your instrument is always ready. "The word 'theatre' comes from the Greeks. It means the seeing place. It is the place people come to see the truth about life and the social situation." - Stella Adler. Embrace this workout as a key to unlocking and portraying *that* truth by letting your voice be the vehicle that transports your audience into the heart of your story.

READ PASSAGE - 30 Seconds [Set Timer]
Speak the passage and take note of its quality. **Tip**: Record Audio to compare afterward.

> "Spring breathes new life into the world. Flowers bloom, birds return, and the earth awakens from its slumber with vibrant energy. The scent of fresh growth fills the air, heralding a season of rebirth and rejuvenation."

RELAXATION - 1 Minute [Set Timer]
Deep Breathing: Sit and Inhale deeply through your nose, filling your lungs, then exhale slowly through your mouth. Imagine stress leaving your body with each breath.

Nay Nay Nay - 1 Minute [Set Timer]
Pick a song and sing the word "Nay" repeatedly. Start with a comfortable pitch and gradually move the sound from your nose to your chest, ensuring each "Nay" is clear and resonant. Stretch your range as best you can to strengthen.

Sustained 'S' - 2 Minutes [Set Timer]
Inhale deeply and then exhale slowly, making a continuous 's' sound. Keep the sound as even and steady as you can. Always push a little longer than you think you can.

Vowel Pronunciation Drill - 2 Minutes [Set Timer]
Slowly go through each vowel sound **(A, E, I, O, U)**, **holding and exaggerating each sound. Combine them with consonants** (e.g., ba, be, bi, bo, bu). Pay attention to the clarity and sharpness of each sound. Repeat a few times before moving to the next.

Lip Trills - 3 minutes - [Set timer]
Close your lips together lightly, like you're going to blow a raspberry. Then, blow air through your closed lips while making sounds. You should feel a tickling sensation. Pick a song and Lip Trill the whole along with it. **Tip**: Stretch your range as much as you can and pick a song you've never listened to.

The Cork Exercise - 4 Minutes [Set Timer]
Place a cork between your teeth and try to read a passage aloud. This forces your articulation muscles to work harder. If you don't have a cork, bite down gently on your thumb. You can use the following text for this exercise:

READ PASSAGE AGAIN - 30 Seconds [Set Timer]
Speak the passage and take note of its quality. **Tip**: Record Audio to compare.

Discovery Journal - 1 Minute [Set Timer]

WORKOUT COMPLETED [ ]

An actor is supposed to be a sensitive instrument.
Marilyn Monroe

SUBTEXT

Subtext is what lies beneath the surface of our words. It's the hidden layer of meaning, driven by the character's internal thoughts, emotions, desires, and motivations. Subtext is one of my favourite things as an actor because so much can be said with one simple line of dialogue. The power of "Hello" can be exciting if you told that person years ago "If I ever see you again, I'll kill you. Maybe it's the most beautiful person you've ever seen. Now, say "hello". *Subtext* shows the audience what your relationship with the characters/places/situations are, without having to explain it. We experience it every day and it is our job to create characters that interact as we do.

VOCAL WORK - 3 minutes - [Set Timer]
Lip Trills: Close your lips together lightly, like you're going to blow a raspberry. Then, blow air through your closed lips while making sounds. You should feel a tickling sensation. Pick a song and Lip Trill along with it. **Tip**: Stretch your range as much as you can and pick a song you've never listened to.

SUBTEXT PRACTICE
Use the line of dialogue provided and practice each of these subtexts **out loud.** Move on to the next, only when you believe yourself. Trust that you will know when *that* is. Before you begin, **pick a spot to look at and imagine** in detail, **who you are speaking with.** **Tip**: *Sometimes* we mean exactly what we are saying. Look for that too. **Extra**: Substitute someone you have a strong relationship with in real life, good or bad, and see it's affect.

Initial Line: "They're starting construction on the new community skatepark."
Your Response Line: "Skatepark? Seriously? I mean, the area's been needing a place like that. A green space can really change the feel of a neighborhood. Do you think it'll be a good addition?"

SUBTEXTS - 6 Minutes [Set Timer]
[ ] Enthusiasm: You're genuinely excited about the positive impact of the park.
[ ] Nostalgia: The construction reminds you of childhood memories in similar parks.
[ ] Cynicism: You doubt the park will live up to the community's expectations.
[ ] Indifference: You don't see the park as something that will affect your life.
[ ] Concern: You're worried about environmental and financial implications.
[ ] Your Own Subtext

RELATIONSHIP SUBTEXTS - 6 Minutes [Set Timer]
[ ] Grumpy Neighbour who is always so negative.
[ ] Your overly excited and exhaustingly optimistic Mother.
[ ] Your excited nephew who just started skateboarding.
[ ] Your crush who you don't know anything about yet.
[ ] A stranger at a bus stop who doesn't blink.
[ ] Your Own Subtext

Discovery Journal

_____
_____
_____
_____

WORKOUT COMPLETED [ ]

Technique is what you fall back on when
you run out of inspiration.
Rudolf Nureyev

EMOTIONS

The 'moment before', **the emotional preparation, is the most important key to a great scene.** If you start any scene *without* an emotional preparation it feels like trying to drive a car in neutral. The preparation is the uphill climb of every rollercoaster; Once you grind all the way to the top, the chains let go and the rest of the ride takes care of itself. "No one wants to see a play or a movie and look at technical proficiency. You want to be moved, you want a human experience, you want to feel less alone" - Viola Davis. **Practice your emotions over and over** so when it's time, you aren't worried "Will I get there?" **You're imagination and emotions should be a tinderbox, so easy to light up. All it take is half a spark.**

EULOGY - 12 Minutes [Set Timer]

Find a quiet comfortable space. Choose someone in your life who is alive and important to you. Create an imaginary reason for why they have died. Now start from the point of the phone call— Imagine who calls, what they say and what you say. Eventually find yourself at the funeral, about to begin the eulogy. See the casket, is it open or closed?? What is that person wearing and any other details for yourself. Before you begin to speak, look into the audience and see who is there- Family, friends etc **Then begin the eulogy. Tip**: Be as specific as you can with everything. **Inside of specificity is where you will find the triggers to your heart.** Let your imagination take you wherever you want in this exercise. **Example**: Placing her favourite sheep stuffed animal in the casket, tucked under her arm like she always held it, then kissing her goodbye one last time.

DISCOVERY JOURNAL - 3 Minutes [Set Timer]

Make sure to **include the specific triggers** you experience because you can use these **TRIGGER MOMENTS** in the future instead of repeating the *entire* exercise.

WORKOUT COMPLETED [ ]

When you hit a wall – of your own imagined limitations – just kick it in.
Sam Shepard

THE CORK EXERCISE - 4 Minutes [Set Timer]

Place a cork between your teeth and read a passage aloud. This forces your articulation muscles to work harder. If you don't have a cork, bite down gently on your thumb. You can use the following text for this exercise:

"In the old town, cobblestone streets wind between historic buildings. The murmur of voices and the clinking of cafe cups blend with the footsteps of passersby, each stone echoing stories from centuries past."

WRITE A LETTER - 10 Minutes [Set Timer]

Get a piece of paper or write this in your device. **Take a moment** to let this situation and relationship sink in. Then let your imagination run wild and **write them a letter.**

Your Character: Emma, a single parent who has recently lost her teenage daughter in a tragic accident.

Other Character: The driver responsible for the accident, who survived but has been living with immense guilt and trauma.

Relationship: Emma has never met the driver before the accident. Their lives became tragically intertwined due to the devastating event. The mix of grief, anger, and the search for meaning in such a loss encapsulates the complexity of Emma's emotions towards the driver.

Context of the Letter: Amidst her overwhelming grief, Emma decides to write a letter to the driver. This letter is an outpouring of her heartbreak, her struggle to cope with the irreplaceable loss of her daughter, and her attempt to process the range of emotions she feels towards the person responsible. It's a confrontation of her pain, a search for understanding, and perhaps a step towards healing.

Discovery Journal - 1 minute [Set Timer]

_____
_____
_____
_____
_____
_____
_____

WORKOUT COMPLETED [ ]

Some people want it to happen, some wish it would happen, others make it happen.
Michael Jordan

VOCAL WORK - 3 minutes [Set timer]

Lip Trills: Close your lips together lightly, like you're going to blow a raspberry. Then, blow air through your closed lips while making sounds. You should feel a tickling sensation. Pick a song and Lip Trill along with it. **Tip**: Stretch your range as much as you can and pick a song you've never listened to.

VERBAL IMPROV - 10 Minutes [Set Timer]

Find a space where you are comfortable and free to express yourself. Take a moment to **let this situation, character and prompt, sink in**. Then let your imagination run wild: **Picture who you are talking to** then **begin with *the prompt*** and **continue to verbalize everything** this character would say. **Tip**: This is exploration! There is no "getting it right". BE BRAVE to explore and discover.

Character: Harper, a renowned chef known for their creativity and ethical sourcing, finds out that their trusted supplier, Jordan, who has always seemed reliable, has been providing ingredients from questionable sources. Harper's commitment to sustainability makes this revelation particularly troubling.

Prompt: "Jordan, I've learned about the true source of our ingredients. We need to talk about your practices."

Who are you talking to:

Describe them in two specific words:

Discovery Journal - 2 minutes [Set Timer]

_____
_____
_____
_____
_____
_____
_____
_____
_____

WORKOUT COMPLETED [ ]

Don't confuse fame with success.
Madonna is one; Helen Keller is the other.
Erma Bombeck

SELF AWARENESS

The more you understand yourself, the more you are able to understand and develop your characters. Like you, your characters have thoughts, beliefs, traumas, passions etc. When you become aware of your own and start to see how those experiences and beliefs have shaped your life, how you operate and view the world, then you can develop your characters that are much more rich and vivid.

PHYSICAL WARMUP - 2 minutes [Set Timer]
Freeform Dance: Put on some music and engage in freeform dancing. Allow your body to move spontaneously and without inhibition. This can help you tap into your creative instincts and develop physical expressiveness. **Tip**: Try music you've never listened to.

CURRENT EMOTIONAL INVENTORY - 3 Minutes [Set Timer]
Write down and **record your current emotions**. Identify what you're feeling at this moment and why. **Tip**: Be as specific as you can, **don't disregard anything.** You can also **scan your body** to see how and where your current emotion is affecting you. Your posture, the way you walk, bouncing foot, sore neck etc

CURRENT EMOTIONAL STATE:

SELF DISCOVERY QUESTIONS - 10 Minutes [Set Timer]
I suggest a journal or writing it in your phone's notes so you don't run out of space here.

What am I most grateful for in my life?

What aspects of my life give me energy, and what drains me? (Extra: Remind yourself of how they feel and take note so you can recreate that)

WORKOUT COMPLETED [ ]

Value your opinion about yourself above
the opinion that others have of you
Daniel Silva

IMAGINATION

We have a lot of tools in our arsenal as actors but I believe imagination is the most powerful. "If you hook into the character's belief system and you believe it 100%, there is no way the audience won't." - Meryl Streep. Everyone has an Imagination but it must be worked out to get stronger. Think of your imagination as a limitless playground. In this space, you can be anyone, go anywhere, and do anything. **Have the courage to allow yourself to play!**

VOCAL WORK - 2 Minutes - [Set timer]

Lip Trills: Close your lips together lightly, like you're going to blow a raspberry. Then, blow air through your closed lips while making sounds. You should feel a tickling sensation. Pick a song and Lip Trill along with it. **Tip**: Stretch your range as much as you can and pick a song you've never listened to.

IMPROVISED STORYTELLING - 5 Minutes [Set Timer]

Speak out the scenario provided and continue the story! Focus on vivid details, character development and how the main character overcomes the main obstacle. **Tip**: Try not to stop speaking so you don't have time to "think". Allow your imagination to keep moving forward without interruption. **Tip:** Record these stories on your device, in case it's great but more importantly to see your progress as you go on.

STARTING POINT: You are Casey, an amateur astronomer and astrophotographer, who captures an unidentifiable celestial object in your telescope one clear night. Intrigued, you start researching and soon realize that the object is not documented in any astronomical records. As you observe it night after night, strange phenomena begin to occur – the stars seem to communicate through patterns—

IMAGINARY WORLD EXPLORATION - 6 Minutes [Set Timer]

Find a quiet space to relax and focus. **Close your eyes** and let your imagination run wild. **Tip:** Engage all your senses to explore this environment. Touch, taste, smell etc and allow your emotions to guide you. **Extra:** After you explore this world with your senses, you could introduce characters and have a dialogue with them. Are they friends or foes?

IMAGINARY WORLD: COBBLESTONE HAVEN - A quaint village with cobblestone streets and charming, ivy-covered cottages. The aroma of freshly baked bread wafts from a nearby bakery, but oddly... No one in the town is smiling.

JOURNAL YOUR EXPERIENCE - 2 Minutes [Set Timer]

_____
_____
_____
_____
_____
_____
_____

WORKOUT COMPLETED [ ]

I always say you can't live on awards, but boy, doesn't it feel great to get them?
Bette Davis

ANCHORING INTO YOUR CHARACTER COLOUR & MUSIC

Anchoring yourself into your character is vital. It's one of the most freeing feelings when you understand their *essence* because everything they do, how they do it and what their purpose is, becomes so clear to you and the audience. Every choice you make after you find your *anchor*, feels easy, because you're acting from who and what your character is at the core. You can call it an essence, an aura, vibe, energy etc. We all have it and feel it from everyone around us. There are many ways into your character but music and colour are my favourite. Music can inform the script, your character, even each scene. Colours, I think you will find, can work incredibly because we as humans respond to colours like frequencies. Colours evoke many feelings and if you pay attention closely, you can see everyone has their own 'colour' that defines their core. An essence that informs how they operate and move through the world.

THEIR COLOUR - 2 Minutes [Set Timer]
Think of **someone you know**, and **define them with a colour**. **Tip**: Trust yourself. Your initial colour is usually close. **Tip**: Start with basic colours then eventually become much more specific. **Example**: Corinna is an earthy green with rays of sunlight flowing through the green. **Extra**: Ask someone who knows *that person* as well, what they think this person's colour is and why. See how close your answers are or not.

YOUR CHARACTERS COLOUR
Read the given character description just as you would an audition, **assign a colour to that character.** Now take that colour you chose and **allow it to infuse into your entire body**, affecting your every move, your speaking, the way you see the world etc. **Take any book** you have, flip to a random page and **read the text as this Colour/Character**. **Tip**: Be specific, choose a colour that excites you and don't be afraid to get creative.

CHARACTER DESCRIPTION: [PARKER] Parker is a charismatic yet enigmatic magician specializing in close-up magic and sleight of hand. Performing in intimate venues and upscale events, they dress in sleek, stylish attire that adds to their mystery. Parker's performances are not just about tricks; they weave storytelling and psychological elements into their act, creating a captivating experience. Behind the scenes, Parker is deeply introspective. A past that influences their art in subtle ways.

CHOOSE THEIR COLOUR - 4 Minutes [Set Timer]
THEIR COLOUR:

CHOOSE THEIR SONG - 4 Minutes [Set Timer]
THEIR SONG:

READ PASSAGE FROM BOOK - 2 Minutes [Set Timer]

FREEFORM DANCE - 2 minutes - [Set Timer]
Put on the selected music and **engage in freeform dancing, anchored in your colour/character,** Allow your body to move spontaneously and without inhibition. This can help you tap into your creative instincts and develop physical expressiveness *while staying in character.* **Tip**: Journal about the differences as opposed to how you normally dance.

JOURNAL YOUR EXPERIENCE - 1 Minute [Set Timer]

WORKOUT COMPLETED [ ]

I tried to be as real as possible.
I had a hell of a time.
Paul Newman

HISTORICAL RESEARCH

We are in the information era and have access to the world and its rich history at our fingertips. This exploration is not about 'learning facts'; it's a journey to the heart of human experience. The empathy and the understanding, especially on the things you disagree with, are incredibly valuable. If you look closely, you'll find the way people think, at different times in history, their attitudes, choices, and the way they move their bodies can teach you so much about us, right now. Fill your toolbox so it's overflowing with information and ideas to pull from so your imagination has so much to play with.

PHYSICAL WARMUP - 2 minutes - [Set Timer]
Freeform Dance: Put on some music and engage in freeform dancing. Allow your body to move spontaneously and without inhibition. This can help you tap into your creative instincts and develop physical expressiveness. **Tip**: Try music you've never listened to.

RESEARCH - 13 Minutes [Set Timer]
YouTube, streaming platforms, the internet or books, **research the given era/person/moment in time,** journal or make notes on your device, so when you want to find this information, it's organized and readily accessible. As you go, **write anything and everything _you_ find fascinating. Tip:** If the topic doesn't interest you, choose your own, or take a chance and still research it, but from a different perspective. Physicalities, voice, ideals, etc. Trust your body that when you see something interesting, you'll know. **Extra**: Speak it out and copy their movements. Our memory recall is massively affected by our bodies. Be specific and when you re-read your notes, you'll be amazed by how much your mind and body remember.

TOPIC:
Rosa Parks' Arrest (1955) - The Perspective of James F. Blake: During Rosa Parks' historic act of defiance against racial segregation in 1955, James F. Blake was the bus driver who confronted her. Blake's role in this pivotal event, although less celebrated, offers a complex character study for an actor. Researching Blake's perspective provides insights into the societal norms of the era and the mindset of an ordinary individual entangled in a significant moment of civil rights history.

___
___
___
___
___
___
___
___
___
___
___
___
___
___
___
___
___

WORKOUT COMPLETED [ ]

I act for free, but I demand a huge salary as compensation for all the annoyance of being a public personality.
Robert Mitchum

BELIEF

Beliefs are the convictions that something exists or is true, especially without proof. That is also the definition of what we do as actors. We play make-believe. Our beliefs shape our world, especially our beliefs about ourselves and it works for the characters you play. Understand your beliefs and how they influence your mind, body and spirit, then you will be able to better understand others, so you can embody them. Allow the beliefs of your character to colour your perception of your world and your interaction with everything in it. "Acting is the best magic trick in the world. We applaud performances not because it's real, but because you made us believe."

VOCAL WORK - 2 Minutes - [Set timer]
Lip Trills: Close your lips together lightly, like you're going to blow a raspberry. Then, blow air through your closed lips while making sounds. You should feel a tickling sensation. Pick a song and Lip Trill along with it. **Tip**: Stretch your range as much as you can and pick a song you've never listened to.

BELIEF WORKOUT
Get your journal or write in here. **Define your personal belief/view** on the given subject. **Grab any book you own,** flip to a random page and **read it out loud,** colouring the words and intention with your belief system. **Tip:** Write trigger words you can hook into in the future: **Optimism-** Always smiling, grateful, opportunity, sunshine yellow.

YOUR PERSONAL BELIEF
Mistakes- 7 Minutes [Set Timer]

_____
_____
_____
_____

READ WITH BELIEF - 2 Minutes [Set Timer]

CHARACTERS BELIEF
Mistakes
Mistakes are the forge of human character, sculpting wisdom from the raw ore of errors. To me, each misstep is a vital chapter in the epic of growth, not a stain but a stepping stone to greater understanding. In embracing my flaws, I find the true essence of resilience and learning.

READ WITH CHARACTERS BELIEF - 2 Minutes [Set Timer]
Forget your personal view and **fully embrace the character's belief.** Read out loud again.

JOURNAL YOUR EXPERIENCE - 2 Minutes [Set Timer]

_____
_____
_____

WORKOUT COMPLETED [ ]

PERFORMANCE STRATEGY
14 DAY REVIEW

TAKE A MOMENT OF REFLECTION AND BREAKDOWN WHERE YOU ARE RIGHT NOW IN YOUR CAREER AND AS AN ACTOR.
THE MORE SPECIFIC YOU ARE THE MORE CLEAR YOU CAN SEE WHERE YOU ARE NOW SO YOU CAN GET TO WHERE YOU WANT TO GO FASTER

★ ★ ★ ★ ★

Chris Gardner: His struggle with homelessness while raising a son was portrayed in the film "The Pursuit of Happiness." He later founded his own brokerage firm.

DATE:

MY WHY
WHY ARE YOU DOING WHAT YOU ARE DOING
BE SPECIFIC

MY MAIN GOALS
IN-ORDER OF IMPORTANCE

1.

   Action Step(s):

2.

   Action Step(s):

3.

   Action Step(s):

FROM THE LAST 14 DAYS
5 STAR RATING

YOUR KEY POINTS AND TAKEAWAYS - WHY THAT AMOUNT OF STAR RATING, LIKES, DISLIKES, THE BIGGEST LESSON YOU LEARNED, GOOD OR BAD:

STRENGTHS:

WEAKNESSES:

IMPROVEMENT STRATEGY
HOW CAN YOU IMPROVE ON THESE AREAS FOR THE NEXT 14 DAYS:

GOAL FROM LAST :
DID YOU ACHIEVE IT?

WHY OR WHY NOT?

GOAL FOR THE NEXT 14 EXERCISES
THE MORE SPECIFIC YOU ARE THE GREATER THE RESULT

   Action Step(s):

To be a character who feels a deep emotion,
one must go into the memory's vault and
mix in a sad memory from one's own life.
Alfred Hitchcock

MY WHY:

GOAL(s):

PHYSICAL WARMUP - ECHO MOVEMENT - 1 minute [Set Timer]
Vibrational Dance: Move to the echoes of your own claps or stomps, creating a rhythm that resonates through your body. **Tip:** Focus on the reverberation of each sound you make and let that guide your dance.

VOCAL WORK - 3 minutes [Set Timer]
Whispered Chants: Choose a simple phrase and whisper it rhythmically, exploring different pitches and tones. **Tip:** Notice how whispering affects your vocal cords differently than speaking or singing.

EMOTIONAL RECALL - 5 minutes [Set Timer]
Joyful Surprise: Recall a moment of unexpected joy, relive the surprise, and the ensuing happiness. **Tip:** Allow your movements to be light and spontaneous, as if reacting to the good news all over again.

ANIMAL WORK - AYE-AYE
Research - 2 minutes [Set Timer]
Delve into the unique behaviours and movements of the nocturnal aye-aye, particularly its distinctive foraging method.

Animal Exercise - 3 minutes [Set Timer]
Adopt the aye-aye's tapping and probing actions with your fingers, as if searching for food, and its skittish, erratic movements. **Tip:** Embrace the aye-aye's solitary nature and peculiar foraging technique to influence your motion and interactions with the imaginary world around you.

Discovery Journal - 1 Minute [Set Timer]
3 Main Characteristics: (Whatever stands out to YOU to embody the essence)

_____
_____
_____
_____
_____
_____
_____

WORKOUT COMPLETED [ ]

Acting is everybody's favourite second job.
Jack Nicholson

SCRIPT ANALYSIS for **RELATIONSHIPS & SPECIFICITY** - 15 minutes [Set Timer]
Choose your character, circle everything in this script you have a relationship with. Including people, places, things, smells, time of day etc. **Write what your relationship with those items are and be specific**. The more specific and fun you have with your relationships, the more interesting your characters will be and the more fun the audience has. **Tip:** Everything isn't in the scene. Use your imagination to create details, only if it's contextually appropriate. **Extra:** Write your > **Objective, win or lose? Consequence of failing?** The **Who What Where When Why.**

Title: **Last Will and Misadventure**
INT. ECCENTRIC LAWYER'S OFFICE - DAY
A cluttered, old lawyer's office. Bookshelves line the walls, HAROLD (eccentric, dry wit) sits behind a disorganized desk. MARGOT (sharp-tongued, stylish), his estranged daughter holds a will—

MARGOT
Uncle Louie left me his fortune...
HAROLD
On one condition.
MARGOT
Right, you said that. What was the condition again?
HAROLD
You have to spend a night in his haunted mansion.
MARGOT
Haunted? Uncle Louie was a con artist, not a ghost hunter.
HAROLD
He was eccentric, that's for sure. But, his rules.
MARGOT
One night?
HAROLD
That's it. Unless you're scared of a few ghosts.
MARGOT
Please. I've basically been living with one for my whole life.
HAROLD
That's the spirit, you little shit!
MARGOT
Dad, what's the catch? There's always a catch with Uncle Louie.
HAROLD
Ah, right, the minor detail. You have to stay in the mansion with... let's call him a companion.
MARGOT
A companion?
HAROLD
Louie's pet parrot, Captain Beaky. Supposedly, he knows where the money is hidden.
MARGOT
So, I have to spend the night in a creepy— Sorry, haunted mansion with a bird that knows where his money is hidden?
HAROLD
You're money. Maybe. But, exactly. Oh, and the parrot talks. Only in riddles.
HAROLD
It's one night, Margot. What could possibly go wrong?
BEAKY
Take me home. Take me home.
Margot jumps! Beaky is here. She looks at Harold, then at the will. Then at Beaky. Sure, let's do it!

WORKOUT COMPLETED [ ]

It took me years to figure out that you don't
fall into a tub of butter, you jump for it.
Claudette Colbert

IMAGINATION

We have a lot of tools in our arsenal as actors but **I believe imagination is the most powerful.** "If you hook into the character's belief system and you believe it 100%, there is no way the audience won't." - Meryl Streep "Imagination is more important than knowledge for knowledge is limited. - Einstein. Everyone has an Imagination but it must be worked out to get stronger. Think of your imagination as a limitless playground. In this space, you can be anyone, go anywhere, and do anything. **Have the courage to allow yourself to play!**

Solo Imaginary World Exploration - 6 Minutes [Set Timer]

Find a quiet space to relax and focus. **Close your eyes** and **let your imagination run wild. Tip:** Engage all your senses to explore this environment. Touch, taste, smell etc. Allow your emotions to guide you. **Extra:** After you establish this world in your imagination, you could introduce characters and have a dialogue with them. Are they friends or foes?

IMAGINARY WORLD: Labyrinthine Library of Infinite Knowledge: Delve into a multi-dimensional library containing universal knowledge.

JOURNAL YOUR EXPERIENCE - 2 Minutes [Set Timer]

_____
_____
_____
_____
_____
_____
_____

Your Characters Filter - 5 Minutes [Set Timer]

Everyone including the characters you play see the world through their own specific perspective/filter. I like to use the word filter because you can take out a filter, clean it, change its style, colour, an optimist or a pessimist, comedian or a nihilist, etc. **Find a quiet space** to focus. **Close your eyes and let go of your personal thoughts and emotions** to make space for your characters. **Open your eyes, and allow the filter provided to effect everything around you. Tip:** Explore wherever you are and interact with the objects. **Extra:** How does *this* character walk and move in their world?

FILTER: Adventurous Explorer: Sees every new place and situation as an adventure.

JOURNAL YOUR EXPERIENCE - 2 Minutes [Set Timer]

_____
_____
_____
_____
_____
_____
_____

WORKOUT COMPLETED [ ]

I don't want people to know what I'm actually like. It's not good for an actor.
Jack Nicholson

CHARACTER STUDY "PEOPLE WATCHING"

Actors are required to portray characters that are believable and relatable. You don't have to agree with them but you have to understand them. Walk like them, talk like them, see the world like them. So, in order to fill our toolbox, we have to **go out into the world and study**. Then practice them over and over so we can "walk in their shoes', comfortably and confidently. Study their movements, mannerisms, the "vibe" they give off, the clothes they wear etc. **Fill your toolbox with the rhythms and idiosyncrasies of human behaviour.**

OBSERVATION CHARACTER STUDY - 15 Minutes [Set Timer]

Find a busy place where you can **sit and observe.** Choose anyone you find interesting. **Write down what stands out about them.** *The way they sit, drink their coffee, walk, talk, interact with others etc.* **Tip**: **Mirror them immediately**. This will help memorize the feeling of that character so whenever you come back to these characters you're discovering, your body will remember. **Extra**: Before you go to sleep, read over the characters from today and reenact their movements.

COLOURS: We as humans respond to colours like frequencies. If you pay attention closely, you can see everyone has their own 'colour' that defines their core. An essence that informs how they operate and move through the world.

WHAT COLOUR ARE THEY:

WORKOUT COMPLETED [ ]

People who are unable to motivate themselves must be content with mediocrity, no matter how impressive their other talents.
Andrew Carnegie

VOICE & DICTION

I wish I had learned this at the beginning of my career. The confidence to communicate clearly and powerfully is a game-changer for you as an actor. **Think of your voice as a musical instrument that needs regular tuning. This workout is your daily tuning session,** ensuring that your instrument is always ready. "The word 'theatre' comes from the Greeks. It means the seeing place. It is the place people come to see the truth about life and the social situation." - Stella Adler. Embrace this workout as a key to unlocking and portraying *that* truth by letting your voice be the vehicle that transports your audience into the heart of your story.

READ PASSAGE - 30 Seconds [Set Timer]
Speak the passage and take note of its quality. **Tip**: Record Audio to compare afterward.

> "In ancient halls, history whispers of bygone eras. Stones speak of past glories, echoes of footsteps resonate, painting pictures of yesteryears. The walls hold memories, each carving and corner a testament to time's passage."

RELAXATION - 1 Minute [Set Timer]
Deep Breathing: Sit and Inhale deeply through your nose, filling your lungs, then exhale slowly through your mouth. Imagine stress leaving your body with each breath.

Nay Nay Nay - 1 Minute [Set Timer]
Pick a song and sing the word "Nay" repeatedly. Start with a comfortable pitch and gradually move the sound from your nose to your chest, ensuring each "Nay" is clear and resonant. Stretch your range as best you can to strengthen.

Sustained 'S' - 2 Minutes [Set Timer]
Inhale deeply and then exhale slowly, making a continuous 's' sound. Keep the sound as even and steady as you can. Always push a little longer than you think you can.

Vowel Pronunciation Drill - 2 Minutes [Set Timer]
Slowly go through each vowel sound **(A, E, I, O, U)**, holding and exaggerating each sound. **Combine them with consonants** (e.g., ba, be, bi, bo, bu). Pay attention to the clarity and sharpness of each sound. Repeat a few times before moving to the next.

Lip Trills - 3 minutes - [Set timer]
Close your lips together lightly, like you're going to blow a raspberry. Then, blow air through your closed lips while making sounds. You should feel a tickling sensation. Pick a song and Lip Trill the whole along with it. **Tip**: Stretch your range as much as you can and pick a song you've never listened to.

The Cork Exercise - 4 Minutes [Set Timer]
Place a cork between your teeth and try to read a passage aloud. This forces your articulation muscles to work harder. If you don't have a cork, bite down gently on your thumb. You can use the following text for this exercise:

READ PASSAGE AGAIN - 30 Seconds [Set Timer]
Speak the passage and take note of its quality. **Tip**: Record Audio to compare.

Discovery Journal - 1 Minute [Set Timer]

WORKOUT COMPLETED [ ]

Acting is a question of absorbing other people's personalities and adding some of your own experience.
Paul Newman

SUBTEXT

Subtext is what lies beneath the surface of our words. It's the hidden layer of meaning, driven by the character's internal thoughts, emotions, desires, and motivations. Subtext is one of my favourite things as an actor because so much can be said with one simple line of dialogue. The power of "Hello" can be exciting if you told that person years ago "If I ever see you again, I'll kill you. Maybe it's the most beautiful person you've ever seen. Now, say "hello". *Subtext* shows the audience what your relationship with the characters/places/situations are, without having to explain it. We experience it every day and it is our job to create characters that interact as we do.

VOCAL WORK - 3 minutes - [Set Timer]
Lip Trills: Close your lips together lightly, like you're going to blow a raspberry. Then, blow air through your closed lips while making sounds. You should feel a tickling sensation. Pick a song and Lip Trill along with it. **Tip**: Stretch your range as much as you can and pick a song you've never listened to.

SUBTEXT PRACTICE
Use the line of dialogue provided and practice each of these subtexts **out loud.** Move on to the next, only when you believe yourself. Trust that you will know when *that* is. Before you begin, **pick a spot to look at and imagine** in detail, **who you are speaking with**. **Tip**: *Sometimes* we mean exactly what we are saying. Look for that too. **Extra**: Substitute someone you have a strong relationship with in real life, good or bad, and see it's affect.

Initial Line: "Did you see that the old theater downtown is showing classic movies all month?"
Your Response Line: "They are? Cool. Classic movies are my favourite. You going to go? It could be fun to catch one. What's your favourite classic?"

SUBTEXTS - 6 Minutes [Set Timer]
[ ] Cinematic Nostalgia: You cherish the timeless appeal of classic films.
[ ] Critical: You find most old movies outdated and prefer modern cinema.
[ ] Excited: You're thrilled about experiencing these classics as they were meant to be seen.
[ ] Uninterested: You've never been much into movies, old or new.
[ ] Curious: You're intrigued to see how these films hold up over time.
[ ] Your Own Subtext

RELATIONSHIP SUBTEXTS - 6 Minutes [Set Timer]
[ ] The Movie Buff Pal: You've shared countless film nights dissecting classics.
[ ] The Skeptical Friend: They always debate old vs. new movies with you.
[ ] The Romantic Interest: You shared a significant moment during a classic movie.
[ ] The Parent who introduced you to these films.
[ ] The Sibling with whom you've never agreed on movie tastes.
[ ] Your Own Subtext

Discovery Journal

_____
_____
_____
_____

WORKOUT COMPLETED [ ]

If you really do want to be an actor who can satisfy himself and his audience, you need to be vulnerable.
Jack Lemmon

EMOTIONS

The 'moment before', **the emotional preparation, is the most important key to a great scene.** If you start any scene *without* an emotional preparation it feels like trying to drive a car in neutral. The preparation is the uphill climb of every rollercoaster; Once you grind all the way to the top, the chains let go and the rest of the ride takes care of itself. "No one wants to see a play or a movie and look at technical proficiency. You want to be moved, you want a human experience, you want to feel less alone" - Viola Davis. **Practice your emotions over and over** so when it's time, you aren't worried "Will I get there?" **You're imagination and emotions should be a tinderbox, so easy to light up. All it take is half a spark.**

EULOGY - 12 Minutes [Set Timer]

Find a quiet comfortable space. Choose someone in your life who is alive and important to you. Create an imaginary reason for why they have died. Now start from the point of the phone call— Imagine who calls, what they say and what you say. Eventually find yourself at the funeral, about to begin the eulogy. See the casket, is it open or closed?? What is that person wearing and any other details for yourself. Before you begin to speak, look into the audience and see who is there- Family, friends etc **Then begin the eulogy. Tip**: Be as specific as you can with everything. **Inside of specificity is where you will find the triggers to your heart.** Let your imagination take you wherever you want in this exercise. **Example**: Placing her favourite sheep stuffed animal in the casket, tucked under her arm like she always held it, then kissing her goodbye one last time.

DISCOVERY JOURNAL - 3 Minutes [Set Timer]

Make sure to **include the specific triggers** you experience because you can use these **TRIGGER MOMENTS** in the future instead of repeating the *entire* exercise.

WORKOUT COMPLETED [ ]

Every role was challenging.
I've never had an easy job.
Heath Ledger

THE CORK EXERCISE - 4 Minutes [Set Timer]

Place a cork between your teeth and read a passage aloud. This forces your articulation muscles to work harder. If you don't have a cork, bite down gently on your thumb. You can use the following text for this exercise:

> "The forest in autumn is a tapestry of colours. Leaves in shades of red, orange, and yellow rustle in the gentle breeze, falling softly to the forest floor, creating a carpet of vibrant hues."

WRITE A LETTER - 10 Minutes [Set Timer]

Get a piece of paper or write this in your device. **Take a moment** to let this situation and relationship sink in. Then let your imagination run wild and **write them a letter.**

Your Character: Jordan, a recent heart transplant recipient.
Other Character: The parents of a young donor who passed away and whose heart Jordan now has.

Relationship: Jordan never knew the young donor or their family personally. However, the life-saving transplant created an invisible and profound connection between Jordan and the donor's parents. This connection is filled with a complex mix of gratitude, sorrow, and the weight of carrying on a piece of someone's legacy.

Context of the Letter: Feeling an overwhelming sense of gratitude mixed with deep respect for the donor's family, Jordan writes a letter to them. The letter is an expression of immense thanks, acknowledgment of their loss, and the emotional journey of living with the heart of someone else's child. It's also a delicate outreach, offering condolences and sharing the impact their child's gift has had on Jordan's life.

Discovery Journal - 1 minute [Set Timer]

_____
_____
_____
_____
_____
_____
_____

WORKOUT COMPLETED [ ]

I'm not handsome.
What I am is charming.
David Niven

VOCAL WORK - 3 minutes [Set timer]
Lip Trills: Close your lips together lightly, like you're going to blow a raspberry. Then, blow air through your closed lips while making sounds. You should feel a tickling sensation. Pick a song and Lip Trill along with it. **Tip**: Stretch your range as much as you can and pick a song you've never listened to.

VERBAL IMPROV - 10 Minutes [Set Timer]

Find a space where you are comfortable and free to express yourself. Take a moment to **let this situation, character and prompt, sink in**. Then let your imagination run wild: **Picture <u>who</u> you are talking to** then **begin with *the prompt*** and **continue to verbalize everything** this character would say. **Tip**: This is exploration! There is no "getting it right". <u>BE BRAVE</u> to explore and discover.

Character: Riley, a dedicated teacher and advocate for equality in education, discovers that their colleague, Alex, known for being competitive, has been altering students' grades for personal gain. Riley's own experience with academic dishonesty during their school years makes this situation deeply personal.

Prompt: "Alex, I've seen the grade changes you've been making. We need to address this now."

Who are you talking to:

Describe them in two specific words:

Discovery Journal - 2 minutes [Set Timer]
_____
_____
_____
_____
_____
_____
_____

WORKOUT COMPLETED [ ]

In the theatre, characters have to cut the umbilical cord from the writer and talk in their own voices.
Irwin Shaw

SELF AWARENESS

The more you understand yourself, the more you are able to understand and develop your characters. Like you, your characters have thoughts, beliefs, traumas, passions etc. When you become aware of your own and start to see how those experiences and beliefs have shaped your life, how you operate and view the world, then you can develop your characters that are much more rich and vivid.

PHYSICAL WARMUP - 2 minutes [Set Timer]

Freeform Dance: Put on some music and engage in freeform dancing. Allow your body to move spontaneously and without inhibition. This can help you tap into your creative instincts and develop physical expressiveness. **Tip**: Try music you've never listened to.

CURRENT EMOTIONAL INVENTORY - 3 Minutes [Set Timer]

Write down and **record your current emotions**. Identify what you're feeling at this moment and why. **Tip**: Be as specific as you can, **don't disregard anything.** You can also **scan your body** to see how and where your current emotion is affecting you. Your posture, the way you walk, bouncing foot, sore neck etc

CURRENT EMOTIONAL STATE:

SELF DISCOVERY QUESTIONS - 10 Minutes [Set Timer]

I suggest a journal or writing it in your phone's notes so you don't run out of space here.

Write out your <u>PERFECT</u> DAY from morning till night. Be specific and hold nothing back.

WORKOUT COMPLETED [ ]

Being an actor is the loneliest thing in the world. You are all alone with your concentration and imagination, and that's all you have.
James Dean

IMAGINATION

We have a lot of tools in our arsenal as actors but I believe imagination is the most powerful. "If you hook into the character's belief system and you believe it 100%, there is no way the audience won't." - Meryl Streep. Everyone has an Imagination but it must be worked out to get stronger. Think of your imagination as a limitless playground. In this space, you can be anyone, go anywhere, and do anything. **Have the courage to allow yourself to play!**

VOCAL WORK - 2 Minutes - [Set timer]

Lip Trills: Close your lips together lightly, like you're going to blow a raspberry. Then, blow air through your closed lips while making sounds. You should feel a tickling sensation. Pick a song and Lip Trill along with it. **Tip**: Stretch your range as much as you can and pick a song you've never listened to.

IMPROVISED STORYTELLING - 5 Minutes [Set Timer]

Speak out the scenario provided and continue the story! Focus on vivid details, character development and how the main character overcomes the main obstacle. **Tip**: Try not to stop speaking so you don't have time to "think". Allow your imagination to keep moving forward without interruption. **Tip:** Record these stories on your device, in case it's great but more importantly to see your progress as you go on.

STARTING POINT: You are Jordan, a young urban explorer who finds an old, abandoned subway station beneath the city. Venturing inside, you discover a train that seems to be from another time.

IMAGINARY WORLD EXPLORATION - 6 Minutes [Set Timer]

Find a quiet space to relax and focus. **Close your eyes** and let your imagination run wild. **Tip:** Engage all your senses to explore this environment. Touch, taste, smell etc and allow your emotions to guide you. **Extra:** After you explore this world with your senses, you could introduce characters and have a dialogue with them. Are they friends or foes?

IMAGINARY WORLD: AURORA CASCADES - A world of vibrant waterfalls that shimmer with the colours of the northern lights. Except one. The water has stopped and its pool below has dried out.

JOURNAL YOUR EXPERIENCE - 2 Minutes [Set Timer]

_____
_____
_____
_____
_____
_____
_____
_____
_____

WORKOUT COMPLETED [ ]

When I'm making a film
I'm the audience.
Martin Scorsese

ANCHORING INTO YOUR CHARACTER COLOUR & MUSIC

Anchoring yourself into your character is vital. It's one of the most freeing feelings when you understand their *essence* because everything they do, how they do it and what their purpose is, becomes so clear to you and the audience. Every choice you make after you find your *anchor*, feels easy, because you're acting from who and what your character is at the core. You can call it an essence, an aura, vibe, energy etc. We all have it and feel it from everyone around us. There are many ways into your character but music and colour are my favourite. Music can inform the script, your character, even each scene. Colours, I think you will find, can work incredibly because we as humans respond to colours like frequencies. Colours evoke many feelings and if you pay attention closely, you can see everyone has their own 'colour' that defines their core. An essence that informs how they operate and move through the world.

THEIR COLOUR - 2 Minutes [Set Timer]
Think of **someone you know**, and **define them with a colour**. **Tip**: Trust yourself. Your initial colour is usually close. **Tip**: Start with basic colours then eventually become much more specific. **Example**: Corinna is an earthy green with rays of sunlight flowing through the green. **Extra**: Ask someone who knows *that person* as well, what they think this person's colour is and why. See how close your answers are or not.

YOUR CHARACTERS COLOUR
Read the given character description just as you would an audition, **assign a colour to that character.** Now take that colour you chose and **allow it to infuse into your entire body**, affecting your every move, your speaking, the way you see the world etc. **Take any book** you have, flip to a random page and **read the text as this Colour/Character**. **Tip**: Be specific, choose a colour that excites you and don't be afraid to get creative.

CHARACTER DESCRIPTION: [KENDALL] Kendall is a gifted but unorthodox music producer, known for blending unconventional sounds and techniques to create unique audio experiences. Their studio is a labyrinth of vintage and modern equipment, a playground for sonic experimentation. Kendall's style is eclectic, often wearing headphones around their neck and sporting a look that's as distinctive as their music. Despite their success in the industry, Kendall remains somewhat elusive, preferring the creative solitude of the studio over the limelight. Their character is a fusion of artistic genius, a rebel spirit.

CHOOSE THEIR COLOUR - 4 Minutes [Set Timer]
THEIR COLOUR:

CHOOSE THEIR SONG - 4 Minutes [Set Timer]
THEIR SONG:

READ PASSAGE FROM BOOK - 2 Minutes [Set Timer]

FREEFORM DANCE - 2 minutes - [Set Timer]
Put on the selected music and **engage in freeform dancing, anchored in your colour/character,** Allow your body to move spontaneously and without inhibition. This can help you tap into your creative instincts and develop physical expressiveness *while staying in character.* **Tip**: Journal about the differences as opposed to how you normally dance.

JOURNAL YOUR EXPERIENCE - 1 Minute [Set Timer]

WORKOUT COMPLETED [ ]

When I was a teenager, I began to settle into school because I'd discovered the extracurricular activities of drama and debate. Art saved me.
Sally Field

HISTORICAL RESEARCH

We are in the information era and have access to the world and its rich history at our fingertips. This exploration is not about 'learning facts'; it's a journey to the heart of human experience. The empathy and the understanding, especially on the things you disagree with, are incredibly valuable. If you look closely, you'll find the way people think, at different times in history, their attitudes, choices, and the way they move their bodies can teach you so much about us, right now. Fill your toolbox so it's overflowing with information and ideas to pull from so your imagination has so much to play with.

PHYSICAL WARMUP - 2 minutes - [Set Timer]
Freeform Dance: Put on some music and engage in freeform dancing. Allow your body to move spontaneously and without inhibition. This can help you tap into your creative instincts and develop physical expressiveness. **Tip**: Try music you've never listened to.

RESEARCH - 13 Minutes [Set Timer]
YouTube, streaming platforms, the internet or books, **research the given era/person/moment in time,** journal or make notes on your device, so when you want to find this information, it's organized and readily accessible. As you go, **write anything and everything _you_ find fascinating. Tip:** If the topic doesn't interest you, choose your own, or take a chance and still research it, but from a different perspective. Physicalities, voice, ideals, etc. Trust your body that when you see something interesting, you'll know. **Extra**: Speak it out and copy their movements. Our memory recall is massively affected by our bodies. Be specific and when you re-read your notes, you'll be amazed by how much your mind and body remember.

TOPIC:
The Launch of Sputnik (1957) - The Perspective of a Soviet Engineer: During the landmark event of the Soviet Union launching Sputnik, the world's first artificial satellite, in 1957, consider the perspective of a lesser-known Soviet engineer involved in the project. This engineer, unlike major figures like Sergei Korolev, played a crucial but unrecognized role in this groundbreaking achievement. Researching this engineer's experience offers insights into the challenges and triumphs of space exploration from the viewpoint of a dedicated but not publicly celebrated individual, highlighting the teamwork and technical ingenuity.

WORKOUT COMPLETED [ ]

The best actors do not let the wheels show.
Henry Fonda

BELIEF

Beliefs are the convictions that something exists or is true, especially without proof. That is also the definition of what we do as actors. We play make-believe. Our beliefs shape our world, especially our beliefs about ourselves and it works for the characters you play. Understand your beliefs and how they influence your mind, body and spirit, then you will be able to better understand others, so you can embody them. Allow the beliefs of your character to colour your perception of your world and your interaction with everything in it. "Acting is the best magic trick in the world. We applaud performances not because it's real, but because you made us believe."

VOCAL WORK - 2 Minutes - [Set timer]

Lip Trills: Close your lips together lightly, like you're going to blow a raspberry. Then, blow air through your closed lips while making sounds. You should feel a tickling sensation. Pick a song and Lip Trill along with it. **Tip**: Stretch your range as much as you can and pick a song you've never listened to.

BELIEF WORKOUT

Get your journal or write in here. **Define your personal belief/view** on the given subject. **Grab any book you own,** flip to a random page and **read it out loud,** colouring the words and intention with your belief system. **Tip:** Write trigger words you can hook into in the future: **Optimism-** Always smiling, grateful, opportunity, sunshine yellow.

YOUR PERSONAL BELIEF

The Purpose of Life- 7 Minutes [Set Timer]

_____
_____
_____
_____
_____

READ WITH BELIEF - 2 Minutes [Set Timer]

CHARACTERS BELIEF

The Purpose of Life

Life is a canvas where dreams colour every corner with vibrant potential. Each moment is a brushstroke of ambition, painting a masterpiece of experiences rich in hope and wonder. In this journey, the pursuit of dreams is the heartbeat of existence, pulsating with the promise of what could be.

READ WITH CHARACTERS BELIEF - 2 Minutes [Set Timer]

Forget your personal view and **fully embrace the character's belief**. Read out loud again.

JOURNAL YOUR EXPERIENCE - 2 Minutes [Set Timer]

_____
_____
_____
_____

WORKOUT COMPLETED [ ]

PERFORMANCE STRATEGY

SIX MONTH
FINAL REVIEW

TAKE A MOMENT OF REFLECTION AND BREAKDOWN WHERE YOU
ARE RIGHT NOW IN YOUR CAREER AND AS AN ACTOR.
THE MORE SPECIFIC YOU ARE THE MORE CLEAR YOU CAN SEE WHERE
YOU ARE NOW SO YOU CAN GET TO WHERE YOU WANT TO GO FASTER

★ ★ ★ ★ ★

" Your story here"

DATE:

MY WHY
WHY ARE YOU DOING WHAT YOU ARE DOING
BE SPECIFIC

THE LAST 6 MONTHS
5 STAR RATING

☆ ☆ ☆ ☆ ☆

YOUR KEY POINTS AND TAKEAWAYS - TAKE A LOOK AT WHERE YOU STARTED AND WHERE YOU ARE NOW. WHAT WAS YOUR JOURNEY and HOW HAVE YOU CHANGE

STRENGTHS:

WEAKNESSES:

IMPROVEMENT STRATEGY
HOW CAN YOU IMPROVE ON THESE AREAS FOR THE FUTURE:

GOAL FROM LAST :
DID YOU ACHIEVE IT?

WHY OR WHY NOT?

GOAL FOR THE NEXT STEPS OF YOUR CAREER
THE MORE SPECIFIC YOU ARE THE GREATER THE RESULT

Action Step(s):

GOING FORWARD

I hope you're incredibly proud of the work you've put in. It doesn't matter how long it took, one year of workouts isn't a small feat. That's 45 more hours you've come closer to perfecting your craft.

My hope for you is you've come closer to knowing yourself as an artist. What works for you, what doesn't. That you've taken pieces from this book or even just an idea and completely changed it to work for you. Whatever it is, just know, I hope your dreams come true.

Never forget **YOUR WHY.**
That fire inside you that makes you, you... *That's* the magic this world needs.

Love in your heart. Fire in your soul.

Victor Zinck Jr

STORIES & FEEDBACK

I WOULD LOVE ANY AND ALL FEEDBACK FROM YOUR EXPERIENCE! HOW IT HELPED, WHAT WORKED AND WHAT DIDN'T. EVEN JUST A HELLO! THIS BOOK IS THE FIRST I'VE EVER WRITTEN LIKE THIS SO IT WILL BE EVOLVING AS IT GOES AND I WOULD APPRECIATE ALL OF YOUR HELP MAKING IT EVEN BETTER.

VICZINCK@GMAIL.COM

RECOMMENDED BOOKS & RESOURCES

The Intent to Live - Larry Moss - Amazing and inspiring insight and a dictionary of great questions to ask for your characters and their backstory.
The Practical Handbook for the Actor - Melissa Bruder, Lee Michael Cohn, Madeleine Olnek - A very powerful and simple explanation of what we do as actors and how to do it. Great reminder to bring you back to the basics for your best performances.
The power of the Actor - Ivana Chubbuck - My favourite for imagination and creative ways to discover your characters and their world.

Surrender Experiment - Michael A Singer > Letting go of the reigns and trusting yourself in every choice you make.
Magic of Thinking Big - David J. Schwartz - The incredible power of our thoughts and our reality.
The Go Giver - Bob Burg and John David Mann - Your Belief system and the unbelievable affect when you always give more than you receive in payment, has on your life.
Think Big and Grow Rich - Napoleon Hill - One of my favourites for the power of who we surround ourselves with and our thoughts and imaginations to succeed.
The Power of NOW - Eckhart Tolle - Living in the present moment and the effect it has on every aspect of your life.
The Compound Effect - Darren Hardy - My favourite for understanding habits and how to apply his strategy to your day to day life.
PEAK - Anders Ericsson - How the best of the best train "purposefully" and how that specific focus can change your career and life.
Moonwalking with Einstein - For memory techniques - Incredible techniques for those of you like me who struggle with memory!
What Every Body Knows - Joe Navarro - FBI interrogator on instincts that drive body language
The Power of your Subconscious Mind - Joseph Murphy - Understanding and changing the way we think.

The Alchemist - Paulo Coelho & The Prophet - Kahlil Gibran - My two favourite novels for a beautifully poetic way to look at the world and experience life simply and profoundly.

THANK YOU MOM, DAD, DANIEL, PHA PHAN, MITTITA, BRITTANY, BILL, LUCAS, VALENTINA

www.ingramcontent.com/pod-product-compliance
Lightning Source LLC
Chambersburg PA
CBHW071330080526
44587CB00017B/2787